Female Fault and Fulfilment
in Gnosticism

STUDIES IN RELIGION

Female
Fault and
Fulfilment in
Gnosticism

Jorunn Jacobsen Buckley

The University of North Carolina Press

Chapel Hill and London

© 1986 by The University of North Carolina Press

All rights reserved

Manufactured in the United States of America

Library of Congress Cataloging-in-Publication Data

Buckley, Jorunn Jacobsen.
Female fault and fulfilment in Gnosticism.

(Studies in religion)
Bibliography: p
Includes index.

1. Women and religion—History.   2. Gnosticism.
I. Title.   II. Series: Studies in religion (Chapel
Hill, N.C.)

BL458.B83   1986   299'.932   85-29020
ISBN 0-8078-1696-5

Chapter 1 appeared in somewhat different form, under the same title, in
History of Religions 24.4 (1985): 328–44. Chapter 2 is based on two
previously published articles: "The Mandaean Ṭabahata Masiqta,"
Numen 28.2 (1981): 138–63, and "A Rehabilitation of Spirit Ruha in
Mandaean Religion," *History of Religions* 22.1 (1982): 60–84. Chapter 5
appeared in a slightly different version, under the same title, in *Novum
Testamentum* 27.3 (1985): 245–72.

-Yes, the women . . . you can believe in the women. . . .

-Oh yes sar, Fuller said, and then after a pause,

-Woman bring you into the world, you got to stick with her.

-Wasn't it woman brought evil into the world, then?

-Sar?

-Yes. When she picked the fruit from the forbidden tree; and gave it to the man to eat?

-So the evil already there provided, and quite naturally she discover it.

-Yes, yes, and she gave it to the man. . . .

-She share it with him, sar, said Fuller. -Thaht the reason why we love her.

William Gaddis, *The Recognitions*

CONTENTS

A s suggested by Eve's ambiguous role in the Creation, the female
has been deeply problematic in the Judaeo-Christian tradition.
The Gnostic sources of late antiquity illuminate this problem: the
majority of Gnostic texts portray female entities as worldly yet
transcendent beings, fertility figures as well as virgins. Frequently, contradictory characteristics are attributed to a single female; thus, paradoxes occur and
categories clash. The present work examines selected Gnostic female figures
that epitomize such dissonance.

More than ten years ago, the female figure Ruha ("Spirit") in Mandaean
Gnosticism caught my interest. More recently, I became intrigued by entities
called "female" in other forms of Gnosticism; ranging from mythological
females to constituent elements designated "female," such entities have no
common denominator other than their attributed femaleness. Contrary to some
scholarly assumptions (both traditional and current), the females in Gnosticism cannot be lumped together in a large, single, and negative camp. The
abundant and routine depreciations of Gnostic female figures seem to me to
rest on the tendency of many scholars to assume a common Gnostic devaluation of earth, married life, sexuality, and propagation—and thus, by implication, of all females. Granted, these pejorative views *are* found in Gnostic
mythologies, but they fail to appear according to any single set of standards or
formulae. Indeed, the surface depreciation of females frequently masks a
profound concern with these figures because they are ambiguous, possessing
outrightly positive—and therefore surprising—qualities.

Gnostic traditions that do not devalue femaleness as such may, as one might
expect, refrain from advocating the stringently ascetic practices that are often
assumed to be part and parcel of Gnosticism. A number of the females
discussed in the present work are characterized by sexual power and by both
dangerous and laudable creative autonomy. Female power to act and to create—whether legitimate or not, whether the female is alone or in partnership
with a male—is a recurring motif in Gnostic texts. Acknowledgment of such
female capacities may lead to the elevation of the female to divine levels:
Gnostic females can be portrayed as *the* One, personified, primary, transcendental principle. In these cases, philosophically sophisticated forms of Gnosticism may describe the female embodiment of ultimate reality in paradoxical
terms. A female figure then represents both positive and negative concepts,

combining in herself the universal totality and constituting the basis for oppositional categories such as good and evil, light and darkness, spirit and matter. "Dynamic monism" might be a pertinent term for what this kind of female embodies.

In sum, Gnostic views of female entities tend to emphasize extremes: the female may be a sinful creatress who possesses illegitimate abilities, or she may be the highest divinity, residing beyond categorization and judgment and accessible to thought only through paradox or *via negativa*.

Mythological females and conceptual entities designated "female" can be mirrored on the human level. Here, they do not symbolize human women so much as they do a female component present in both male and female human beings. According to some Gnostic traditions, the soul (*psuchē*) is a female, human constituent that needs to be transcended; in such cases, the female must transform herself into—or merge with—a male partner. I present examples of Gnostic rituals that have precisely such aims. A ritual change from female into male may represent a transformation of the earthly into the spiritual, and such a conversion of human constituents may be required if an individual is to achieve otherworldly goals. Significantly, a number of Gnostic traditions insist that these goals must be reached while the celebrant still remains in the earthly world; that is, Gnostic ritual does not necessarily emphasize achievements in the world beyond, the "Lightworld," after death, as many scholars have claimed.

Such rituals put the speculative dualism so prevalent in Gnosticism to creative use, for they actively transform speculation into a springboard for propulsion into the Lightworld. These rituals do not jar with conceptual, Gnostic dualism; rather, they harness this dualism to the conditions and goals of human life. By engaging in ritual activities, Gnostics creatively contribute to their own salvation, manipulating opposing forces towards positive ends.

The question of salvation is central to the study of females in Gnosticism, and the texts I have chosen deal consistently with the problem of redemption for the female entities. If they can be saved, what precisely constitutes their liberation? This depends, of course, on the ideological framework of the specific Gnostic texts. Interpretations of and embellishments on the creation story in Genesis 2 and 3 (and Gen. 1, to a lesser extent) crop up frequently in Gnosticism. For some Gnostics, the first part of Gen. 2 expresses the salvific ideal acutely: liberation is represented by a unified human being, Adam, in his pristine state prior to his separation into male and female. Gnostics who so elevate this presexual human entity do not, generally, put much stake in sexual life and earthly procreation. On the other hand, some Gnostics see marriage as an earthly prerequisite for a higher, Lightworld unification of male and female. Still others advocate (as noted above) the outright abolition of the female. In most cases, however, salvation seems to entail a balance between "spiritualized" genders,[1] a condition in which the female *as* female is subjugated and transcended and the male is no longer male in the usual sense of the term.

I have selected six different Gnostic texts or traditions that illuminate female figures, or elements denoted "female," each of which will be treated in depth in a separate chapter. A concluding, seventh chapter offers a summary of important parallels, divergencies, and themes regarding the female entities encountered in the first six chapters.

The first chapter focuses on *The Book Baruch* (*Bar.*), a source transmitted by the church father Hippolytos of Rome. This text paraphrases the Genesis creation accounts, and it presents a female divine entity, Eden. The only female in a divine threesome, Eden represents earth. In certain ways, she fills the role of a female, creative principle, the sort of deity eagerly sought by a number of feminist scholars of the Biblical tradition. In the second and third chapters I deal with two females who have much in common: the Mandaean Ruha ("Spirit"), and personified Wisdom, Sophia, in *The Apocryphon of John* (*Ap. John*). Both are sexually active, lack a legitimate partner, and thus demonstrate threatening female autonomy. But in their higher forms these females become revealer figures.

The challenge of female autonomy is solved, as discussed in the fourth chapter, by the idea of a single, male entity that has enclosed and subjugated the female within himself. Here, the text is *Excerpta ex Theodoto* (*Exc. Thdot.*), a source that deals with the problem of salvation ingeniously, by advocating a backwards move: the female taken from Adam's rib must return into the male. In the fifth chapter I concentrate on logion 114 of the more outspoken *Gospel of Thomas* (*Gos. Thom.*), which deals with the female as a stage to be left behind. I argue that the gospel as a whole exhorts its adherents to transform the female, not only into the male, but into the spiritual Adam, the "living soul" of Gen. 2:7.

The text for my sixth chapter, *The Gospel of Philip* (*Gos. Phil.*), exhibits strong ideological links with *Gos. Thom.* Central emphasis is placed on Mary Magdalene, Jesus' female partner. I argue that the gospel identifies Magdalene with female entities that possess double characteristics: earthly and otherworldly, creative and destructive. Paradoxes abound in this text. Far from designating either male or female as "fallen," the gospel treats marriage positively, making it a requirement for participation in the ritual that establishes the Lightworld in the earthly realm.

These six chapters comprise a sequence, or progression, discussed in the concluding chapter. The first two chapters present ambivalent and ambiguous female figures, strongly connected with—but not solely blamed for—the presence of evil. Female ambiguity and propensity for sin appear, again, in the Sophia of *Ap. John*, which moves the scene of action from an earthly level back to the beginnings in the Lightworld and to the female's role there. In the beginning, Sophia's autonomous activity appears as a central, negative issue and her need to belong in a salvific pair-relationship becomes an acute concern. This concern is evident in the traditions treated in the next three chapters. In *Exc. Thdot.*, anthropology parallels mythology: soul and spirit in the human being are merged to become an asexual, angelic entity, just as female Sophia and male Christ are needed to complement one another. The female as a stage to be left behind emerges both in *Exc. Thdot.* and in *Gos. Thom.* In the latter text, as well as in *Gos. Phil.*, Jesus' female followers become paradigms of the saved: they are images of the Savior's Lightworld spouse and they lead double (even triple) lives. *Gos. Phil.* demonstrates a full-blown philosophical system in which the female shows herself as Truth becoming manifest in the lower world.

The female as an earthly as well as a spiritual force—sinful, powerful, and ambiguous—has dominated the Judaeo-Christian view of human women ever since God pointed out the forbidden tree in the garden of Eden. My work attempts to broaden the scope of the study of female imagery by centering on some Gnostic paraphrases of the canonical creation accounts.

Unlike many works on Gnosticism, mine does not attend to the question of Gnosticism's origin, its influence on early Christian thought, and the like. I am simply taking the Gnostic texts and traditions as givens, asking not, "where do they come from?" but "what do they mean?" Inquiring about sense—whether pragmatic or symbolic, whether in terms of philosophy, mythology, or ritual—I ask questions that should interest students of Gnosticism, of early Christian literature in general, and of religious symbols of the female. Identifying myself as a historian of religions, and therefore brandishing a nonapologetic flag, I address myself specifically to colleagues concerned with the interrelationships of thought, myth, and ritual, and to those who still deem it worth while to think about theory and method in the study of religions. In dealing with the chosen texts, I have tried to let the texts influence the method of interpretation, rather than to lower a constricting, square frame called "my method" on them.

ACKNOWLEDGMENTS

Growing up on the grounds of a mental hospital, I became attuned to alternative realities at a tender age. Gnosticism started to interest me during the late sixties, and in the Netherlands in 1973 Gilles Quispel, fascinated by female revealers in Gnostic texts, spurred me to continue studying such figures. In the Divinity School at the University of Chicago I learned primarily from my esteemed teacher Jonathan Z. Smith, who had the good sense to let me find my own way in studying the female entity Ruha in Mandaean Gnosticism.

A fellowship at Harvard made this book possible. Most of it was written in the lower regions of Andover Library, during my tenure there (1981–82) as a lecturer and research associate in the Divinity School's Program of Women's Studies in Religion. Profound thanks are due to the eminently capable and enthusiastic director of the program, Constance Buchanan, and to my fellow research associates: Kari Børresen, Cheryl Gilkes, Jo Ann Hackett, and Barbara Pope. I also benefited from conversations with members of the Divinity School's faculty, especially Krister Stendahl and the late George MacRae, and am grateful for the genuine interest the female faculty showed in my project.

I thank the Research Council at the University of North Carolina at Greensboro for a grant supporting travel back to Harvard in the fall of 1983. Thanks are also due my wonderful colleagues in the Department of Religious Studies at the University of North Carolina at Greensboro for their unfailing professional and moral support. I owe much to oral and written communications, over several years, with Elaine Pagels, Judith Van Herik, and Deirdre J. Good, and I pay homage to my husband, Thomas Buckley, who has endured my occasionally absent-minded company while I wrote the book. Finally, a nod of acknowledgment goes to the scholars of Gnosticism whose theories I disagree with, for their work made much of mine possible.

Female Fault and Fulfilment
in Gnosticism

Transcendence and Sexuality
in *The Book Baruch*

INTRODUCTION

In his *Refutation of All Heresies*, the church father and heresiologist Hippolytos (early third century) relates the contents of a book, *Baruch*, by the Gnostic Justin. According to Hippolytos, Justin is the most vile of all heresiarchs;[1] nevertheless, or perhaps precisely for that reason, he gives a detailed account of the blasphemous content of *Bar.*, Justin's principal book.[2]

It is of course dangerous to rely completely on church fathers as informants on Gnostic systems of thought, but in the case of *Bar.* Hippolytos's rendering seems remarkably coherent and faithful. For long stretches, Hippolytos appears almost carried away with Justin's fascinating, though repugnant, story—but whenever he remembers to check himself, he inserts "he [Justin] says," so as to distance himself from the text. Thus, Hippolytos's own voice does not seriously disturb the account, for he refrains from constantly interrupting the story in order to heap up counterarguments of his own. In short, Hippolytos seems too interested in *Bar.* to disparage it repetitiously.

I am intrigued by *Bar.*'s way of presenting the problem of the origin of good and evil, and my particular concern is to investigate the relationships between the three main powers portrayed in it. The lowest of these three powers is female and could therefore automatically be taken to signify evil; but the text itself discourages such a conclusion, I think, for its message is more complex on the issue of determining a culprit for the introduction of evil. I propose, then, to examine the possible answers to the origin and the problem of evil as *Bar.* poses these matters and, next, to discuss various scholarly interpretations of the text in this regard.

First, a detailed presentation of Hippolytos's text is in order. Here, I will emphasize and explore the problem spots of the text. The second main part of this chapter is divided into three sections, devoted to each of the three powers in *Bar.* I will consult previous scholarship in each of these three sections, the last of which sums up the issues pertaining to the role, evaluation, and particular force of the female power in Justin's book.

To a large extent, Hippolytos appears to be quoting *Bar.* directly. Quite often, the heresiologist inserts "he says" or "they say" into his account, which strengthens the impression that he is working from a text lying in front of him. These insertions are particularly prominent in the beginning and at the end of the account.[3]

Justin's story is, essentially, a Genesis-based creation account. In the beginning, there were three powers, two male and one female. All three are called "power of the All" (*Bar.* 26.1). "The Good," the more exalted of the two male powers, is the only one that possesses foreknowledge; the second male has the title "father of all things created" (26.1). The third, female power, who is half woman, half serpent, is "irascible, of double mind and double body, in all respects resembling the one in the fable of Herodotus" (26.1).[4] This double-ness is to be kept in mind in the following, for one might expect anything from such a composite figure. The "father of all things created," like the female, does not possess foreknowledge, and this lack, too, might indicate unpredictability.

The female is, next, identified as Eden and Israel, and the three powers are said to be the origin of all things. The "father of all things created" is no other than Elohim, who, on seeing Eden, becomes desirous of her. Apparently, Elohim's desire arises because of his lack of foreknowledge; this lack is not repudiated, but simply stated.

Eden experiences a compatible desire for Elohim, and the two unite "in heart-felt love" (26.2). It is worth noting that there is no negative evaluation of this first mating. Still, this first union paradoxically becomes a separation, for Eden and Elohim's offspring, the twenty-four angels, are divided into two groups: twelve angels are paternal, that is, they belong to Elohim, while the other twelve are Eden's. All twelve Eden-angels carry names that evoke demons or archons, such as Babel, Achamoth, and Naas. Only five Elohim-angels are named: these are Michael, Amen, Baruch, Gabriel, and Esaddaios (26.3).

Although the angels seem to originate in both parents, they strictly belong to, and work for, their respective master/mistress only. But the division goes even deeper, for the father Elohim *"begot for himself* from Eden" his twelve angels, while the maternal angels are those *"whom Eden made"* (26.3; my

emphasis). This demarcation appears to reflect the important idea of a difference between "male" and "female" birth, and possibly a difference in evaluation of the two kinds of offspring.

Loyal assistants to their respective "parent," the angels connote Paradise.
Justin ingeniously interprets "God planted a paradise in Eden . . ." (Gen. 2:8)
to mean that Elohim made Eden pregnant (26.5).[5] The angels are, indeed, the
trees of Paradise, and two of them are mentioned specifically: the tree of life is
Baruch, the third paternal angel, and the tree of knowledge of good and evil is
Naas, the third maternal angel. Naas's name may be a reference to his mother's
snakelike appearance, and Eden's double-mindedness may be discerned in the
double nature of her angel's capacity: good and evil. On both parental sides,
then, the third angel seems destined to play an important role.

Bar. stresses that the paradise—that is, the angels—came about "out of the
mutual good pleasure of Elohim and Eden" (26.7). The text obviously wishes
to emphasize a positive attitude towards their union, despite obvious and
looming separations and discrepancies.

Elohim's angels create man, and they use their mother, Eden, for creation
material. She is identified as the earth. Selective, the angels choose as their
matter "the human and civilized regions of the earth above the groin" (26.7).[6]
Here, one notes that the paternal angels create man, but Elohim seems unin-
volved in the creation (despite his epithet "father of all things created") for he
lets the angels create on his command. Elohim presumably has reasons for not
wanting direct implication in the creation process. It is his own spouse who
furnishes the material for creation, and man is made from her "better" parts.
Here is the second evaluative standard for the two parts of Eden: her "animal"
portions are used to form the "beasts and other living creatures" (26.7). *Bar.*
does not specify who it is that undertakes this second creation.

Even if it is the paternal angels who have made man, the next section states:
"They made man, then, as a symbol of their unity and love" (26.8). It is
unclear whether this "unity and love" is that of the angels, or of Elohim and
Eden. The latter seems the more reasonable view, for the angels have not been
referred to as either "unified" or "loving"—on the contrary, the two groups of
angels are strictly separated.

Eden, far from lifeless after having been used as creation material, supplies
the human being with a soul, and Elohim furnishes the spirit. Again, Adam—
the man—is said to be "a seal and love-token and eternal symbol of the
marriage of Eden and Elohim" (26.8). This constant, positive reiteration
starts, perhaps, to wear thin, and one begins to expect the worst. For there are
abundant actual and potential separations: the grouping of the angels, the
difference in creation material, spirit and soul, the two trees.

Another creation ensues: Eve is made in the same manner as Adam—that is, one supposes, from the same matter. Like Adam, she receives a soul and a spirit, but in addition to being a seal and a symbol, Eve is "a seal of Eden to be preserved for ever" (26.9). This indicates a differentiation in the symbolization of the two sexes: Eve bears a special relation to Eden, which resembles the relationship of the maternal angels to their mother. Still, both Adam and Eve are symbols of Elohim and Eden's love.

Next the human pair is commanded to "increase and multiply, and inherit the earth" (26.9). Here, the Gen. 1:28 command is combined with a version of the Gen. 2–3 story of Adam and Eve. There is, as yet, no prohibition; rather, one finds an encouragement. The earth to be inherited is interpreted as Eden, which could be a clue to further events: that is, one wonders what this might mean with respect to more spiritual yearnings.

The next section gives an exegesis on the origin of the "paternal law" of dowry from women to men. This duty is enjoined upon women, who, in imitation of Eden, ought to give to their men "all [their] power" (26.10). What power, if any, might Eden still retain in herself?

So far, the story has been preparing for some power-play between Eden and Elohim. The previous separations now have an added dimension, the ceding of power from Eden to Elohim. As a prelude, one hears of the evil aspects of the mother's angels (these aspects have already been indicated by their negative-sounding names). Divided into four parts, the maternal angels make up the four rivers of Paradise; they also connote the zodiac-spirits that malignantly influence human life. Here, in *Bar.* 26.11–13, one finds the first extended portrayal of the mother's angels as unquestionably evil.

The zodiacal powers are nevertheless necessary, for a specific reason. Evidently, it is not by chance, or even by fate, that these powers dominate human life on earth: their installation—by Eden, one assumes—came about because Elohim deserted Eden. After "Elohim had established and formed the world out of mutual good pleasure, he wished to go up into the lofty parts of heaven and see whether anything was defective in the creation, taking his own angels with him" (26.14).

Here Elohim is credited with the creation, which is a view different from that given above in 26.7–8. Neither the angels nor Eden are mentioned as cocreators, though Eden may be included through the formulation "out of mutual good pleasure." In order to gain a bird's-eye view, as it were, Elohim ascends to inspect his creation. On this tour, he brings his own angels aloft, but he leaves Eden behind because, since she is earth, "she did not wish to follow her consort upwards" (26.14). The text does not say that she was unable to ascend, although this seems implied. One clue may be that Eden's element, the soul, is less eligible for ascent than is Elohim's spirit. Although Elohim and Eden gave their respective elements to the human being, both male and female, they themselves do not possess one another's element. Eden's lack of spirit may cause her to remain below.

Before Elohim can start his inspection from above, he discovers something unexpected: ascending to the limit of heaven, he sees a light superior to the one he has created below. He declares, "Open the gates to me, that I may enter in and make confession to the Lord; for I thought that I was Lord!" (26.15). A voice from above promptly states that this is the gate of the Lord by which the righteous enter (26.16).[7] Leaving his angels outside, Elohim, presumably eligible, enters and sees "what eye has not seen and ear has not heard and has not entered into the heart of man" (26.16).[8]

Gone is Elohim's concern for possible defects in his own world, gone is any thought of his spouse below. Even his angels cannot follow him into the superior light over which presides "the Good." This supreme power, which possesses foreknowledge, invites Elohim to sit at his right hand (26.17).[9] Perhaps feeling unworthy, Elohim instead pleads with "the Good" to let him go back down in order to destroy his own world. He now realizes that his own spirit is caught in the human being, and he wants to retrieve it. Apparently, there were more faults with his creation than Elohim at first imagined.

Elohim's insights here remind us of those belonging to a good Gnostic. That the spirit is "bound in men" (26.17), as Justin has it, has not been put in such negative terms before. Seeing that his own creation is vastly inferior, and even damaging, Elohim wants to undo it. Does this include Eden? one wonders. Here, echoes of Gen. 6:6–7 reverberate: God regrets his creation and wishes to obliterate it.[10]

One might expect that Elohim's wish to undo his creation would favorably impress "the Good." Not at all, for "the Good" objects, saying, "You can do nothing evil when you are with me, for it was out of a mutual good pleasure that you and Eden made the world. So, let Eden have the creation so long as she will. But you stay with me" (26.18).

It seems remarkable that "the Good" defends the lower creation, and even expressly states that destruction of the world would be sinful. Only Elohim's presence above hinders the execution of such a plan; allowed below, he would, in all likelihood, carry it out. "The Good" defends the creation as positive. (The "mutual good pleasure" seems, increasingly, like a formula, recurring again and again in Justin's book.) Eden is allowed to rule over the world, its life and organization. Is this a compromise on the part of "the Good," or a happy declaration?

Elohim, relieved of his responsibility towards his world, is also caught:

ironically, he cannot liberate his own spirit in the human beings. His own salvation into the upper world is, at the same time, an incarceration.[11] That ascent should equal imprisonment must be the height of Gnostic sarcasm. Elohim is unable to interfere in the affairs of the world. His suspicions of defects were well founded, it turns out, but there is nothing he can do about this from his elevated prison. Defects discovered from the faraway vantage point must remain defects.

Down below, Eden feels deserted and reacts with revenge, giving full rein to her grief over her husband's departure. She beautifies herself, hoping to lure him down[12]—little suspecting that her spouse is unable to move downwards. She then summons one of her angels, Babel—identified with Aphrodite—to cause disloyalties and divorces among human beings (26.20).[13] The particularly wicked purpose of this is to punish the spirit of Elohim in mankind and thereby to harm Elohim, too. Acting in this "eye for an eye, tooth for a tooth" manner, Eden seeks to balance the grief that Elohim has caused her. Her own unhappiness may not be ameliorated by this, but it spreads the misery, making both male and female human beings suffer. Is Elohim, at this point, beyond the capacity of being directly hurt?

Bar. condemns Elohim, who "contrary to the compacts made by him forsook his consort" (26.21). Elohim seems to have broken his part of the marriage-contract. Again, why did not Eden go with him? Is it, perhaps, because of the power Eden has brought to Elohim that she cannot rise? Or does she not want to? If all Eden's power now belongs to Elohim, he seems to have misused it. A more specific question is whether it is Elohim's own powers that have enabled him to ascend, or whether his ascension is due to the Edenic part of his powers.

In any case, Elohim, alarmed, observes Eden's punishments—aimed at him—upon mankind, and he dispatches Baruch to help the hapless spirit. (The angels on both Eden's and Elohim's sides appear to have more mobility and abilities than either of their parents.) Appearing in the midst of Eden's angels, Baruch utters to man the command not to eat of the tree of knowledge of good and evil—that is, of Naas. This is the first prohibition in *Bar.* Naas and Baruch, the two trees, are now pitted as opponents, vying for the human being.

Baruch, somewhat surprisingly, tells man to "obey the other eleven angels of Eden" (26.22), the information about the evil influences of these angels notwithstanding (26.11–14).[14] But the explanation is that while the eleven have passions, Naas, alone among Eden's angels, also has transgression. This means either that the passions are left unrepudiated or that there is nothing man can do to offset their influence, for they are necessary evils.

The information that Naas is, potentially or actually, sinful prepares one for what follows: Naas commits adultery with Eve and a homosexual act with Adam. These are the first illegal sexual acts. Heterosexual activity between man and wife is not censured; on the contrary, Adam and Eve have been told to multiply (26.9).

That Naas is responsible for "adultery and paederasty" (26.23) can be seen as a link back to the phrase, "The necessity of evil, however, came about on some such ground as this" (26.14). For, immediately after blaming Naas, *Bar.* says: "From that time both evil and good held sway over men, springing from one origin, that of the father. For by ascending to 'the Good,' the father showed a way for those who are willing to ascend, but by departing from Eden he made a beginning of evils for the spirit of the father which is in men" (26.23–24).[15]

Several issues need consideration here. The whole story told between 26.14 and 26.23 offers the explanation for the necessity of evil. The evil occurring in these sections is largely due to the workings of Eden and her angel Naas; *Bar.*, however, blames neither of these; the fault is Elohim's. Elohim's ascent may have been undertaken in good faith—or even naively—but it is the cause of the tragedy of evil. Still, the book tries to show the equivocal nature of Elohim's situation: if he had not ascended, there would be no model for the salvation of man's spirit; on the other hand, by leaving Eden, he exposed his own spirit to the evils for which he alone is responsible. There are no easy answers as to "correct action" here; the story deliberately lets any decision hang. Spiritual life will have to bear the cost of earthly unhappiness. Earthly life, again, leaves something to be desired for the spirit.

The angel Baruch now starts his principal career: he is sent out successively to a series of prophets who, by his inspiration, proclaim "the Good." But Naas constantly interrupts and obscures Baruch's message. Baruch relates to Naas as the spirit to the soul, and the two are forever fighting for control. A mouthpiece for Elohim, Baruch tries to speak to the prophets—from Moses to Heracles—but they all fail in their task, due to Naas's (that is, the soul's) interference. Here, in section 26, the creation is, for the first time, called "evil." Strong words are also used further on, where Heracles, the last of the unsuccessful prophets, is sent "that he might prevail against the twelve angels of Eden and liberate the father from the twelve wicked angels of creation" (26.27). Elohim appears to suffer, directly, in the human being.[16]

Naas prevents the prophetic message from being heard, and the soul, both in the prophets and in their audience, distorts the meaning. Trouble abounds because "the Good's" message cannot be directly transmitted, for it is Elohim who equips the prophets to preach "the Good." That is, neither "the Good" nor Elohim speaks in an unmediated fashion: the message has to filter through too many faulty conveyers.

After Heracles has miserably failed at his mission by being seduced by Omphale ("Babel or Aphrodite" [26.28]), Jesus, the last of the prophets, finally succeeds. Called "son of Joseph and Mary" (26.29)—in good Jewish-Christian tradition, *not* "son of God"!—Jesus hears Baruch tell of the depressing results of the earlier prophets' attempts at proclaiming "the Good." The twelve-year-old shepherd Jesus vows to succeed in his preaching on "the things concerning the father and 'the Good' " (26.30).

Naas, enraged at his inability to sway Jesus, has the prophet crucified. "But he left the body of Eden on the Cross and went up to 'the Good.' Saying to Eden: 'Woman, you have your son!' (John 19:26), that is, the psychic man and the earthly, but himself yielding the spirit into the hands of the father . . . he went up to 'the Good' " (26.31–32).

Here, several points need clarification. First, the body called "Eden" is, essentially, the same as the woman to whom Jesus speaks when he ascends. For the text identifies Jesus' psychic and earthly body, that is, his soul, and possibly his material body, with Eden. As soul, Jesus is the son of Eden, who here takes the place of his mother Mary. Shedding his lower element(s), Jesus surrenders his spirit to Elohim, and ascends to "the Good." (It is worth noting how the two, Elohim and "the Good," are kept apart here.) One assumes that Jesus is the first man who has succeeded in imitating Elohim. Whether he has succeeded in making many converts, *Bar.* leaves to the imagination. In any case, the prophets' message seems to have included directions for ascension. By accomplishing his mission, Jesus has effected his own salvation.

Immediately after the story of Jesus' ascent, comes a highly unexpected piece of information: "the Good," it turns out, is no other than the god Priapus, the principle of fertility and procreation. *Bar.* attempts an etymological explanation for this equation: Priapus "created before (Greek: *prin*) anything existed" (26.32); therefore "the Good" carries the name of Priapus because he was the first creator. Revered by everyone, Priapus has his statue in every temple; he is a universal god. The cause of creation, he probably also confirms and guarantees Eden's and Elohim's creation. In stark contrast to the previous judgment of the creation as evil,[17] the tone is again positive, for the god of fruitfulness has no criticism for Eden's and Elohim's activities, and "the Good" has declared that Elohim's plan to destroy his creation would be an evil act (26.18).[18]

Bar. goes on to enumerate several Greek myths (e.g., that of Leda and the swan) as examples of the universal validity and truth of Eden's and Elohim's union. Being allegories, these myths in reality speak of the story of Eden and Elohim. The Old Testament, too, testifies to this universal truth, for *Bar.* next adduces Biblical parallels.

The Old Testament quotations are presented with a slightly different perspective, however, for here the concern is not so much with the actual mating of the two powers as with the spiritual dimension of the union. Moreover, the possibility of mankind's ascension comes into focus. Thus, Isa. 1:2, "Hear, O heaven, and give ear, O earth, for the Lord has spoken," is interpreted as follows: heaven is Elohim's spirit in man; earth is the soul, Eden; the Lord is Baruch.[19] Going to Isa. 1:3, *Bar.* says that the text "Israel did not know me" refers to Eden, "for if she had known that I [i.e., Elohim] am with 'the Good,' she would not have punished the spirit in men because of the paternal departure from thence" (26.37).

The Isaiah exegesis implies that Eden, too, ought to hear the message from the upper world. This would mean that she, as soul, might be eligible for salvation. *Both* heaven and earth are admonished to incline their ears: soul and spirit alike can hear the preaching and, consequently, rise up. Isa. 1:3 shows that Eden did not know of Elohim's goal; now, however, the human soul may possess this saving knowledge. But could Eden have known? Not even Elohim really knew what lay ahead of him at his ascent; his motive had nothing to do with his reward, and his salvation seems almost by chance. One might recall, here, that both powers lack foreknowledge. The conclusion is that the human beings—furnished with both spirit and soul—seem to be vastly better equipped for salvation than either Elohim or Eden. And yet Jesus, although a human being, did not save his soul, but left "Eden" behind!

Paragraph 27 gives a brief, but crucial, account of a ritual to be performed in imitation of Elohim (Jesus is not mentioned any more, whether as a model for ascension, or otherwise). The goal of the mystical ritual is to be "perfected with 'the Good' " (27.1) by swearing an oath. Hippolytos says that Justin does not teach the mystery until "he has bound his dupe by an oath," and the initiate is admonished to "neither . . . publish nor abjure these doctrines."[20] Himself an intruder into secrecies, Hippolytos gives the oath as follows: "I swear by him who is above all things, 'the Good,' to preserve these mysteries and to declare them to no one, neither to turn back from 'the Good' to the creation" (27.2).

Elohim swore this oath, and he, too, kept quiet after beholding "the Good."[21] More importantly, he did not regret having sworn the oath. *Bar.* here adduces Ps. 110:4 as reference: "The Lord has sworn and will not repent" (27.1). In the present setting this verse takes on a particular hue, for the information is given in the context of a mystery-initiation, and the candidates are exhorted not to succumb to doubts or regrets about swearing the oath. The emphasis on repentance shows ambivalence at having abjured earthly life, and having promised to leave one's "Edenic" part behind. Elohim *might* have regretted the oath—he repented his own creation!—but the initiates are not to do so, because their model did not.

The admonition suggests a warning against suspecting a mystery-religion of lacking efficacy. Holding up Elohim as the pattern, *Bar.* states that the oath will cause the initiate, like Elohim before him, to "see what eye has not seen and ear has not heard and has not entered into the heart of man" (27.2).[22] Thus, the ritual has two stages: the oath is the prerequisite for the vision. Next, the initiate performs a kind of "inner baptism"—that is, he drinks from the spiritual waters coming from above the firmament. Elohim, too, undertook this baptism and, the text assures us, did not repent.

This is the second time *Bar.* has stressed Elohim's lack of repentance, so this must be a tricky point as regards the appeal of the mystery. Neither the vow to leave the earth, nor the cleansing, is to be regretted. To emphasize the possibility of regret, however, demonstrates an acute anxiety about the decision to join in the mystery. The chance that one might regret one's membership or, even worse, become an apostate, links up with *Bar.*'s pervasive conflict, or "double-mindedness," regarding the abandonment of earthly life in favor of a spiritual one.

The last of the scriptural exegeses in *Bar.* concerns Hos. 1:2. The line, "to take to himself a wife of harlotry, because the land will go a-whoring from the following of the Lord" (27.4), speaks of the relationship between Eden and Elohim. Unlike the Greek myths referred to in 26.34–35, which spoke of the union of Eden and Elohim in positive terms, the verse from Hosea supports the mystery; that is, it advocates the spiritual life by referring to the defective relationship between God and Israel. The Old Testament references in 26.36–37 had yet another focus: soul and spirit were exhorted to listen to the message from above, and to ascend to "the Good." The Hosea reading offers the most negative exegesis of Eden's and Elohim's relationship. The differences in the use of Greek and Biblical materials show, once more, the ambivalence towards life on earth. The mystery-ritual attempts to solve the conflict, but it is nevertheless performed in a mood of strong ambivalence.

Thus, whatever one chooses, regret may set in; it seems that one cannot pursue both earthly and spiritual life simultaneously. Encouraging spiritual salvation, Justin holds up Elohim, the culprit of the story in *Bar.*, as a model for human insight and ascent. A negative, but redeemed, figure, Elohim seems to mediate between Eden—earth, "of double mind and double body"—and the transcendent "Good," who is, puzzlingly, identified with Priapus. All three powers, then, appear to be complex; none seems to belong clearly to a negative or a positive category.

"The Good."

Perhaps the most perplexing figure of *Bar.* is "the Good." Some scholars have found it well-nigh impossible to accept the identification of "the Good" with Priapus. E. Haenchen, for example, in his introduction to *Bar.*, says that the kingdom of "the Good" ". . . has nothing in the least to do with our world," and the identification of "the Good" with Priapus is an "alien interpolation." Transcendence and procreative power simply cannot be permitted in the same figure. Allowing for the Gnostic predilection for finding cryptic parallels in various mythological traditions (e.g., seeing Eden's and Elohim's marriage expressed in Greek myths), Haenchen nevertheless refuses to accept an other-worldly entity to be represented by a phallus in front of every temple. The identification is "from the basic gnostic point of view nothing short of blasphemy."[23] Undoubtedly, this would be so from Haenchen's viewpoint also.

It seems to me that Haenchen has too rigid a notion of what "gnostic" implies. In Gnosticism, as in other religious traditions, divine entities do not always remain within their spheres, they perform unexpected acts and even carry unfamiliar identifications. But Haenchen observes that " 'the Good' may not intervene in earthly events, since his goodness is not consonant with that";[24] as Priapus, however, "the Good" would appear precisely to interfere constantly on earth. "Goodness" should not be taken in its elevated, metaphysical sense, but rather as the power furnishing bounty on earth. In his earlier article, Haenchen calls "the Good" "peculiarly anemic," compared to Elohim; he also speculates on "the Good's" putative lack of dealings with the world and, not wishing the upper principle to be stained by the world, he defends "the Good's" pure transcendence: "the Good" becomes an otiose deity.[25]

Elohim, Haenchen feels, has impinged on "the Good's" prerogatives, for to impart the "divine" spirit is properly the task of "the Good," not of Elohim. (But *Bar.* does not explicitly call the spirit "divine.") In spite of Haenchen's high regard for "the Good," he surprisingly blames this very principle "for the misfortunes of man."[26] This conclusion is based on the information that "the Good" prevents Elohim from descending to save his spirit in man. Trying to cling to a "pure" image of the upper god, Haenchen is unable to achieve a coherent portrait of this figure. These discrepancies and logical impossibilities in "the Good" should then perhaps be blamed on the Gnostics, who created troubles for subsequent interpreters.

Several commentators on *Bar.* have criticized Haenchen's view of "the

Good." R. M. Grant, for instance, sees the identification of "the Good" with Priapus as positive, for the equation points to the creative powers in the upper principle.[27] (Curiously, in a more recent article Grant completely disavows Priapus, saying that this entity has no place in Justin's story.[28]) A more thorough discussion of Haenchen's interpretation comes from M. Olender: noting that scholars, in general, have resisted the Priapus/"the Good" equation, Olender sees it as one of his tasks to uncover Priapus-texts that may explain the role of Priapus in *Bar.*[29] Olender feels that one cannot simply accuse Hippolytos of absentmindedness when he inserted the identification into his account of Justin's system. Thus, Olender disagrees with Haenchen's interpolation thesis.[30]

Priapus is a god of light and sexual power,[31] and Olender compares him to the Eros figure in the Gnostic text *On the Origin of the World.*[32] He adduces Priapus inscriptions that deserve attention. One of these, dating from the first or second century, hails Priapus as creator of the world, as Nature, and as Pan. Further, Priapus accomplishes his tasks on earth, in heaven, and in the ocean; he is the creative principle of the universe and of the most important gods, Bacchus, Venus, and Jupiter. In light of all this, Olender finds no reason for artificially dividing the transcendent from the lifegiving aspects of "the Good," Priapus.[33]

M. Simonetti, observing the transcendence and unknowability of "the Good," admits that the identification with Priapus fits badly, but he adds that this equation should not cause astonishment; one may expect such things in a Gnostic text, he says.[34] Sounding a sobering note, then, Simonetti allows for otherworldliness and life-affirming exuberance in the same divine figure.

The Relationship of Elohim to
"the Good" and to Eden

As noted, Elohim occupies a peculiar position, filled with tensions. *Bar.* has squarely blamed him for the miseries of mankind following his desertion of Eden. And yet, Elohim becomes a paradigm for salvation. H. Jonas observes Elohim's similarity to the Manichaean Primal Man, who must free and recover his own spirit (pneuma). The same scholar notes the "extraordinary Gnostic significance" of a rehabilitation of the demiurge *precisely because of* this figure's turning toward his own creation.[35] This fits Elohim who, saved from his work below, now resides with "the Good" above. A middle and, seemingly, a mediating being, Elohim makes the dualism explicit and tangibly real.[36] He is the cause of the separations, and he is the first to realize the implications of these; his own trapped spirit perfectly parallels his imprisoned life in the upper world.

Haenchen raises the tricky question of how Elohim could recognize "the Good," of whom he had no previous knowledge.[37] K. Kvideland, for her part, wonders why *Bar.* introduces, as the reason for Elohim's ascent, the inspection of the creation. She sees this as a superfluous addition, for as Elohim's work is completed, his rightful place is above. Kvideland views God's rest on the seventh day (Gen. 2:2) as the rationale for Elohim's ascent: his work as creator is done, and his function is now soteriological. As long as he remained on the creator-stage, he was ineligible for ascension, not equal to "the Good." Now, though, he is perfected, and shows the way for the human spirit.[38]

Haenchen, using blunter words, states that Elohim becomes a savior for egoistical reasons.[39] Kvideland seems less attuned to the dynamics of *Bar.*, to the function of Elohim's ascent in relation to the other characters in the story. The parallel to Gen. 2:2 may be valid, but it is of little help in understanding the complexities surrounding the ascent according to *Bar.* Haenchen notes that evil starts only after Elohim's departure.[40] He does not, however, directly accuse Elohim for the introduction of evil, for he has, as seen above, already decided that "the Good" is the culprit.[41] Grant, on the other hand, concludes: "Evil was not due precisely to Elohim's departure, but to Eden's consequent frustration"[42]—but her agony came about after her husband's ascent, so here again one is confronted with the problem of placing the guilt.

In line with his observations on Eden's troubles, Grant states that man "desires to come to 'the Good,' but in his desire he causes frustrations for others."[43] However, it is not just to others that ascending man causes harm, but also to himself, to his purportedly earth-bound soul. (The repeated assurances of Elohim's lack of regret might be recalled at this point.) Whichever life one chooses, the worldly or the otherworldly, some part of oneself will suffer.

Simonetti outrightly interprets the spirit's—that is, Elohim's—rising as the cause of evil.[44] He supports a somewhat strange exegesis of Elohim, however: stressing Elohim as a degraded divine principle in the material world, and also as a savior, he adopts the view that Elohim descended *in illo tempore*, voluntarily giving up his position with "the Good" in order to unite with Eden! The apparent train of thought—that what goes up must first have come down— does not always, as logical law, hold in Gnostic myth. Simonetti's view becomes problematic when one recalls his statement that evil is due to Elohim's departure. Does this mean that Elohim should not have come down at all? Apparently not, for toward the end of his study Simonetti states that the (postulated) descent is not to be viewed negatively.[45]

Simonetti makes the valuable observation that Elohim utters "I thought I was god" *after* he has ascended, *not*, in the manner of other Gnostic demiurges, while on earth, engaged in creative activities. Concluding that Elohim was simply ignorant, not filled with the hubris of more unsavory creators, Simonetti tries to keep him from disintegrating into too many irreconcilable fragments. He holds Elohim responsible for evil (*contra* Haenchen) and notes that Elohim can be restrained from further evil only by staying with "the Good."[46]

Elohim's relationship with Eden evokes another set of reactions from commenting scholars. R. van den Broek takes note of Justin's favorable view of marriage, a view that accords with Jewish-Christian, Elchasaite, and Mandaean evaluations.[47] Simonetti, too, remarks on the lack of condemnation, finding it significant that Adam and Eve's marriage took place before Elohim's disappearance.[48] Therefore, human as well as divine marriages are approved.

Referring to the angels, Grant concludes that "[p]assion in itself is not evil." And yet, further on, he claims that Baruch wants mankind to give up "marriage and love, which though good are subject to frustration, to the higher heavenly marriage and love to be found with 'the Good.' "[49] It appears to me, however, that *Bar.* (and Baruch!) shows great ambivalence on this point; moreover, there is no hint that the envisioned relation to "the Good" in any way connotes a heavenly marriage. No sexual imagery occurs in the initiation to the mystery in *Bar.* 27.1–2.

Haenchen speaks of Elohim and Eden's marriage as an "apparent harmony" that turns to catastrophe.[50] He concludes his introduction to *Bar.* by reprimanding Hippolytos for neglecting to discern "the weakness that Gnosis betrays precisely in this book: it knows no goal for which life is worth living. One's nearest, and therefore one's love, has not come into sight as such a goal."[51] It depends, of course, on which kind of love Haenchen refers to; *Bar.* treats carnal as well as spiritual love, and is of two minds about both. Haenchen appears to attack *Bar.* for not advocating some other kind of (orthodox) love-ideal. But his argument seems to miss the point: the goal of life is *both* here on earth *and* up above with "the Good."

Simonetti notices the positive, optimistic tone in the description of Elohim and Eden's marriage. To the question of whether Eden could have ascended with Elohim to "the Good," he assumes that the very earth-nature of Eden would have prevented her from doing so. But he also thinks that Eden might have made a conscious choice, for elsewhere he stresses that she may tilt both ways, to good or to evil; she is, originally, a neutral figure.[52] In contrast, G. C. Stead simply states that Eden refused to follow Elohim upwards.[53]

Eden

"As the myth unfolds Eden becomes the source of evil, both physical and moral," Stead judges, referring to the evil committed by Eden's angels.[54] No doubt, the maternal angels do evil, yet their acts are responses to their mother's commands. At some distance, Eden directs the punishments bestowed on the spirit. But *Bar.* 26.23–24, as seen above (p. 9), squarely puts the blame for evil on Elohim for having deserted Eden; by deserting her he has set off a chain reaction of deplorable acts for which he must bear the guilt.

Eden, Simonetti says, is "less complex, but no less ambiguous" than Elohim. She represents the earth in its eschatological aspect. Characterized by doubleness, and comparable to the Sophia figure, she is not, originally, evil or negatively evaluated.[55] Haenchen, voicing stronger opinions, says of Eden that she is "not just nature in its innate vitality, but also the personification of seduction and evil."[56] This seems exaggerated, an imputation to *Bar.* of too much negativity. In like manner, Haenchen can interpret the words of "the Good," "Let Eden have the creation," as the only solution for mankind.[57] And Grant thinks that "Eden is too emotional for her own good, or for the good of mankind";[58] she is to blame for the disorderliness of human existence.

The commenting scholars, then, tend to put Eden in the role of the destructive force, evil's very source. The interpretations wobble, however, because *Bar.* itself gives ambiguous answers to the problem it poses. The marriage of the divine pair turned sour only later, at which point the contract, for all practical purposes, was dissolved. For human beings, the solution is twofold: either to remain ruled by the life on earth, the procreative forces, or to ascend, like Elohim. In either case, one loses something. It is this very insight that so confuses investigators into *Bar.* Instead of definitively equating evil with the earth, and good with the beyond, the text tells us in mythic imagery why such easy answers would be insufficient and dishonest.

Eden is the lower principle, along with Elohim, and like both Elohim and "the Good" she is unbegotten and eternal—and yet she is, more or less automatically, taken to be evil. Is this because she is the only female in the triangle? Scholarly interpreters often appear to side with Hosea, rather than with Priapus. The Priapus figure has, of course, been hard to accept, but I think there is an overlooked link between Eden and Priapus. Both denote fertility: Eden supplied material for human beings and animals, and Priapus is the god of plant and animal life.[59] Olender remarks on the ithyphallic character of Priapus,[60] and here I discern a clue to Eden's shape: the phallic Priapus is akin to the snakelike Eden.

Naas perpetuates his mother's figure, and he, too, possesses a sexual character. Partaking in both good and evil, he influences Adam and Eve to do the same. Only Naas's transgressions, his unnatural sexual acts with the human pair, are repudiated—heterosexual activity between spouses is not. Right after telling of Naas's sin, *Bar.* expressly names Elohim as the origin of good and evil. Elohim's possibly *perverted* spiritual ascent—it was unintended qua ascent, because he knew nothing of "the Good"—depicts the shrinking from earthly responsibilities. Now, he washes his hands, as it were, and wants to destroy all life, in order to save some part of it, his spirit. No wonder that "the Good," Priapus, denies him that outlet.

In a twisted way, Eden, not Elohim, is the one who does effect a sort of destruction. By sending her angel Babel to wreck human marriages, she violently expresses what Elohim has done to her. Elohim's wish to destroy has not been granted; one does not know whether Priapus agrees with Eden's particular form of revenge against her spouse, but it would seem doubtful. Eden's sending of Babel ruins the human marriage-contract, in an exact parallel to Elohim's breach of the divine contract.

All ties between Eden and Elohim appear cut, but they both, in different ways, retain a relationship with "the Good." Elohim *represents the damaged tie between Eden and Priapus*, the procreative elements, and he is to blame for the continuing, imperfect, suffering life on earth. In her revenge, Eden punishes herself, too, and "the Good" can prevent further damage only by forbidding Elohim's descent. Captive, Elohim is unable to intervene on earth; his salvation becomes a prison, a reminder of his failure as a divine husband and his imperfection as shepherd of his own spirit in human beings.

Elohim's regret at having left his spirit below is ironically juxtaposed with the repeated assurances in the mystery-ritual: he did not repent his ascent. But the text itself almost contradicts this. Had Elohim not ascended, he would have had no cause to feel sorrow for his spirit. Having gone upwards, he valiantly assures himself that he does not regret having ascended to "the Good." He keeps quiet,[61] guarding the secrets of the upper realm. In like manner the initiates modeling themselves on Elohim, are sworn to secrecy. The real secret may be that salvation is double-edged; if one ascends, one has lost earthly pleasures and given up the carnal life devoted to Eden and to Priapus; one's spirit will thus be saved, but at a painful cost.

However, to discover, having arrived above, that the procreative power is also the transcendent, ineffable "Good" furnishes the punch line in *Bar.* The human being cannot pursue the life of the earth and that of the spirit simultaneously, but "the Good" is the very cause and condition for *both* kinds of life, effortlessly balancing transcendence and sexual power. Only the foreknowledgeable "Good" knows how to perform this task, which seems beyond the capacities of mankind. Once above, the human being may realize the truth of "the Good's" doubleness, but it is then impossible to put this knowledge into practice on an earthly level. Perhaps the reward for entering the mystery is precisely this insight. The silence of the initiate may indicate not only guarded secrets, but amazement, for the paradoxical identity of "the Good" is inexpressible.

Appearing in two (as it seems) diametrically opposed worlds, "the Good" is not diminished by its procreative facet on earth. Nor does the transcendent character of "the Good" deny the life-affirming, earthly one. The divine principle, beyond gains or losses, does not appear impoverished on earth and perfect up above, but constitutes the very reason for life in both realms.

The link between "the Good" and Eden remains undisclosed to outsiders, to those uninitiated into the mystery. That the highest principle, "the Good," maintains a positive connection with the lower, female entity demonstrates a constellation found in Mandaeism, where Ruha, personified spirit and personified earth, makes up the element required for human life. Because the upper principle—in Mandaeism, it is the Lightworld—remains, ultimately, responsible for the creation of earth and of the human being, the presence of the spiritual, female entity is not categorically condemned. Like Eden, Ruha is an ambiguous figure but a necessary component in the scheme of creation, its maintenance and development.

CHAPTER 2

The Salvation of
the Spirit Ruha in
Mandaean Religion

INTRODUCTION

Mandaeism differs from many other Gnostic traditions: it has a vast literature (in an East Aramaic dialect), its complicated cultic systems correlate with a rich mythology, and its proponents live today, as their ancestors did, along the rivers and waterways of southern Iraq and Khuzistan, Iran. *Manda* means "knowledge," and so the Mandaeans are Gnostics who call themselves "the knowledgeable ones" (they are known as *Ṣubbi,* "baptisers," to outsiders). The religion is characterized by a framework of dualism: good and evil, light and darkness, male and female, right and left. These entities stand in opposition to one another, and yet intertwine and cooperate; human beings, as well as figures in the Mandaean mythology, may thus be composites, possessing both positive and negative traits.

One Mandaean mythological female figure, Ruha ("Spirit"),[1] has long been viewed as completely evil. Citing passages from Mandaean texts, scholars generally interpret this figure as a leader of the dark forces opposed to the Lightworld and its envoys.[2] It is certainly true that Ruha, at times called Ruha *d*-Qudša, seems like a devalued Holy Spirit: she is the mother of the evil planets and of the zodiac-spirits, as well as the consort of the negatively evaluated Adonai. In some of the Mandaean creation accounts Ruha tempts and leads astray the ambiguous demiurge Ptahil, and she also endangers the earthly human being who lives under Ruha's encroaching rule.

A considerable number of Mandaean tractates do, however, present a much more complex, and even positive, picture of Ruha. In these she resembles a fallen Wisdom-figure, wobbling between Light and Darkness, and on occasion uttering proclamations and revelations unsuitable for an evil being. In *The Canonical Prayerbook of the Mandaeans* (*CP*), for instance, one finds Ruha crying, "My Father, my Father, why didst thou create me? My God, my God, my Allah, why hast thou set me afar off and cut me off and left me in the depths of the earth and in the nether glooms of darkness so that I have no strength to rise up thither?"[3] This passage evokes both Ps. 22:1–2 and Jesus' last words on the cross. At least one surprised scholar has wondered whether the words are meant maliciously;[4] another has called the "distortion" of the words on the cross "spiteful."[5] But in the Mandaean context the words are Ruha's own, and they appear as part of a lengthy hymn recited by Mandaean priests. In this text, the evil powers—including Ruha—are overcome by the Lightworld, to which they immediately offer praise. Ruha's utterance thus, in some sense, suits the context. But the problem remains: what is the significance of an allegedly evil figure yearning for liberation? And what is the possible legitimacy of this yearning?

The ambiguous figure Ruha is paralleled by the middle component—spirit, *ruha*—in the human being. Situated between body and soul, the spirit, always regarded as female, wavers between good and evil, between higher and lower instincts. The two upper elements, soul and spirit, are imaged as siblings, and they abide only temporarily in the body; at the body's death, the two are supposed to leave the material part behind.[6] It is important to note that the soul cannot ascend to the Lightworld alone; it needs the companionship of the spirit, its "sister." Because of the spirit's wobbly nature, however, a successful ascent for the two upper components is far from assured.

The joining of spirit and soul is the primary aim of the Mandaean death-mass (*masiqta*), a ceremony carried out, from ancient times to the present day, for every newly deceased Mandaean. Both spirit and soul are necessary for the creation of a new, Lightworld body (*'uṣtuna*) for the deceased. Only the priests, the religious elite, who embody the Lightworld beings (*'utria*) on earth, are capable of piloting the spirit and soul up through the planetary spheres to the Lightworld, and only they are able to establish the conditions for a new creation of a "heavenly" body.

The salvation of the spirit, then, can be discerned on two levels in Mandaeism: the *masiqta* aims at joining spirit and soul in such a fashion that the spirit acquires the nature of the soul, and the mythological figure Ruha, too, seems ultimately eligible for salvation. Here one should note the tripartite schema, for the ambiguous Ruha wavers between good and evil as does the human component by the same name. Tripartite models, generally, allow for more movement and dynamic than do static, dualistic ones where two opposed principles have no clearly stated mediating element. Ruha and *ruha*, then, both "betwixt and between," are situated in the middle, and may tilt either to good or to evil. However, the mythology of Ruha, as well as the ritual of the *masiqta* that centers on the joining of soul and spirit, can be shown to support the thesis of an ultimate salvation for both spirit entities.

THE MYTHOLOGICAL FIGURE RUHA

GR 5.1 tells of a Lightworld envoy, Hibil-Ziwa ("Light-Hibil"), who journeys to the underworld, the world of Darkness, before the creation of the earthly world, Tibil (*GR* 5.1, pp. 150f.). Certain rumors have reached the Lightworld: it seems that the underworld aspires to wage war with the Lightworld, and Hibil is sent out on reconnaissance to try to prevent such an attack. A long, complex story of Hibil's experiences and feats in the underworld follows; however, I see this part of the account as partially covering up the underlying message in the tractate, for what at first seems a side issue turns out to be a most important part of the story—namely, the part concerning Ruha.

In the first underworld (there are seven) Hibil finds Ruha, but the text says nothing about how she arrived here, or whether the underworld is, in fact, her true home. Hibil promises Ruha that he will take her to her parents; this must mean that her underworld parents are not her real parents. Taking Ruha upwards, out of the darkness, Hibil encloses her in a world between darkness and the world to come, the earthly world. Here, in limbo, Ruha utters Sophia-like complaints, and eventually gives birth to the monster 'Ur. Mother and son spend myriads of years trying to escape their prison, while Hibil, seemingly detached, visits them now and then.

One text explains why Ruha, at this stage, is unfit to ascend to the promised parents: "[Hibil speaks] 'How can we rise up towards my Parents when the creatures that I brought are not like Us, nor is their appearance like that of the 'uthras, the children of Light? My Parents will not now desire to have them in Their presence!' "[7] It is worth noting that this text assumes Hibil's and Ruha's common parentage. Other tractates refer, in a more or less veiled fashion, to Ruha as a potent element, who seems to incorporate the powers of the underworld.[8] Thus, *she* embodies the underworld power that the Lightworld sought to conquer. At the same time, Ruha appears, ultimately, to belong to the Lightworld proper.

Ruha's son 'Ur wants to fight against the Lightworld, but his mother advises him to attack the underworld instead![9] Hibil defeats 'Ur, and reassures Ruha that he, Hibil, has come to destroy 'Ur only (*GR* 5.1, p. 173.16–17). Obviously, Ruha has been brought up from the darkness for some crucial purpose, for why else would a Lightworld envoy liberate a purportedly evil figure?

Embodying the powers of darkness, Ruha, it turns out, is going to furnish the earthly realm as well as the human being with her spirit element, the life-force. This is why she has been removed from the darkness.

GR 3 offers a long and entertaining description of the relationship between Ruha and the unsuccessful Mandaean demiurge Ptahil (*GR* 3, p. 98.22ff.). Pitted as opponents, these two are uneasy coworkers, each one striving for control over the creation. It is not only Ptahil who is troubled by his first, failed attempt at creating (*GR* 3, p. 100.1–7)—Ruha, too, is disappointed at the ungainly offspring she bears to her son 'Ur: the zodiac-spirits and the evil planets (*GR* 3, pp. 99.23–28 and 101.2–5).

Ptahil and the planets create Adam, but he remains lifeless. According to one text, a soul from the Lightworld then enters Adam, but this soul is accompanied by "the Evil Spirit" (*ATŠ*, pp. 215–16).[10] This spirit is responsible for introducing deceit and falsehood into the body. There is a significant reason for allowing this to happen: the soul is not supposed to dominate the spirit (ibid.). Elsewhere, the text voices the tripartite schema in this way: "For when the Body was formed, a Soul (*nishimta*) was formed, and when the Soul took shape in the Body, the Body formed the Vital Spirit (*ruha*)" (*ATŠ*, p. 164 [218]).

In *GR* 10, after Ptahil has succeeded in creating the world, he creates Adam after his own image and Hawwa (Eve) after Adam's image (*GR* 10, p. 242.26–27). Here Ruha does not figure independently, but Ptahil injects his own spirit (*ruha*) element into Adam. In an alternative account, Ptahil declares to Ruha that he will ". . . form my image as man and your image as woman. We shall call the man Adam and the woman Hawwa" (*GR* 11, p. 266.20–22). That Ruha is found worthy as a pattern for the creation of Hawwa is highly significant; it indicates a clearly positive view of woman, earthly life, and marriage. This evaluation is characteristic of Mandaeism to the present day.[11]

Ruha's role as revealer comes through in an episode in which Adam bar Adam, a son of the first man, is seduced by Ruha and her planets, Ruha having disguised herself as his wife/sister Hawwa. Surprisingly, Ruha reveals to him the necessity for the separation of the sexes, saying, "If there were no unevenness, then we would have only one nature . . . and they would have created us as one *Mana*. But, as unevenness exists, they have made you a man and me a woman" (*GR* 3, p. 130.5–14; *Mana* means "vessel" or "garment"). Here the temptress is the revealer who informs that the original imbalance—perhaps present even in the Lightworld—explains the creation of the two distinct sexes.

The relationship between the sexes is portrayed in *ATŠ* as well. Here the mythological imagery is more florid; earth represents the female, Jordan (i.e., running water), the male.

> For Earth called Jordan (living water) "My Father" when its mysteries fell into her. And she cried aloud to Jordan "Do not penetrate me" and said to it "Answer me, my father, answer me" and "Raise me up, (O) great Son of the Mighty (Life), father of a son of Life!" And then the jordan spoke: it cried aloud with its voice, and came and clothed all her mysteries, covering her aridities with green foliage. And her baser mysteries he drew upwards, he steadied her babbling tongues, cleared her vision and turned the spheres. (*ATŠ*, p. 173 [243])

Elsewhere, *ATŠ* explicitly identifies Ruha with earth:

> For Earth is a spirit (or Ruha), which holdeth and entangleth all mysteries and any being who doth not seek to depart from her. . . . This is the Earth of the Parents: She raised up physical life and she is the Great Mother, from whom all swarming creatures, burgeonings and increase proceeded and (by her) were maintained. (*ATŠ*, p. 239 [137])

According to an as yet unpublished manuscript, *Diwan malkuta ʿlaita*, the candidates for priesthood, though having been "nurtured in the lap of Ruha," have for their father the Pure Ether in the Lightworld.[12] The candidates exhort, "Woe to those who . . . did not turn away from Earth, nor came forth from within their Mother."[13] Priests are said to have passed from the Mother, the earth, to the Father, the Lightworld, even while they paradoxically remain on earth fulfilling their duties to the Mandaean community.

Ruha, like the human spirit component, wobbles between her present status and her envisioned one. For the time being, however, she is earth, and rules earth, the middle world between darkness and Lightworld. In her dealings with Mandaean saviors and envoys from the Lightworld one discerns, again, her capricious and ambiguous nature. For example, when Ruha and her seven sons, the planets, wish to erect the city Jerusalem, the Lightworld sends its ambassador, Anoš-ʿUtra, to foil Ruha's plans (*GR* 15.11, pp. 336f.). The city built, and the Jews, Ruha's followers, thriving, Anoš appears in the city and wins converts to Mandaeism. A battle ensues, and Anoš declares that he will destroy Jerusalem. Ruha pleads with him, but then, suddenly, she turns against her subjects and offers to help Anoš instead: "Please, give me permission; I will bring down the gates of the walls upon them [the Jews] so that they die on the spot. The Jews who sinned against your disciples shall be killed" (*GR* 15.11, p. 342.35–39). Anoš accepts no such offer from a former adversary, and he successfully puts an end to Jerusalem, singlehandedly.

This unexpected turnaround demonstrates Ruha's inner knowledge that the Lightworld has legitimate claims. In another text, a prayer recited daily by Mandaean priests, Ruha addresses herself to the Lightworld messenger:

"Thou camest from the House of Good Beings. (O) would that Thou hadst not come into corruption. Into the evil and falsity of this world! Would that Thou hadst not come into corruption. And hadst not been seen by my eyes!" [The Light-being answers] "If verily I came, if verily I appeared, Thine eyes are eyes of falsehood, Whilst my eyes are eyes of truth. Lying eyes are darkened utterly. If thou wishest to see, Ruha, Go to the house of him who knoweth Me, Those who know Me, For I dwell amongst them, In the hearts of my friends, And the thoughts of my disciples." (*CP*, p. 123[14])

Bewailing the bad luck of the envoy, Ruha apparently wishes that the salvific knowledge had remained hidden to her. Ambivalent, she is at once attracted to the messenger, and wishes that she had not realized the implications of his message. In another text, Ruha has requested gnosis from the Lightworld, but her wish has not been granted.[15] Another tractate of the same book, however, says that Hibil has given Ruha salvific instruction, and this act, seen as a betrayal, has caused dissent in the Lightworld (*JB*, p. 15).

Ruha expresses insights and longings that one does not associate with thoroughly devilish beings in Gnostic mythologies. The Lightworld's motive for instructing her, and the solution to the question of whether she is, indeed, a worthy recipient, are now closer at hand. Ruha does, it seems, belong to the Lightworld; like a malfunctioning Gnostic on earth, she remains turned, however ambivalently, toward her legitimate home on high.

Ruha's self-revelations and her identifications with female Light-beings demonstrate her real identity. In an unusual text—*GR* 6, the *Book of Dinanukht*—one finds a composite being, half book, half human, who reads in himself (*GR* 6, p. 206.11f.).[16] This being, Dinanukht, is approached by another book, Disai, who speaks unsettling, prophetic words. Attempting to destroy Disai, Dinanukht twice fails, and then leaves the disturbing little book alone. Next, Dinanukht falls asleep, and has the following vision:

Then came Ewath, the Holy Spirit, to me in my *škina* ["dwelling"] and says to me, "Why are you lying there, Dinanukht? Why do you like to sleep? I am the life that was from the beginning, I am the Kušṭa ["Truth"], which was even earlier in the beginning. I am the radiance, I am the light. I am death, I am life. I am darkness, I am light. I am error, I am truth. I am destruction, I am construction. I am blow, I am healing. I am an elevated man, who is older and who was there before the builder of the heaven and the earth. I have no peers among kings and there is yet no crown in my kingdom. There is not a single human being who could give me a message in the foggy clouds of darkness." (*GR* 6, p. 207.32–42)

Ewath is Ruha, whose words have already been uttered, in part, by Diṣai. Diṣai left out the proclamative "I am" phrases, but otherwise the book supports Ruha's assertions. The dichotomies in Ruha's revelation defy any simple philosophical principle of contradiction.

Immediately after this proclamation, Dinanukht is taken to the upper worlds, where he proceeds through the purgatories (*maṭarata*). The third one, he discovers, is Ruha's abode, and here she is revealed as a demonic seductress (*GR* 6, p. 219.9–10). In the last purgatory, the House of Abatur, Dinanukht sees "the Life that was from the beginning . . ." as described by Ewath/Ruha in the earlier dream (*GR* 6, p. 207.32–40). Abatur's house is the storage place for the opposed elements mentioned by Ruha; it is also the realm of preexistent souls not yet sent down to earth.

Wishing to ascend even further, Dinanukht is disappointed to hear that this is impossible because he must return to earth to preach his vision (*GR* 6, p. 211.20–21). Back down below, tainted by insanity, he behaves strangely, but carries out his duty.

In this text Ruha appears in a variety of places. First, Diṣai proclaimed the dichotomies, and Ruha turned out to *be* these opposed principles. In another guise, Ruha was found in the third *maṭarta,* and then, in oppositional form, she appeared in the House of Abatur, on the threshold of the Lightworld. The message is thus present on various levels, in a variety of fashions, but *one* personage incorporates these composites.

The Book of John (*JB*) testifies to the image of Ruha on the edge of the Lightworld. Under the name Kanath-Niṭufta, Ruha waits for her liberation into the Light. She has come up from the underworld, approaching the savior Manda *d*-Hiia ("Knowledge-of-Life"):

Kanath-Niṭufta sat for sixty-two years at the outer wall until the scent of Life settled, and a messenger came to her, saying, "Arise, arise, Kanath-Niṭufta, you whom Life has constructed and created. Arise, Barath-Niṭufta, whom the Life has heartily loved. Arise, Pirṣath-Niṭufta, and ascend to your father. Arise, Šarrath-Niṭufta, and become a support for the Life. Arise, Pearl-Niṭufta, you pure pearl, whom Life loves and for whom it became a creator. Arise, Simat-Haije-Niṭufta, whom the great Planter has created." (*JB*, p. 228.11–20)

Mythologically, this section links up with *GR* 5.1, where Hibil left Ruha in the middle world, before the creation of the earth (*GR* 5.1, p. 163.10; see p. 22, above). Now, Ruha has come further, and she is invited to ascend, having found favor with the Lightworld and its envoys.

Another text, *Diwan Abatur* (*Diw. Ab.*), gives several names for Ruha, of which one is Niṭufta and another Simat,[17] as in *JB* (p. 228.11–20). Simat is the name of the female counterpart of the Great Life in the Lightworld. In both *Diw. Ab.* and *ATŠ* (p. 211) Ruha is also identified with Qin, her "mother" in the underworld.[18] It is significant that Ruha can be equated both with the highest mythological female figure, Simat, and with the lowest one, Qin. She spans both worlds, and everything in between. Therefore, she may have two "mothers," diametrically opposed. Depending on the realm in which Ruha appears, she may carry a "dark" or a "light" name.

ATŠ mentions the perverted "sign of the left" as that of Ruha (*ATŠ*, pp. 138–39 [107]), the opposite of the sign of the right used by Mandaean priests in religious rituals. This information can be linked with another *ATŠ* text:

> Behold, Light and Darkness are brothers. They proceed from one Mystery and the Body (*'uṣṭuna*) retaineth both and for each sign in the body (*pagra*) there is a corresponding sign belonging to the Darkness. Were it not marked with the mark of Darkness, it would not be established, nor come forward for baptism and be signed with the Sign of Life [the sign of the right].[19]

Importantly, the deficient sign of the left, that of the spirit, is no less than *the* prerequisite for final eligibility for the Lightworld, to which belongs the sign of the right.[20] This thought, eminently applicable to Ruha's own situation as middle element and earth, expresses that it is necessary to live the earthly, material life for one's allotted time.

In *Diw. Ab.* Hibil declares that "Ruha and all her creatures are brought into complete subjection and the seal of Life hath been placed upon them" (*Diw. Ab.*, p. 19).[21] The so-called "evil" beings have been redeemed. In a related vein, *CP* speaks of the blessing bestowed on human beings who correctly commemorate their dead. This blessing is compared to that given to Simat-Hiia, that is, Ruha: "Simat-Hiia was blessed when she arose . . . (And) came from the worlds of darkness" (*CP*, p. 279).[22] However, her liberator, Hibil, remains impure because he has been tainted by the underworld. Baptised, he is, nevertheless, "(still imbued with) the hue of darkness *until Simat-Hiia arose*" (*CP*, p. 281 [my emphasis]). Moreover, Simat blesses Hibil! (ibid.). Even the Lightworld envoy cannot be restored to his previous position until

Ruha/Simat is fully redeemed; the upper world depends on the lower one for its own restoration. Finally, the *'utria* are said to raise Simat to the Lightworld (ibid.).

As a last piece of evidence, one might recall Ruha's complaint in *CP* 75[23] (see above, p. 21): this lament reminds us of the last part of Ruha's revelation in *GR* 6, which portrays her as still stranded in isolation (*GR* 6, p. 207.32–42). *CP* 75 is the only clue we have to any "fall" of Ruha's, to any image resembling the "fallen Sophia" traditions in other Gnostic texts. The lament, "Why hast thou set me afar off and cut me off and left me in the depths of the earth and in the nether glooms of darkness," implies that the Lightworld at some point expelled Ruha. The reason is never clearly given, but the expulsion must have been necessary so that she could accomplish her tasks in the world-to-be, the earth. But she spans all three worlds, and was at first sent to the very bottom, the underworld, from which she ascended to form the conditions for the earthly creation; for earth is, as noted, Ruha herself. Her final absolution, her redemption from her own confinement as earth, is at least a feeble attempt at an answer to Ruha's agonizing question. A fully adequate reply is, however, never supplied.

Scholars have had much trouble with the positive, and positively ambiguous, statements pertaining to Ruha.[24] Both E. S. Drower[25] and K. Rudolph[26] tend to view Ruha in the underworld (in the *CP* passage) as an allegory of the imprisoned soul. However, these judgments ignore that the issue is the liberation of the spirit, not of the soul. With respect to both *CP* and *JB* it is necessary to take into account that the earthly world—as a putative prison for the soul—is not yet created! Accustomed to associating any jailed component with a soul element, scholars ought first to consult the text to see whether there may be components other than a "soul" that might be in need of salvation.

Settings in which Ruha appears include: underworld (from which she is rescued), earth (which she impersonates and to which she gives her spirit-life), the *maṭarata*, and, finally, the Lightworld itself. As a boundary-breaking revealer, she reveals her identifications with female Light-beings. All-present, and still elusive, she shows up in all realms, now suffering, now elevated above all definitions. As mythological figure and as component in the human being, she plays her most important role in the earthly, human realm.

The earth, however, has its own higher image, with which it will eventually merge. Like Ruha, who is identified with Simat, the earth, Tibil, possesses its *dmuta* ("ideal counterpart") in the upper world of *Mšunia Kušṭa*.[27] This realm—"geographically" a part of the Lightworld—is the blueprint for the earthly world. If the earth is female, one could perhaps see Mšunia Kušṭa as male, for this upper world was created by the Lightworld fathers, and is untainted by any interference from the lower, demonic forces (*Diw. Ab.*, pp. 13–14). Everything and everybody has an ideal counterpart in this pure world.

The *dmuta* expresses, moreover, the paradoxical fact that entities may show themselves as both good and evil, may possess both higher and lower characteristics. Not only human beings, but also defective Lightworld beings[28]— Ruha among them—have their upper images in Mšunia Kušta. The *dmuta* furnishes a solution to the static, dualistic model: it lends a dynamic feature to Mandaean mythological thought as well as to the anthropological speculations. The wide scope of activities of a figure like Ruha can be understood in light of the *dmuta*, because this higher image is the very condition for Ruha's varied appearances and activities in the different worlds. All these varieties are bound together in *one* identity, the *dmuta*.

Of course, one consequence of this idea is that it becomes impossible to predict the behavior and the "moral" character of any figure appearing in the lower worlds. Accustomed to the dualistic doctrine in Gnosticism, students of the vacillating Ruha-figure might be apt to despair at such indefinite possibilities for roles. As an alternative to rigid dualism, however, the idea of the *dmuta* is instructive precisely because it allows for the often observed, but rarely appreciated, variations within a single figure in Gnostic mythology. Definite designations like "good" or "evil" become, then, subject to the law of transitoriness. Particularly with respect to the middle beings—creators and defective Light-beings—the *dmuta* idea furnishes new insights. Early on, H. Jonas made the shrewd observation that "what the middle beings were to 'mediate,' was exactly the realization of otherwise merely abstract dualism."[29] About Gnostic creators in general, Jonas comments, "The basic thought of atonement for the demiurgic entity—precisely because of his bent towards creation—is of extraordinary (Gnostic) significance."[30]

It would seem that the ultimate redemption for demiurges and other devalued figures in Gnostic mythology expresses something entirely different from "cheap," mythological solutions. Ultimately positively evaluated, everything and everyone appearing in the lower worlds is eligible for final salvation. The idea of the *dmuta* furnishes, in Mandaeism, the clue to an understanding of a dualism which, *without* an all-encompassing image like the ideal counterpart, would remain totally abstract and purely metaphysical.

To strike a final note in this section, one may contemplate a little-noticed remark of Drower's about Ruha: the negative judgments of Ruha have, more often than not, been based on her equation with Ruha *d*-Qudša, a devalued "Holy Spirit." This derogatory title for the spirit never occurs in the Mandaean sources of the most esoteric type, but mainly in the polemical tractates.[31] The esoteric literature—that is, to a large extent, the ritual texts—is uninterested in the evil Ruha, being much more concerned with her possible salvation in the form of the human spirit, *ruha*.

THE SALVATION OF THE SPIRIT, *RUHA*,
IN THE HUMAN BEING

It is not only the mythological figure Ruha who awaits salvation into the Lightworld: her counterpart, *ruha*, in the human being also anticipates its elevation into the beyond. Parallel to the mythological concern for Ruha's liberation, one finds the same, but much more central, interest in *ruha* in the Mandaean *masiqta* ("raising up"), the mass for the dead. At the death of the body it is the Mandaean priests' obligation to try to save the spirit along with the soul. Drower explains the *masiqta* as follows:

> The *masiqta* ("raising") affects the two non-material parts of a human being which survive death; the *nishimta* and the *ruha*. The *nishimta* . . . is pre-existent and when destiny attached it to its earthly partners, the *ruha* (spirit) and the *pagra* (body), it associates with them reluctantly and yearns for its home in the "world of light." The *pagra* dies and is integrated back into mother earth. The *ruha* is . . . swayed by emotion and strongly affected by bodily instincts and yet is drawn upwards by the *nishimta*. After purification in the after-life, the *ruha*, which is still linked to the *nishimta*, unites with it . . . and they rise "as one" into the "ether-world" or "world of light."[32]

Because the body cannot rise, the *masiqta* focuses on the two upper elements. The goal of the *masiqta* is fourfold: to join the spirit with the soul, to create a Lightworld body (*'uṣṭuna*) for this joined entity, to incorporate the newly deceased Mandaean into the community of ancestors in the Lightworld, and to assure that the living and the dead remain in communion.

Thus, the *masiqta* is carried out for every Mandaean community-member, and it is the priests, the religious specialists, who perform the ritual. The main part of the *masiqta* remains hidden to the laity and other outsiders. This rule illuminates the idea, previously noted, that the priests have already passed from the Mother to the Father[33]—that is, the priests are, indeed, *'utria* on earth, and they alone are capable of piloting the soul and spirit upwards through the hostile planetary spheres, *maṭarata*, into the Lightworld.

There are several kinds of *masqata* (pl. of *masiqta*); here, however, I will present only a very brief account of the most secret[34] part of the ritual proceedings, those that pertain especially to the joining of soul and spirit.

Elaborate preparations are required for the *masiqta*, starting the day before the ritual proper. On the day of the main ritual, the celebrants—a varying number of priests—start to impersonate the dead person and to utter prayers in his name.[35] Before the priests retire into the cult-hut, *mandi*, where the secret ritual takes place, there is an important sacrifice, which must be performed in public:[36] a priest and his helper, *šganda*, kill and prepare a dove, called *Ba*. As he is killing it, the priest tells the dove that it will rise with the soul,[37] for the dove symbolizes the spirit.

Part of the dove's meat is shredded and put on the *tariania*, the trays that are required for the ritual, one for each celebrant. These trays contain, in addition to the dove-meat: a certain number of *fatiria*—that is, small, half-baked, saltless biscuits, the total of which must be sixty; a small water-bottle; a cup of sesame oil, *miša*; a drinking bowl containing four raisins mixed with pounded dates; shreds of quince, grape seeds, pomegranate, date, coconut, almond, walnut, citrus; and a myrtle twig. The food *tariana* represents the spirit, and is placed in front of each priest, to his left; to the right, symbolizing the soul, stands another tray, which holds fuel, a fire-basin, and incense.[38] The priests, fully clothed in ritual garb, start the ritual and remain hidden inside the *mandi* until the end of the *masiqta*.

Throughout the lengthy and complex proceedings, the prayers express the envisioned goal of the ritual; they also speak of the performed action, so that words and action mutually reinforce one another. In addition there are ritual commentaries that explain the effects of the combined words and action—for example, "When you do action A, and say sentence X in prayer Y, the effect on the soul and spirit is Z." Thus, the *masiqta* can be interpreted on several levels, and these levels may be read in parallel so that a full picture of the proceedings emerges.

First, water is poured from the water-bottle into the drinking bowl, and the raisins are mashed into the water. While doing this, each priest recites the second *masiqta*-prayer, *CP* 33. The water cleanses sins, and the prayer likens the water poured on the raisins to rain fertilizing the earth.[39] Next, incense is wafted onto the *tariana* holding the foodstuffs, and this signifies the pleasant odor of the Lightworld enveloping the earthly elements. One must remember, however, that even though these are earthly, they will, in fact, ascend. *CP* 35 here includes the words, "(*though*) spirits and souls sit (*here*) as guilty, (*yet*) . . . they shall rise as innocent" (*CP*, p. 36).

During the recitation of specific words in *CP* 75, "spirit and soul are estranged from hatred, envy, dissension and evil thought" (*ATŠ*, p. 241 [144]). At the end of this prayer, "soul and spirit take hands and are heartened" (ibid.). A formula in *CP* 9 has this effect: "the spirit moveth towards the soul and saith

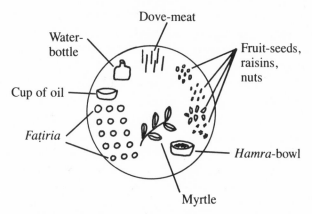

(Adapted from E. S. Drower, *Water into Wine*
[London: Murray, 1956], p. 250)

to her, rejoicing, 'By thy life, my sister in Kušṭa, this is my day of days! Mine eyes are no longer dazzled and fleshly sloth is removed from my heart" (ibid. [146]).

(One notes that here the spirit calls the soul her "sister." The two are often thought of as brother and sister. In *GL* 3, for instance, the spirit says, "By your life, my sister, bring me with you when you ascend"; referring to the spirit as "my brother," the soul at first refuses, calling the spirit "a lying spirit," but later gives in, to the spirit's great joy and relief—and the two are successfully brought together in the upper world.[40])

The priest, who has been wafting incense onto the left *ṭariana*, has also held a myrtle twig in his left hand. He now twists this into a tiny wreath, *klila*. The *šganda* gives him a piece of dough, *pihta*, and eight *pihta*-prayers ensue. The first of these "open[s] the great Door of nourishment to the soul and spirit" (*ATŠ*, p. 242 [148]). Significantly, the eight prayers "[represent] the eight months in which an infant is formed in the womb" (*ARR*, p. 16); this clearly refers to the envisioned rebirth of soul and spirit in the Lightworld.

The priest next "fertilizes" the water-and-raisin mixture, *hamra* or *mambuha*, by dipping his priestly ring, Šum Yawar Ziwa,[41] into it. A commentary on one of the *mambuha*-prayers, *CP* 45, stresses that the "mingling (seasoning) hath taken place" *in* the priests as personifying the deceased, *through* them as celebrants, and *in* the spirit and soul themselves (*ATŠ*, p. 243 [152]; my emphasis); thus, the effect is triple and we have here a trivocal symbolic act. After this, the *klila*-prayers are said to interweave soul and spirit (ibid. [153]).

Now comes the most crucial part of the *masiqta*, the recital of the long prayer, *CP* 49 (*CP*, pp. 43–46). The priest puts down *klila* and *pihta* on the *tariana* and starts to pray, "This, the glory and light of life, is to bring forth the spirit and soul from the body and to clothe the living soul in a living garment" (*CP*, p. 43). The prayer mentions Ṣauriel, the angel of Death, who releases the spirit and soul from the dead body.[42] Spirit and soul are now put to the ultimate test: they are weighed in the scales of Abatur (*CP* 49, p. 45), who reigns in the *matarta* on the threshold of the Lightworld and "weighs works and wages. He weighs and joins the spirit with the soul. Whoever shows himself worthy in weight is carried aloft and a support is secured for him in the Life" (*GL* 1.4, p. 451.25–29).[43]

During the recitation of *CP* 49, the priest folds the *pihta* around the *klila*, but he does not let the two ends of the dough-fragment meet. This act is called "clothing the wreath."[44] Holding aloft the *klila* so arranged in his left hand, the priest, using his right hand, puts on each *fatira*, one at a time, a piece of each kind of fruit, seed, and nut from the *tariana*. He also includes a shred of the *Ba*. Each *fatira* thus treated becomes a *qina*, an "arrangement."[45] Now the priest signs each *fatira* with the sesame oil, the *miša*, making three passes over the biscuit, moving from left to right.[46]

Meticulous rules apply to this procedure. The oil-signings must be performed at particular phrases in *CP* 49, not randomly. If the signings are done correctly, among their effects is that "the eyes of the soul turn towards and gaze at the spirit, and she reacheth her hand towards her and embraceth her with all her strength" (*ATŠ*, p. 244 [154]). This particular effect comes about at the words, "the spirit of N. hath gone and become of (*the same*) nature as the soul."[47]

All allotted prayers and passes must be performed for all *fatiria*.[48] The completed *fatiria*, or *qinata*, are then stacked up in a heap. After more prayers, the *klila* and *pihta* are separated and the wreath is put down on the heap of *fatiria*.[49] According to *ATŠ*, the wreath is "an inner heart situated in the breast" (*ATŠ*, p. 246 [166]). This exegesis associates *Ba* and *klila*, for the breast of the *Ba*, the dove, supplied the meat for the *fatiria* ritual, and both *Ba* and *klila* are spirit-symbols.

The *pihta* and *klila* are now detached, and the priest breaks off a part of the top and bottom *fatiria* in the heap (*ARR*, p. 18). This breaking off is called "the mouth which ye opened for the soul" (*ATŠ*, p. 246 [166]). Then, the two biscuit-pieces together with a slice of the *Ba* are pressed into the *pihta*, which is folded up. Next, water is poured from the bottle into the *mambuha*: this signifies the "union of the cosmic Father and Mother . . . a mingling of water and wine."[50] The bowl has now become "the Divine Womb."[51] Dipping the folded-up *pihta* into the water and "wine" mixture, the priest accomplishes this: "spirit, soul and body are firmly integrated and ye have girt them with a single girdle" (*ATŠ*, pp. 246–47 [166–67]). The priest then swallows the moist *pihta whole* and drinks the *hamra* as well as the *hamra*-bowl's rinsing-water, which is provided by the *šganda*. Other prayers and hymns ensue and the priests conclude by offering one another the ritual handshake, *kušṭa*, saying, "May *Kušṭa* strengthen you, my brother-ʿuthras! The living have been joined in communion, just as ʿuthras in their *skintas* are joined in communion!" (*ARR*, p. 21).

There follows immediately a second part of the *masiqta*, in which six separate *faṭiria* are treated in much the same manner as the previous sixty. The entire ritual is repeated with a few notable changes—most importantly, avoidance of oil-signs at specific phrases in *CP* 49, 51, and 52.[52] The dangerous words, at which the priests must be careful not to sign, refer to the spirit. In these prayers the expression *ma d-bh* (pronounced "ma de-ba"), "that which is with her," refers to the spirit (the spirit is "with her," that is, with the soul). The pun—bh pronounced ba—allows the intimation of the spirit without directly naming it.

ATŠ warns, "if thou makest a 'pass' at the 'that which is with her,' thou neglectest (*dost pass by*) the soul" (*ATŠ*, p. 246 [163–64]).[53] The point here is that the proceedings must not halt the soul on the spirit's level, because the goal of joining soul and spirit would then be hampered and the spirit would not attain to the level of the soul.[54]

ARR explains the necessity of "the *masiqta* of the sixty" and the separate treatment of the six *faṭiria*: "For these sixty . . . keep the (*unborn*) babe safe: thirty for the days, and thirty for the nights during which it breathes not (yet) the breath of life" (*ARR*, p. 38). And *ATŠ* says, "For they (the Parents?) are the source (head) of the body, and these sixty *faṭiria* are like a body without a head" (*ATŠ*, p. 239 [138]). The last six *faṭiria*, evidently, supply the head, and thus complete the Lightworld body, the *ʿuṣṭuna*.

However, not even these two parts of the *masiqta* are enough to secure the joined spirit and soul in the above. Called the "Mother-*masiqta*," the *masiqta* that combines the sixty plus six *faṭiria*-ceremonies must be set in conjunction with the yearly "Father-*masiqta*." On the last day of the five-day festival, Panja, right before New Year's, the Mother- and Father-*masiqta* are celebrated together: they make up the "*masiqta* of the Parents," the *Ṭabahata*.[55] This is the time of open, unhindered access to the Lightworld, when no evil forces can intercept the ascending soul and spirit. Impure deaths are "corrected" during Panja in the *Ṭabahata-masiqta*, which fulfils the purpose only partially achieved by the *masqata* during the previous year. It seems, too, that the

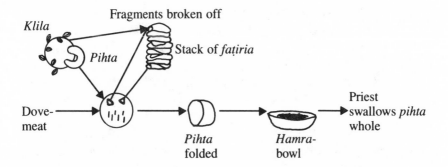

Ṭabahata-masiqta includes the commemorating of any soul suspected of being hampered in its upwards course, whether the death has been impure or not.[56]

In the *Ṭabahata, all faṭiria*—in the part for the six *faṭiria*—receive signs, and thus the "open-ended" acts (that is, those lacking signs) in the Mother-*masiqta* are completed, "closed." It is significant that in the *Ṭabahata* the *klila*-prayers *CP* 46 and 47 are left out, and these omissions openly express that the spirit no longer has its separate existence apart from the soul; the two are now, inextricably, one. When the priests reach *CP* 71 in the Father-*masiqta*, they are assured that "judgement together with prosecution is finished with at that moment" (*ARR*, p. 45).

The meticulousness of the described *masiqta* seems both puzzling and awesome. That the joining of soul and spirit should necessitate such detailed, time-consuming handling of tangible, even gross, materials, appears perhaps as excessive. For a Gnostic religion in particular, these ritual embellishments may strike a reader as almost alien.[57] But the symbolism of the *masiqta* is coherent. This becomes clear if one takes into account the prayers, ritual commentaries, and exegetic texts together with the prescribed action of the ritual.

For an interpreter, matters become complicated when the two elements, soul and spirit, are represented by more than one symbol each. In addition, one particular item may symbolize two different entities. For instance, the killed dove offers a parallel to the deceased human being: death down here is a prerequisite for life up there. Sacrifice attempts to control the event of death. The specific requirements of the victim, the dove—male sex, perfect, of proved fertility—suggest that the bird signifies an ideal human being, perhaps a priest. On the other hand, the dove represents the ascending spirit. A manipulable spirit is required for the priests' work in the ritual, for neither words alone nor fervent hopes suffice for a successful ascent.

Not only the dove, *Ba*, but also the *klila* symbolizes the spirit. The wreath is enveloped by the soul element, the *pihta*, and here it is noteworthy that the soul is represented in a "raw" state: the dough is only half baked. Once in the Lightworld, incorporated in the *'uṣṭuna,* one expects that the soul will be fully "baked," as it were. The "clothing of the wreath"[58] anticipates the joining of soul and spirit, or more specifically, that the spirit will acquire the nature of the soul.

The *pihta* is a soul; but the *faṭiria,* too, represent souls. There is a difference, however, for the *faṭiria, fully baked,* symbolize the full-fledged souls. These are the Mandaean souls who have already successfully ascended, and they are set up as models for the present soul and spirit. Adding to the complexity, the myrtle wreath laid on top of the *faṭiria*-heap is "clothing which preserves the soul" (*ARR*, p. 42). The spirit, in its ascending aspect when connected to the *pihta*, becomes a life-giving force to the ancestors in the Lightworld. The constant interconnections between the presently treated spirit and soul and the already ascended forefathers speak of the *laufa,* the vital connection between the living and the dead. This is no less than *the* lifeline in Mandaeism. The *klila* thus mediates between the two worlds.

The phrase used of the *klila*—that it is an "inner heart"[59]—expressly connects *klila* with *Ba*, whose breast-meat furnishes the spirit elements wrapped into the *pihta*. On the way upwards, however, the spirit is transformed and acquires the nature of the soul. In its *klila*-aspect, the spirit gives "life" to the ancestors, while the *Ba* furnishes the new *'uṣṭuna* with the spirit in the Lightworld. That the spirit is necessary on earth as well as in the Lightworld is of the utmost importance, for the evergreen myrtle demonstrates the "surviving" spirit element, so to speak. The *Ba*, digested by the priest, is integrated with the soul, and therefore loses its distinct, separate identity. The new *'uṣṭuna* is "fed" by the ancestors, that is, by the pieces of *faṭiria* stuck into the *pihta*. Nourishment comes from the departed Mandaeans, while new life comes from the "pregnant" priests.[60] Gradually, the priests cause the new life to come about and the *pihta* will, in its turn, become a *faṭira,* an ancestor.

The persistently "pregnant" language in the priests' prayers indicates that a birth is to take place. The celebrants act as both parents and midwives to the ascending companions; a successful rebirth in the Lightworld depends crucially on the priests' correct actions on earth, in the ritual. It is also worth remembering that the celebrants impersonate the dead, throughout the *masiqta*. Thus, they have multiple identities as long as the ritual lasts.

The vital connection between the earth and the Lightworld, the *laufa,* is perceived as a movement from below to above, in constant interchange.[61] Another directional symbolism is also present in the *masiqta*, the movement from left (earth) to right (Lightworld). The priests know how to balance these realms because they are essentially citizens of both. The incense represents the *laufa* in its aspect of moving from above to below; the earth, the left *ṭariana*, is enveloped by the scent from above, the right *ṭariana*. Also, the *klila* and *pihta* are held in the priest's left hand, but the *faṭiria* are treated with the right hand. Oil-signings go from left to right, anticipating the successful rise from earth to Lightworld. *'Utria* on earth, the priests, in parallel to their Lightworld counterparts, are able to perform creations *from below*. These activities have an effect in the Light-realm, thus breaking the dividing line between the two realms.

CONCLUSION

The concern with the salvation of the element *ruha* by elevation into the Lightworld is reflected in the mythologies of the figure Ruha's final liberation. As we have seen, Ruha is earth, and the earth is the human realm in which contact with the upper world is possible, *via ritual*. The element *ruha* can be manipulated in the *masiqta* ritual, and at the same time the Ruha-figure can be said to be partially restored through this freeing of each human spirit. Not until the end of the earthly world will Ruha find her final redemption, but every saved human spirit anticipates the earth's, Ruha's, own salvation into the Lightworld.[62] Here, the idea of the *dmuta* is central on all levels of creation, for human being as for the earth itself.

Any life and creation on the earth-level depends on Ruha, who mediates between the lower and the upper worlds. Ambiguous, she may turn to good or to evil, but she remains the condition for the *laufa*'s upward direction. The metaphysical dualism in Mandaeism is regularly broken by ritual means. That the ritual is so central to the religion indicates a more positive evaluation of the earthly realm than one might expect in a Gnostic system, and the ambivalent and even positive views of Ruha fit this positive concern with the earthly realm.

Ruha, in Mandaean mythology, and *ruha*, in the anthropology, have parallel functions: both make mediation possible between seemingly opposed worlds. Thus, the middle component is ultimately seen in a positive light, although, at times, uneasily so. But the mediator also separates, for Ruha as earth is posited between underworld and Lightworld, and the element *ruha* sits between body and soul. This paradoxical function of Ruha and *ruha* demonstrates a tension in which the dichotomous principles are kept in contact.[63]

Scholars of Mandaeism have tended to stress the negative side of Ruha, both because her positive traits do not suit the metaphysical dualism, and because she is an unpredictable, female figure. Females in Gnostic texts have often, a priori, been evaluated negatively, as if femaleness as such must be a negative attribute. This kind of judgment stems from ideals that allow only for a pattern of starkly opposed entities; more often than not, this means that male means positive, female negative. The role of Ruha (and *ruha*) in Mandaeism, however, breaks such a static model, for the religion permits an inclusive "both-and" typology, rather than a dualistic "either-or." The fact that the paradoxical symbol appears as a female figure and element should not surprise investigators; for even as humanity is one, the sexes are two, and as humanity resides on earth, so does it partake of ambiguities. To identify earth and Ruha, then, is an expression of the paradox of human life. A concluding remark may be taken from Drower's principal Mandaean informant in Iraq, Hirmiz bar Anhar; he says, "Now Ruha is the breath of life in the created world, and our breath is from her."[64]

Mandaeism's concession that Ruha will finally be saved demonstrates that her home was originally in the Lightworld. Her cry of despair in *CP* (see above, p. 21), indicates her origin as well as her goal. H. Jonas notices that this lament resembles the Sophia-traditions in Christian Gnosticism.[65] In fact, bewilderment, passion, and despair characterize Sophia in *Ap. John*. At the same time that she appears in this negative light, Sophia (even more than Ruha in Mandaeism) is explicitly identified with female entities in the Pleroma, the equivalent of the Mandaean Lightworld. A proliferation of females—and of female androgynes—populates the worlds in *Ap. John*, and Sophia somehow includes them all, signifying the female principle that suffers both from fault and from exorbitant power.

CHAPTER 3

The Apocryphon of John:
Sophia, Adam, and Yaltabaoth

INTRODUCTION

The *Apocryphon of John* (*Ap. John*)[1] presents a plethora of Gnostic mythological figures. Of these, I will primarily be concerned with the Wisdom-figure Sophia and with the first human being, Adam. I suspect that there are previously overlooked links and parallels between these entities. Both suffer from the lack of a partner, whom they finally acquire. A subtheme in *Ap. John* is furnished by the speculations concerning Sophia's son Yaltabaoth, who marks a negative, though ambivalent, parallel to both Sophia and Adam. This son also desperately seeks for something he lacks, that is, the spirit element that he unwittingly lost to Adam.

An investigation of Sophia in *Ap. John* is complicated by the fact that she carries several names and identities. Similarly, but in a more limited way, Adam possesses both a heavenly, Pleromatic image and an earthly one. Doubleness is also found in the peculiar problem of androgyny in the text; for instance, how does one explain an androgynous figure who is said to lack a partner? Is that not a contradiction in terms?

I will deal with some of the apparent inconsistencies and contradictions in *Ap. John* as they pertain to Sophia and to Adam. In so doing I assume that the text indeed possesses a certain systematic, "logical" line of thought. To wit: the information that the light-element descends more than once into the lower world does not, I think, indicate that the author of *Ap. John* has forgotten what he wrote on a previous page.[2] It is necessary to discern the reasons for the multiple transmissions of the salvific element; what look like duplications and repetitions may instead mark a thickening, mounting plot that demands repeated Pleromatic intervention.

First, I will present *Ap. John*'s account of the upper, female, androgynous entity in the Pleroma. This active figure—many-named and many-faceted—operates both by herself and in relation to her mate, her *syzygos*. At significant points in the text she is identified with Sophia, who will be investigated next.

Undertaking a creation without her partner, Sophia gives birth to Yaltabaoth. I will follow his activities especially as they relate to Adam. Adam will be treated in the next two sections. He is associated with Sophia, who is increasingly identified with Adam's female Life-giver, First Thought, Thought (Pronoia, Ennoia). This female is no other than the primary female Pleroma-figure.

Adam's spiritual partner, Pronoia/Ennoia/Sophia, is seen apart from his earthly wife, Eve, who plays only a minor role in the text. Both Adam and Sophia (in her imperfect aspect) remain in need of completion—that is, redemption—until the coming of the savior. The fact that they both possess higher, Pleromatic selves accounts for their eligibility for salvation; indeed, they seem already to have acquired a modicum of completion. Yaltabaoth is the only one who never seems to attain to any spiritual life, although he is, strictly speaking, *psuchē* ("soul") incarnate. His imperfect conception and birth affect both the Pleroma and the human world (the latter is created and ruled by Yaltabaoth) so that, for the time being, impairment characterizes both the upper and the lower realm. The awaited perfection of Sophia and Adam symbolizes the healing of the two regions. An absolute dualism, insisting on a radical division between the two worlds, will not hold: neither of the two figures belongs entirely to one or the other region; rather, both straddle them.

After the two sections on Adam, I will conclude by attending to the disciple John's question to the savior regarding the salvation of souls. This issue concerns Yaltabaoth, too, because he is *psuchē* par excellence. As Sophia's son, he would appear to belong among the offspring, σπέρμα, a term whose meaning in *Ap. John* needs some attention. If Yaltabaoth is included in this term, he would seem to be eligible for salvation; if not, the text is inconsistent with respect to its concern for the salvation of souls.

Most succinctly, Adam signifies Sophia's offspring because he must attribute his *real*—that is, spiritual—life to her. She, in turn, saves herself insofar as she saves her offspring. As the spiritual principle in humankind, Sophia both completes humanity and fulfils her own lack. The final healing in *Ap. John* includes a near-comprehensive scheme of redemption both in terms of spiritualized, sexual partnership and in the identification of a figure's lower with its higher, Pleromatic image. The question remains, however, whether the personified soul belongs in this scheme.

THE FEMALE ENTITY IN THE PLEROMA

In the beginning of *Ap. John* the risen Christ appears to the disciple John (brother of James), instructing him. Christ utters, "I [am the Father], I am the Mother, I am the Son" (p. 99, 2.10–15).[3] After a long monologue characterized to a great extent by negative theology concerning the "Monad" (p. 100, 2.25–30), the upper Pleromatic principle, Christ speaks of the Monad's—that is, the Father's—first action:

> He [gazes upon] his image which he sees in the spring of the [Spirit. He] puts his desire in his light- [water, that is] the spring of the [pure] light-water [which] surrounds him. And [his Ennoia performed a] deed and she came forth, [namely] she who had [appeared] before him in [the shine of] his light. This is the first [power which was] before all of them (and) [which came] forth from his mind, that [is the Pronoia of the All]. Her light [is the likeness of the] light, the [perfect] power which is [the] image of the invisible, virginal Spirit who is perfect. [The first power], the glory, Barbelo, the perfect glory in the aeons, the glory of the revelation, she glorified the virginal Spirit and praised him, because thanks to him she had come forth. This is the first thought, his image; she became the womb of everything, for she is prior to them all, the Mother-Father, the first Man, the holy Spirit, the thrice-male, the thrice-powerful, the thrice-named androgynous one, and the eternal aeon among the invisible ones, and the first to come forth. (P. 101, 4.25–5.15)[4]

The Father and the Spirit can be equated (p. 100, 2.30–35). When the Father is reflected in the water, his thought, Ennoia, manifests herself as an autonomous figure.[5] She is both the Father *and* herself. It is worth noting Ennoia's active performance: she "[performed a] deed" even before she came forth. One notes, too, her names "Barbelo" and "Pronoia."

The Father's "mind" should, rather, be translated "thinking," for the term is not νοῦς, but πε]ϥμεεⲩе.[6] After Ennoia has been designated "womb,"[7] her epithets become increasingly otherworldly and paradoxical. "Mother-Father"[8] expresses her androgynous nature; she is also identified as "First Man" (πϣορπ ⲛ̄ⲣⲱⲙⲉ), as well as "holy Spirit"—that is, the Father—and "thrice-male." In short, Ennoia is one (herself), two (herself and the Father, her creator), and three (herself, the Father, and First Man). Christ's self-revelation "Father, Mother, and Son" reverberates here.[9] All three beings seem to be facets of the same, ineffable entity.[10]

Ennoia now starts to address a series of requests to the virginal Spirit. First, she asks for "Foreknowledge," generally understood as Prognosis.[11] At the

end of the requests, when the "five-aeon" is listed, the five can be made out to
include: 1. Barbelo = Pronoia; 2. thought (ⲧⲉⲙⲉⲉⲩⲉ) = Prognosis; 3. inde-
structibility; 4. eternal life; 5. truth (p. 102, 6.1–10).[12] But all four entities in
the first two aeons can be identified with one another, because Pronoia[13] and
Ennoia have already been equated. According to *Ap. John* (p. 102, 6.5–10)
and to BG,[14] the five-aeon is androgynous, but at the same time it is designated as a "ten-aeon," identified with the Father. Thus, according to a bisexual
model, there are five aeons, but following a syzygous pattern, there are ten.
Depending on one's point of view, then, one may see the aeon as five androgynes, or as a collection of five couples. It is important to keep in mind the
bisexuality of the aeons, for especially Ennoia often speaks and acts as both
male and female—or as male only.[15]

At the instigation of the Father, Barbelo becomes impregnated and gives
birth to the Only-begotten Christ (Autogenes). One may note that this is the
first syzygial creation in *Ap. John*. So far, the Father has created Barbelo who,
in turn, asked for the five-aeon (which includes herself). The Only-begotten
alone explicitly has two parents, the Father and Barbelo. Christ's subsequent
"fellow-worker," for whom he asks, is brought forth, but no information is
given as to the gender of this fellow, whose name is "mind" (νοῦς).

F. Wisse's translation, "And the mind wanted to perform a deed through
the word of the Invisible Spirit" (p. 102, 7.1–10),[16] is unfortunate, for the
"mind" here is not Christ's fellow-worker, νοῦς, but "thought," ⲧⲉⲙⲉⲉⲩⲉ, the
Barbelo-figure. This recalls Ennoia's deed in the beginning (p. 101, 4.25f.),
and seems not to refer to any creation on the part of Christ (notwithstanding the
pronoun "his" in Wisse's translation, for Ennoia is both male and female!).

Aided by the invisible Spirit and Autogenes, Pronoia—possibly through
"mind," νοῦς—brings forth the Perfect Man (ⲡⲣⲱⲙⲉ ⲛ̄ⲧⲉⲗⲉⲓⲟⲥ).[17] The virginal Spirit calls him Adam;[18] he, like Sophia (another aeon), is placed
together with Christ. *Ap. John* then says of Adam:

> And the invisible one gave him an intelligible, invincible power. And he
> spoke and glorified and praised the invisible Spirit, saying "It is thanks to
> thee that everything has come into being and everything will return to
> thee. And I shall praise and glorify thee and the Autogenes and the aeons,
> the three: the Father, the Mother, and the Son, the perfect power." (P. 103,
> 9.5–15)

Two points about heavenly Adam are worth noting: he possesses an invincible power, and he repeats the triadic formula already encountered twice.[19]
Next, Adam is said to place his son Seth in the second aeon. Evidently, no
female mate is needed to give birth to Adam's son. The only syzygial creation

so far is Christ; Adam's own birth from Pronoia is ambiguous with respect to any "father" for Adam. Pronoia, being also the invisible Spirit, can be seen as both mother and father of Adam. Conception occurs explicitly only in the instance of Christ's birth. We need not, however, infer a negative attitude toward autonomous creations, without a mate, in *Ap. John*: the five-aeon (which is also the ten-aeon) is both male and female as distinct entities, and male and female as united, androgynous figures. So far, the text has repudiated no birth or creation by single entities.

SOPHIA

And the Sophia of the Epinoia, being an aeon, conceived a thought from herself with the reflection of the invisible Spirit and foreknowledge. She wanted to bring forth a likeness out of herself without the consent of the Spirit—he had not approved—and without her consort and without his consideration. And though the personage of her maleness had not approved, and she had not found her agreement, and she had thought without the consent of the Spirit and the knowledge of her agreement, (yet) she brought forth. And because of the invincible power that is in her, her thought did not remain idle and a thing came out of her which was imperfect and different from her appearance, because she had created it without her consort. And it was dissimilar to the likeness of its mother for it has another form. . . . She cast it away from her, outside that place, that no one of the immortal ones might see it, for she had created it in ignorance. And she surrounded it with a luminous cloud, and she placed a throne in the middle of the cloud that no one might see it except the holy Spirit who is called the mother of the living. And she called his name Yaltabaoth. (Pp. 103–4, 9.25–10.20)

Sophia's creation is the first repudiated act in *Ap. John*. Personified Wisdom does not, like Barbelo, petition to have creations brought forth, but creates autonomously. S. Giversen explains the expression "the Sophia of the Epinoia": "It would be in order to characterize Sophia as the one who is joined with ἐπίνοια: thoughtfulness, plan, consideration." He continues, "If Epinoia were not feminine, it would be natural to regard Epinoia as a syzygy to Sophia, but this is not acceptable because both Epinoia and Sophia are feminine terms."[20] The identities of the two will, indeed, become inextricably intertwined later on in *Ap. John*. A *syzygos* need not be of the opposite gender to its partner, however, for the text contains a doubleness in its view of pairs: those of opposite gender, and those who combine upper and lower images of each other.

Sophia's connection to Epinoia indicates that the former is included in the Pleromatic world, even while she admittedly appears as one of the later (lower?) aeons. But guilt is never outrightly ascribed to her,[21] despite the passage's repeated condemnation of her acting without her mate. Other scholars have been quick to point out that Sophia's sin is due to her being the last aeon—the one most remote from the Pleroma.[22] But there is no doubt that she *is* an aeon, and she stays with Christ *inside* the upper world.[23] Nor is she the lowest or last, for heavenly Adam was created after her, and the last-mentioned aeon would be Adam's son Seth. Another point: why was not Adam, if sole creator of *his* son, condemned for having created in isolation?

Wisdom's creation comes about by a "reflection." But this translation of *Enthumesis* seems ill chosen, for it conjures up "reflection in water," or something of that sort (a motif often encountered in Gnostic texts, which even turns up later on in *Ap. John*). Giversen translates: "with the invisible (ἀόρατος) Spirit's (πνεῦμα) Enthymesis (ἐνθύμησις) and Prognosis (πρό-γνωσις)."[24] This means that Sophia employs the influence of upper entities—male and female (and androgynous!)—for her bringing forth. "That Sophia with these powers thinks out a thought does not seem by itself to be wrong," observes Giversen.[25] But he does not think that these entities *agree* with what Sophia does. Whether they agree or not, it is significant that Sophia is fully capable of using the influence of these figures in order to realize her plan.

Y. Janssens explains, "la pensée de Sophia *est* de penser *à* l'Esprit et à la Prognose. Et c'est dans cette pensée qu'elle veut 'émettre' la copie, la 'ressemblance' "[26] ("the thought of Sophia *is* to think *of* the Spirit and of Prognosis. And it is in this thought that she wishes to 'emit' the copy, the 'image' "). It is natural for Sophia's thought to center on the two beings to whom she owes her existence; imitating these entities, she acts, but does not meet with approval. *Why* her alleged consort does not concede, is never explained. "The personage of her maleness"[27] may be an allusion to Wisdom's own androgynous nature, or to Christ, who may be her rightful "mate."[28] But if Sophia is identified with Epinoia, then this is her consort, since Epinoia is bisexual. Thus, Sophia would have no need of a distinct, male partner.

Sophia's "invincible power"[29] marks an exact parallel to Adam, as noted above. I take this power to be her Pleromatic, creative abilities. BG, stressing the negative view of Wisdom, offers an interesting variant: Sophia's special power is not "invincible," but it is a "lust," προύνικον.[30] This negatively judged capacity gives a very different flavor to the BG passage from the corresponding one in C II.1. N. A. Dahl observes that Sophia's alleged lewdness is no central theme in any of the *Ap. John* versions.[31] Janssens thinks that it is *because* Sophia was unable to find her partner in BG, that she started to act "lewdly."[32] Dahl attributes Sophia's epithet *Prunikos* to the "duplication or multiplication of Mother Wisdom,"[33] that is, to the separation of Epinoia from Sophia.

In regard to the general myth that Yaltabaoth has a form different from that of his mother, G. C. Stead observes that he is "formless, because fatherless,"[34] although *Ap. John* does not explicitly portray the son as "formless." A "lion-faced serpent" (p. 104, 10.5–10),[35] Yaltabaoth evidently does not resemble anything else encountered so far in the text. Realizing that her son is unfit for contemplation by the immortal aeons, Sophia ejects him; but is the cloud, his hiding-place, outside or inside the Pleroma?[36] Yaltabaoth is created by Sophia, ironically, in "ignorance."[37] That Wisdom acts ignorantly marks a Gnostic sense of humor, not to be underrated.

Despite the information that Sophia did not want any of the immortal ones to lay eyes on Yaltabaoth, *Ap. John* tells us that the Holy Spirit sees him. This Spirit is, of course, identified with both the Mother and the Father on high. And because it is equated with Epinoia, so also with Sophia herself![38] BG's first sentence of the corresponding section starts, "Our sister, the Sophia, being an aeon. . . ."[39] According to Schottroff, Christ, the revealer, must be the consort and "brother" of Sophia.[40] The noun "our" reveals that Christ speaks on behalf of other aeons, too. Despite her action, Sophia seems still to belong to the Pleromatic world (although she stays with Yaltabaoth in his cloud).

Ap. John describes Yaltabaoth and his activities in detail. The text continuously repeats that the illegitimate son obtained a power from his mother; evidently, this is the "invincible power" mentioned earlier. *Ap. John* wavers conspicuously as to whether Yaltabaoth has obtained this power with Sophia's consent, or whether he has outrightly stolen it. It is this "mother"-power that enables Yaltabaoth to make and populate his own world.

In a fitting negative parallel to the primary Father and Mother, *Ap. John* states that Yaltabaoth "joined with his madness . . . and begot authorities for himself" (p. 104, 10.25–30).[41] The madness, $\dot{\alpha}\pi\acute{o}\nu o\iota\alpha$, of course evokes the opposite of Epinoia/Sophia.[42] If the madness is Yaltabaoth's mate, she does not figure in the subsequent creation account, for the archon seems mostly to create on his own accord. The Pleromatic world above is his model in the creations he undertakes, although it remains unclear whether he has ever seen this upper realm. Perhaps his mother's power in him accounts for this "blueprint" as well as for his creative capacities. Cunningly, Yaltabaoth keeps his mother's power to himself, but he shares his other element, fire, with his cohorts (p. 104, 11.5–10; p. 105, 12.1–10). Mixing light with darkness he has, ominously, weakened the light, Sophia's power (p. 104, 11.10–20).

The account returns to Sophia: "Then the mother began to move to and fro. She became aware of the deficiency when the brightness of her light diminished. And she became dark because her consort had not agreed with her" (p. 106, 13.10–20). Here, John interrupts the revealer to ask what "moved to and fro" means. Laughing, the savior explains:

> Do not think it is as Moses said, "above the waters." No, but when she had seen the wickedness which had happened, and the theft which her son had committed, she repented. And forgetfulness overcame her in the darkness of ignorance and she began to be ashamed. (IV 21, 13–14 adds: And she did not dare to return, but she was moving) about. And the moving is the going to and fro. (P. 106, 13.15–30)

The text once more mentions that Yaltabaoth took his mother's power, stressing that he knows of no other higher beings except her. Then,

> And when the mother recognized that the cover of darkness was imperfect, then she knew that her consort had not agreed with her. She repented with much weeping. And the whole pleroma heard the prayer of her repentance and they praised on her behalf the invisible, virginal Spirit. (IV 22, 5–7 adds: And he consented, and when the invisible Spirit had consented,) the holy Spirit poured over her from their whole fullness. For her consort had not come to her, but he came to her through the pleroma in order that he might correct her deficiency. And she was taken up not to her own aeon but above her son, that she might be in the ninth until she has corrected her deficiency. (P. 106, 13.30–14.15)

Sophia's moving "to and fro" starts right after Yaltabaoth's blasphemous proclamation that he is the only God (p. 106, 13.5–10). Perhaps it is this utterance that prompts Sophia to realize her deficiency (ϣⲧⲁ). Her diminishing light can be explained as resulting from Yaltabaoth's "theft."[43] However, *Ap. John* also gives a second reason: Sophia's darkness is due to the lack of agreement from her mate.

The disciple John's interruption gives the revealer an opportunity to offer the esoteric exegesis of "Moses' " utterance about the mother's moving.[44] Clearly, Gen. 1:2 is invoked here,[45] as *Ap. John* again associates Sophia and "the spirit of God," the Holy Spirit. The "wickedness which had happened" probably refers both to Sophia's condition and to her offspring's hubris.[46]

The sequence of Sophia's actions and emotions seems strange. Repenting (μετάνοεῖν), she moves,[47] but then she is overcome by forgetfulness "in the darkness of ignorance," and *then* becomes ashamed. Usually, shame follows the "awakening" from forgetfulness.[48] *Ap. John* expressly states that the "darkness of ignorance" is nothing but Yaltabaoth himself.[49] (The themes of forgetfulness, ignorance, and shame should be kept in mind for *Ap. John's* later account of earthly Adam; he, too, is characterized by these traits.) Giversen's translation of the passage seems clearer than Wisse's: "she repented (. . .), and (when she had seen) that an oblivion had come over her in the darkness of ignorance, she began (. . .) to be ashamed while she moved."[50]

The next section interprets Sophia's repentance as a result of her realization that "the cover of darkness" is imperfect. One may reasonably equate "the cover of darkness" with Yaltabaoth.[51] Sophia's next insight—that her consort has not agreed with her[52]—is not presented as a logical extension of her realization of Yaltabaoth's imperfection.

Evidently, Yaltabaoth's imperfection cannot (immediately) be healed; but Sophia's own lack is remedied by the intervening Pleroma. These powers ask the virginal Spirit to save Sophia.[53] C IV's addition is significant, for it emphasizes the Spirit's consent: this is precisely what has been sorely lacking in Sophia's undertakings! *Ap. John* explicitly equates the virginal and the holy Spirit[54] in this section, and one recalls that this entity is both Sophia's female, higher self and, in the traditionally syzygial sense, her mate.

Wisse's translation "from their fullness" seems unfortunate and inconsistent, for it is the Pleromatic essence that is poured on Sophia.[55] The next— seemingly contradictory—sentence is a crucial one: "For her consort had not come to her, but he came to her through the pleroma in order that he might correct her deficiency." Giversen has, "for (. . .) her partner did not come to her, but (. . .) from the Pleroma (. . .) came something to fulfill her want. . . ."[56] Whatever the "something" is, it evokes an element more diffuse, less personalized, than Wisse's "he."

Giversen notes that Sophia is not immediately restored, but that the Pleroma's intervention "aims at a situation where this restoration can occur."[57] That Sophia is put *above* her son's realm would indicate her superiority to him (Giversen, however, has "in," not "above"[58]). In any case, she is temporarily forgiven for her transgression, though the palpable result of her sin, Yaltabaoth, is still actively at large. In addition to having acted without her mate, then, there is a second aspect to Sophia's deficiency: her "objectified" transgression, her son. Because this deficiency can not be made to vanish, Sophia seems denied a return to the Pleroma.

BG offers a clearer impression of the *syzygos's* partial salvation of Wisdom: "After the invisible Pneuma had granted (a hearing to her pleas), it poured over her a Pneuma which derived from the Perfection. Her Consort descended to her to remedy her deficiency by Pronoia."[59] It seems clear that Pronoia is healing Sophia—even though it was *through* Pronoia that Sophia's sin was committed! Pneuma and Pronoia seem equated as Sophia's regained, higher image. Janssens explains, "πνεῦμα παρθενικόν mâle étant d'autre part *un* aspect de Pronoia ('devenue Premier Homme,' BG 27), il est possible que 'par une πρόνοια' exprime encore son intervention dans le redressement de Sophia" ("the male πνεῦμα παρθενικόν, being elsewhere *one* aspect of Pronoia ['become First Man,' BG 27], may now, possibly 'by a πρόνοια,' express his renewed intervention in the rehabilitation of Sophia").[60] Always mindful of Pronoia's identity as "First Man," Janssens now finds this equation useful and illuminating for understanding this puzzling passage about Sophia's *syzygos*. The ambiguities and androgynies of the Pleromatic beings are once more demonstrated in this section: Sophia's Pleromatic image, Pronoia, reveals herself both as female, higher self and as Sophia's mate, "First Man." It is even possible that there is a connection between Pronoia as "First Man" and Adam as "Perfect Man."

Summing up this section on Sophia, one must bear in mind the ambivalence with which *Ap. John* treats this figure. She is—strictly speaking—still an aeon (as is her son!), despite the misuse of her creative, spiritual power. The text's insistence on Sophia's lacking male partner begins to wear thin: syzygial partnership is not a prerequisite for creation in *Ap. John*. Sophia's consort is both herself *and* a separate entity, Pronoia and "First Man"—in fact, it may even be Adam in his earthly aspect: he bears a strong resemblance to Sophia and enters into intimate contact with her.

ADAM: THE BEGINNING OF HIS LIFE

Right after *Ap. John*'s statement that Sophia must stay "in the ninth" until further notice, a voice comes from the aeons, proclaiming, "The Man exists and the son of Man" (p. 106, 14.10–20). Perhaps this message is intended for Sophia, as encouragement[61] or consolation.[62] In any case, Yaltabaoth hears it and thinks it is his mother speaking. Next appears the voice's owner: the Mother-Father who reflects her/himself into the lower regions, revealing the "First Man" image in human form.

Trembling and thrown into great confusion by this image, Yaltabaoth speaks to his cohorts: "Come, let us create a man according to the image of God and according to our likeness, that his image might become a light for us" (p. 107, 15.1–5). Agreeing, Yaltabaoth's authorities add: "Let us call him Adam, that his name might become a power of light for us" (ibid. 10–15). Then follows a lengthy section enumerating the "angels" involved in creating Adam's body. The Powers complete the "psychic and material body" (p. 109, 19.5–10), but they cannot make it live and move about.

Janssens says of the image that it is Sophia's consort, "(= Premier Homme) qui descend au secours de Sophia. Les archontes voient cette image et se disent entre eux: 'Faisons un homme . . .' " ("[= First Man] who descends to the rescue of Sophia. The archons see this image and say to each other: 'Let us make a man . . .' ").[63] Giversen emphasizes that the revealer instructs (τcεβο) the archons.[64] Of course, the revelation *is* the teaching, because it proves the utterance, "The Man exists. . . ."

One should keep two points in mind here. First, there are two (intended or unintended) audiences to the proclamation and to its revelation: Sophia's consort comes to console her and perhaps to reassure her about her future redemption, but the archons think the image is for them, for it teaches them about itself. Second, the Mother-Father's image is that of First Man; for the first time, First Man and heavenly Adam (Perfect Man) are expressly identified. This means that the heavenly image of man and the highest Pleromatic entity are indistinguishable from one another: the divine figure has been revealed as man. And Sophia's mate and "higher self" have been revealed as being one and the same.

Yaltabaoth's expression "a light for us" is mimicked by his archons. "Nach der Meinung der Archonten verbürgen der göttliche Name und die göttliche Gestalt, dass ihr Gebilde leuchten wird" ("According to the opinion of the archons, the divine name and the divine form guarantee that their image will shine"), says H.-M. Schenke.[65] Of course, the archons seem predestined to name their creature "Adam." Giversen stresses that the archons' decision stems from Adam's connection to light, not to earth.[66] According to BG 35.9f. the first Adam was appointed lord over the first aeon of light, and BG's account of Adam's creation by the archons emphasizes that Adam is the *soul*, made in imitation of the projected image from above.[67] Both C II.1 and BG underline the point that the archons are unable to raise Adam up: the soul (*psuchē*) and the material element do not suffice to make a living being. The powers exert no command over the spirit element that is necessary to make Adam a true copy of the image from Pleroma.

Ap. John continues,

> And when the mother wanted to retrieve the power which she had given to the chief archon, she petitioned the Mother-Father of the all who is most merciful. He sent, by means of a holy decree, the five lights down upon the place of the angels of the chief archon. They advised him that they

should bring forth the power of the mother. And they said to Yaltabaoth, "Blow into his face something of your spirit and his body will arise." And he blew into his face the spirit which is the power of his mother; he did not know (this), for he exists in ignorance. And the power of the mother went out of Yaltabaoth into the psychic soul which they had fashioned after the image of the One who exists from the beginning. The body moved and gained strength, and it was luminous. (P. 109, 19.15–20.1)

Sophia—herself characterized by a "lack"—lets Adam have her power, via Yaltabaoth. Has Sophia now started to fulfil her need? As noted above, she darkened after giving birth to her son, because her consort had not agreed. *Now* it is the pneuma-infused Adam who becomes luminous: Sophia's light in him immediately works.

Observing that they have been tricked, the archons punish Adam—who is now superior in intelligence, or wisdom,[68] to his creators—by throwing "him into the lowest region of all matter" (p. 109, 20.5–10).

But the blessed One, the Mother-Father . . . had mercy on the power of the mother which was brought forth out of the chief archon. . . . And he sent, through his beneficent Spirit and his great mercy, a helper to Adam, luminous Epinoia which comes out of him, who was called Life. And she assists the whole creature, by toiling with him and by restoring him to his fullness and by teaching him about the descent of the seed (and) by teaching him about the way of ascent, (which is) the way he came down. And the luminous Epinoia was hidden in Adam, in order that the Archons might not know her, but that the Epinoia might be a correction of the deficiency of the mother. (Pp. 109–10, 20.5–30)

The archons' attempt to enmesh Adam further in matter warrants renewed intervention by the light-forces. His endangered luminosity needs fortification by *luminous* Epinoia, his helper.[69] Epinoia's title recalls Gen. 2:18, where Eve is called "helper"—but Eve has not yet made an appearance in *Ap. John*.[70] The epithet "Zoe" associates back to the previous mention of her, namely, in the section where the holy Spirit is the only one to behold Yaltabaoth in his cloud.[71] Epinoia's luminosity can be seen as a second manifestation of the light-power blown into Adam; now this light becomes "life," Zoe, for him.

That "the purpose of Epinoia is to be a restoration of the mother's want," as Giversen says, must be connected to the restoration mentioned above (p. 106, 14.5–10),[72] which comes from the holy Spirit: Sophia's healing through Adam will be a realization of her previously promised restoration. Giversen goes on: "Whether AJ has made a distinction between the mother-figure whose light-strength diminished, the loss of which is to be restored, and the light-strength concealed in man who is in the world of darkness, sometimes seems vague."[73] I think any such vagueness can be dispelled, though *Ap. John* leaves it up to the reader to work out the parallels and intertwinings of Wisdom and earthly Adam. *Ap. John* speaks of a salvation process for both figures, but treats them, increasingly, as *one* entity.

Wisse's translation of *pleroma* as "fullness"[74] obfuscates the restoration *to* the Pleroma, and *of* the Pleroma. This "fullness" is not just a localized environment to which Adam will eventually return, but a not-yet-achieved state in himself. However, Epinoia appears continuously to be working for this fulfilment in Adam. Here, again, one notes *Ap. John*'s vacillation between present and future salvation, or perhaps the text simply refuses to speak of redemption on only one level, in only one dimension of time.

R. McL. Wilson discerns Wisdom-traditions in the emphasis on Epinoia's relationship to Adam.[75] In BG Epinoia not only toils with and teaches Adam, but she sets up the whole creation "in her own perfect temple."[76] Paradoxically, this instructress both comes to Adam from the outside, *and* already dwells in him. The expression "luminous Epinoia who comes out of him" does not make it clear who "him" is (nor do any of the translations or comments). Epinoia is no other than the first spirit that Yaltabaoth unwittingly breathed into Adam. But now her coming to him again signifies a second instalment, because Adam remains endangered by the archons' schemes.

Both Sophia's and Adam's lacks are supposedly restored, and yet the story does not end. The restoration must become complete, and consciously so for those involved. Lack, as well as light, is associated with both Wisdom and human being.[77]

Scholars hold different views on the Adamic components. Adam has a material body and a *psuchē*—both according to the archons—but his spirit, pneuma, comes from elsewhere.[78] Ironically, Adam's first endowment of the spirit came from Yaltabaoth, who could not himself make full use of this element. W. Foerster, at first, seems to agree with this three-part schema, but then he merges "Lebensgeist" ("life-spirit") and "Seele" ("soul").[79] However, these two must be kept apart, for Yaltabaoth consciously imparts the soul to Adam, but he only unwittingly endows him with the precious spirit.

It is W.-D. Hauschild who most seriously misrepresents *Ap. John*'s evaluation of the pneuma transmitted by Yaltabaoth. He cannot accept that the archon could transfer any positively designated entity to Adam; he therefore devalues this pneuma, and sets it apart from that provided by Light-Epinoia.[80] Wishing to discern a theme of competition between the two "pneumas," Hauschild tries to sort out different pneuma-traditions in *Ap. John*.[81] This draws an unnecessarily complicated picture of the text's teaching about the pneuma. That Yaltabaoth is able—albeit unconsciously—to transmit the spirit to Adam belongs to the numerous Gnostic, sophisticated "jokes" that appear regularly in texts like *Ap. John.* Such Gnostic humor should be savored, not relegated to the category of bad source redaction.

When the alarmed archons notice that Adam is about to assert his superiority once more, they try to re-create him, to make him lose all connection with the light-element. Furnishing Adam with their "opposing spirit,"[82] the archons now render him mortal.[83] The opposing spirit is designated "the bond of forgetfulness," which echoes one of Sophia's characteristics as she was moving about.[84] *Ap. John* nevertheless sounds an encouraging note, assuring us that Epinoia is still in Adam.

Adam is never quite vanquished by the archontic forces, but he needs repeated "transfusions" of light in order to resist his creators. The archons seem to have no direct access to the pneuma, which is the element that they would like to quench in Adam, and to gain power over for their own sakes. The image reflected in the beginning did, after all, show itself to the lower powers, too, and one is left to wonder about the reasons for the image instructing the archons. Does the spirit have a mission among them as well? If so, all three entities—Sophia, Adam, and archons—have a lack that requires healing.

ADAM: PARADISE AND BEYOND

Adam is, next, placed in Paradise. As one might suspect, the garden is a "counter"-Paradise, because it belongs to the archons. This garden contains a tree of the *archons'* life—that is, death—of which they want Adam to eat.[85] To balance the presence of the archontic tree, the tree of knowledge of good and evil is also in the garden. Not unexpectedly, this tree is equated with the Epinoia of light (pp. 110–11, 22.5–10). According to Wisse's translation the archons position themselves in front of the Epinoia-tree in order to prevent Adam from looking at it.[86] If he were to look at the tree, Adam would perceive his own imperfection, his being "naked" of the Pleroma.

At this point Christ, the revealer, tells John that it was he, Christ, who made them (note the plural, although earthly Eve has not yet entered the story) eat of the Epinoia-tree. The savior distinguishes between the lesson taught by the snake and that delivered by him: the snake (Yaltabaoth!) taught lust, begetting, and wickedness. Gazing at the Epinoia-tree, Adam knows that he has disobeyed the archon, "due to the light of the Epinoia which is in him" (p. 111,

22.15–20). So Adam does fall, but it is a "heilsamer Sündenfall" ("salvific fall"), as Schenke terms it.[87]

Realizing that the superior power is still at work in Adam, Yaltabaoth wishes to extract it from him by bringing "a forgetfulness over Adam" (p. 111, 22.20–25). One may recall that forgetfulness overcame Sophia "in the darkness of ignorance,"[88] and that the antimimon pneuma in Adam marks a "bond of forgetfulness" (p. 110, 21.10–15). Offering an esoteric interpretation of "Moses' " account, Christ instructs John that it is not sleep, but a deadening of his perception, that is brought upon Adam. The corresponding passage in C III has, instead of "forgetfulness," "ἔκστασις," as G. MacRae points out.[89] Both versions, then, stress that in what immediately follows, Adam is not his normal self, but in some "altered state."

> Then the Epinoia of the light hid herself in him (Adam). And the chief archon wanted to bring her out of his rib. But the Epinoia of light cannot be grasped. Although darkness pursued her, it did not catch her. And he brought a part of his power out of him. And he made another creature in the form of a woman according to the likeness of the Epinoia which had appeared in him. And he brought the part which he had taken from the power of the man into the female creature, and not the way Moses said, "his rib-bone."
>
> And he (Adam) saw the woman by him. And in that moment the luminous Epinoia appeared, and she lifted the veil which lay over his mind. And he became sober from the drunkenness of darkness. And he recognized his counter-image and he said, "This is indeed bone from my bones and flesh from my flesh." Therefore the man will leave his father and his mother and he will cleave to his wife and they will both be one flesh, for they will send him his consort, and he will leave his father and his mother {. . .}
>
> And our sister Sophia (is) she who came down in innocence in order to rectify her deficiency. Therefore she was called Life which is the mother of the living. Through the foreknowledge of the sovereignty and through her they have tasted perfect Knowledge. I appeared in the form of an eagle on the tree of knowledge, which is the Epinoia from the foreknowledge of the pure light, that I might teach them and awaken them out of the depth of sleep. For they were both in a fallen state and they recognized their nakedness. The Epinoia appeared to them as a light (and) she awakened their thinking. (Pp. 111–12, 22.25–23.36)

This is the second time the text tells of Epinoia being hidden in Adam.[90] But *Ap. John* evidently wishes to emphasize that even now, when Adam is anesthetized, Epinoia has not vanished. Even as the text says that Epinoia cannot be grasped, it concedes the archon some success, for he manages to bring a part of Epinoia out of the drugged Adam.[91] Just as Yaltabaoth made Adam on the model of First Man's (= Ennoia's) reflection, so he now creates the earthly woman. One recalls the androgyny of First Man, so the model presents no problem with respect to gender.

It is significant that the raw material for the woman comes out of Adam. But this "power" has nothing to do with Adam's hylic and psychic nature, for the woman is not (yet) said to possess these elements—she seems a wholly spiritual creature. Giversen notes this "positive importance the creation of woman has for man, thanks to the Epinoia of light which is placed in her."[92]

It is important that the woman is not created to furnish a helper for Adam, but to aid the archon in his persistent schemes to regain the pneuma he lost when vivifying Adam. The text closely connects the woman with Epinoia in the passage beginning "And he (Adam) saw the woman by him." Here, the woman is really double, for on the one hand she is Adam's future earthly companion, and on the other she is his spiritual savior, Epinoia. The words "And in that moment the luminous Epinoia appeared" underscore the impossibility of totally separating the two women at this point.

Lifting the veil from Adam's mind, Epinoia awakens him from intoxication. The "veil" recalls Yaltabaoth being "the cover of darkness,"[93] and I think one could interpret this passage to mean that Yaltabaoth's power is lifted from Adam. Again, this presents a parallel to the previous part of the Sophia-myth, for recognizing the veil as veil renders it impotent.

Wisse's translation "counter-image" seems unfortunate, because it conjures up opposition, as in "counter-spirit" (antimimon pneuma). Adam's recognizing his image, ⲉⲓⲛⲉ,[94] echoes Gen. 2:23–24. *Ap. John* also follows Genesis in Adam's utterance about leaving one's father and mother. Here there is a repetition in the text, but Wisse's brackets together with the shift to a new paragraph give the impression of a lacuna. Giversen's treatment makes more sense of the passage by connecting it with the immediately ensuing information about Sophia: "because they namely (γάρ) shall send him his fellow and he shall leave his father and his mother {. . .}, namely (γάρ) our sister Sophia (σοφία) who came down in innocence. . . ."[95]

I take this to mean that *Ap. John* is speaking of Adam's fellow, Sophia/Ennoia.[96] Realizing that Sophia came down to rectify her fault, Adam recognizes in her his rightful consort. She furnishes him with what he has been lacking, and in so doing, she corrects her own deficiency. BG has an interest-

ing sentence right after Adam's Genesis paraphrase: "Because the Consort of
the Mother was sent forth to remedy her deficiencies, Adam gave her the name
'Mother of all Living.' "[97] Commenting on this passage, Janssens concludes
that Adam and Eve's marriage is based on the image of the relationship
between Sophia and First Man.[98]

Ap. John next identifies Sophia with Zoe, who has been mentioned before,
carrying the name of Holy Spirit.[99] One notices the expression "our sister
Sophia," which shows her doubleness—or quadrupleness, as A. Orbe sees it,
for she is both mother (= sister of the aeons) and daughter (= wife of
Adam).[100] As Epinoia, Sophia is mother, but as runaway aeon, she is disobedient daughter. But there is even a doubling in this daughter-image: she is
"born" out of Adam's side, and in that respect she is his child, while also
becoming his mate. In short, as Wilson sums up, "We have thus at least four
different entities—the Spirit, Sophia, the Epinoia of Light and created Eve—
who have somehow to be discovered in the narrative of Genesis."[101]

Giversen lets Pronoia name Sophia "the mother of all living,"[102] and in
Wisse's edition it seems to be "foreknowledge" (but the term is Pronoia, not
Prognosis![103]) and Sophia who instigate the human beings to taste the knowledge. Yet another actor intervenes, for Christ asserts that it was *he* who
appeared as an eagle on the tree of knowledge. The tree is associated with
Epinoia,[104] and Christ seems to encroach on her territory![105] He, not Epinoia,
is going to awaken the human beings. *Ap. John* wavers with respect to the
salvific tasks of Christ and Epinoia: BG has the latter, not Christ, as the eagle
on the tree.[106]

In a renewed attempt to gain power over Epinoia, Yaltabaoth throws Adam
and Eve out of Paradise (this is probably not a pure calamity, because the
garden is an archontic environment). Clothing the human couple in darkness,
Yaltabaoth perceives that the light-element is still present in the woman.
Because the archon is planning to seduce Eve, Pronoia "sent some and they
snatched Life out of Eve."[107] It is unclear what "some" refers to, but Zoe's
escape is made explicit. Here Epinoia and Eve are split, for the author could
not let Eve be seduced by the archon while Epinoia was still present in her.[108]

Two sons, Eloim (= Cain) and Yave (= Abel), result from this liaison. *Ap.
John* credits the chief archon with the subsequent sexual desire in the human
beings.[109] In contrast to Yaltabaoth's relationship with Eve, Adam's sexual
encounter occurs not with her, but with "the likeness of his own foreknowledge," that is, with Prognosis.[110] With her,

he begot the likeness of the son of man. He called him Seth according to
the way of the race in the aeons. Likewise, the mother also sent down her

spirit which is in her likeness and a copy of those who are in the pleroma, for she will prepare a dwelling place for the aeons which will come down. (P. 112, 24.35–25.5)

In parallel to the previous account of the heavenly Adam, Perfect Man,[111] and his son Seth, earthly Adam now imitates his upper image. Seth's conception requires a heavenly spouse—but recall that no female was needed for the birth of the first, Pleromatic Seth!

Ap. John does not specify the time of the aeons' descent. For the moment, Adam and the human beings remain under the sway of archontic powers, drinking the "water of forgetfulness": "Thus the seed remained for a while assisting (him) in order that, when the Spirit comes forth from the holy aeons, he may raise him up and heal him from the deficiency, that the whole pleroma may (again) become holy and faultless" (p. 112, 25.5–20).

One may assume that this will be the final descent of the spirit. Only in this future event will the human being—and thereby Sophia—be healed of deficiency. Truly significant is the information that the Pleroma, too, remains lacking until this salvific moment: the lacks in Sophia and in the human beings are emblems of the fault in the Pleroma.[112]

Yaltabaoth's constant search for the spirit-element seems not to have met with success. He gains no power over Epinoia by seducing Eve, for the woman has been split, and Adam has acquired Epinoia as his proper mate. Adam's deficiency has been healed and Yaltabaoth has lost out. The promised, full healing will come about at a future moment, but does Yaltabaoth have a place in the scheme of salvation? Adam and Yaltabaoth stand opposed to one another, as does Epinoia to Eve, and Seth to Cain and Abel. The final sorting out of the "seed" with respect to its eligibility for full redemption has not yet been specified.

CONCLUSION

Toward the end of *Ap. John*, John inquires about the destinies of the various kinds of souls. These soul-groups are: the perfect ones; those who were enlightened but did not carry out their duties; those who did not know to whom they belonged; and, finally, the apostates. Christ states that the souls in the first three groups will be saved, but that for the apostates there is no hope.

Giversen is puzzled by the text's concern with the salvation of the soul. He seems to feel that *Ap. John* ought to concentrate on spirits, not souls.[113] I think one may connect Sophia, Adam, and even Yaltabaoth with the text's preoccu-

pation with the souls' fate. Even as Sophia seems more connected to the upper
spirit principle than to the psychic element—traditionally the "wobbly," middle entity—her troubles and vacillations demonstrate that the spirit-element,
too, has its tribulations; the pneuma is not so lofty as to be exempt from trials.
Adam, both psychic and pneumatic, ironically obtained his spirit from Yaltabaoth, who seems to be soul incarnate. And *Ap. John*'s central theme is
precisely Yaltabaoth's numerous attempts to gain access to his own lost spirit.
One recalls, too, that the archon's origin and home would appear to be in the
upper realms, not in the lower ones that he rules.[114] It may be that both spirit
and soul belong in the Pleroma; if this is so, does Yaltabaoth also have a
chance of final redemption?

The account of the various souls' fates leads to John's question about the
origin of the "despicable spirit" (p. 114, 27.30f.). No immediate answer
follows, but Christ starts by saying, "The Mother-Father who is rich in mercy,
the holy Spirit in every way, the One who is merciful and who sympathizes
with you (pl.), i.e. the Epinoia of the foreknowledge of light, he raised up the
offspring of the perfect race" (p. 114, 27.30–28.5).[115] One assumes that "the
perfect race" refers to the first group of souls mentioned above. But because
there are two further categories of souls eligible for redemption, the "offspring"—broadly understood—may include more than just this first group.

Ap. John gives a short account of the flood that Yaltabaoth caused to
obliterate his creation. He does this in *repentance* "for everything which had
come into being through him" (p. 114, 28.30). (One may ask whether this
repentance of the archon implies his final forgiveness by the Pleroma.) Noah is
the hero of the flood story; he and his family escape into "a luminous cloud"
(p. 114, 29.10–15), an exact parallel to the cloud that hid Yaltabaoth in the
beginning![116] And, as Sophia was with Yaltabaoth in his cloud, so now
Pronoia stays with Noah in his hiding place.

Yaltabaoth still strives for power over the spiritual element. He and his
cohorts make more attempts to catch it: they try to mate with the daughters of
men—the Gen. 6:1f. theme—but they do not succeed. Next, they seem to re-
create the antimimon pneuma. Only now does Christ come to the gist of the
answer that John sought above. This new antimimon pneuma is effective, it
seems, for the whole creation is subjected to the archons "until now," says
Christ (p. 115, 30.10).

At this point BG offers an interesting conclusion to the parallel passage in
C II.1: "The Highly-Praised, however, the Father-Mother of Mercy, takes
shape in their descendants (σπέρμα)."[117] To this S. Arai asserts that "Sophia
nimmt in Christus menschliche Gestalt an" ("Sophia takes on human form in
Christ").[118] But Arai's judgment seems misguided, for the text speaks, not of

Christ as the vessel, but of Sophia, the Mother-Father, as taking form in humanity.[119] Arai has another, more useful insight, however, when he states that χι μορφή, "taking form," can also mean the formation or re-creation of the Pleroma.[120] This would support my view that Sophia's defect has indeed affected the Pleroma, and consequently, that the human beings' shortcoming has implications for that upper realm.

Christ now identifies himself with Pronoia: "I, therefore, the perfect Pronoia of the all, changed myself into my seed, for I existed first, going on every road. For I am the richness of the light; I am the remembrance of the Pleroma" (p. 115, 30.10–20). Here, the text of C II.1 contradicts Arai's judgment of Sophia as taking form in Christ; and, just as the Mother-Father in BG was said to take shape in humanity, so now Christ proclaims it as *his* activity.[121] Immediately after Christ's saying, in BG, that the "Mother appeared before me again,"[122] comes this statement about her: "What she accomplished in the world was the remedy of her deficiency."[123] To this, Arai admits that the restoration of Sophia includes that of humankind, her seed, σπέρμα.[124] I would add, more specifically, that by appearing in Adam as his mate, Sophia fills out the lack in him, and thereby saves herself.

Christ next relates how he descended three times (p. 115, 30.15f.),[125] of which the narrative moment is the third. Again, he proclaims that he *is* the three entities—the Father, the Mother, and the Son—and so the end of *Ap. John* now neatly ties in to Christ's initial revelation. The intervening story that makes up most of *Ap. John* has been shown to substantiate the claim that Christ includes the three entities.

It remains to take a closer look at the occurrences of the term "seed" or "offspring" (σπέρμα) in *Ap. John*, for in this term may lie a clue to the promised, near-comprehensive salvation. *Ap. John* refers to σπέρμα in the following passages: (1) 20.20–25, where Epinoia teaches Adam about the descent of his seed—that is, Adam's Pleromatic image has come down as human being to the lower realm; (2) 25.10–15, the seed, humanity, "remained for a while assisting (him)" (that is, the archon); (3) 28.1–5, "the Epinoia of the foreknowledge of light" raised up the σπέρμα of the perfect race; and (4) Christ's proclamation, "I changed myself into my seed" (30.10–15). Only in BG do we have the sentence, "What she accomplished in this world was the remedying of her deficiency."[126] In regard to the last passage, one ought to consult Janssens's translation, "Voici encore les choses qu'elle a faites dans le cosmos: elle a redressé sa descendance (σπέρμα)" ("Here, again, are the things that she has accomplished in the cosmos: she has rehabilitated her offspring (σπέρμα)")[127]: it is not the deficiency that has been raised up, but the offspring, that is, humanity.

If the offspring is the human race, what then of the first offspring, Yalta-baoth? As it turns out, the archon was not even first, for heavenly Adam takes this position. Adam, as both heavenly and earthly offspring, stands, as son, in opposition to Yaltabaoth, the flawed aeon. In a certain sense Sophia has two sons: Adam and Yaltabaoth, the first created in partnership (in his heavenly, first fashioning) and the second an illegitimate child of the androgynous, autonomous Sophia.

Again, if one substitutes "spirit" for Adam, and "soul" for the archon, a possible reason appears for *Ap. John*'s concern with the salvation of the soul, so mystifying to Giversen.[128] As personified *psuchē*, Yaltabaoth is the soul who cannot make use of, or attain to, the spirit. Would Yaltabaoth belong in any of the groups of souls mentioned above? Evidently not, for when Christ speaks of the spirit, saying, "For the power will descend upon every man, for without it no one can stand" (p. 113, 26.10–15), he alludes—negatively, I think—to Yaltabaoth. Being soul, Yaltabaoth is still no man, that is, he does not stand erect. Instead, he is a lion-faced serpent. His condition demonstrates his lack of spirit, and this lack does not seem ever to be healed. One recalls, too, that in the beginning, Yaltabaoth was said to possess a form different from that of his mother—again, a possible reference to his earthbound posture.

Yaltabaoth's tragic loss of spirit when he infused it into Adam should perhaps be seen as his just deserts. By unwittingly squandering the spirit—at the instigation of the Pleroma!—Yaltabaoth destroyed any possibility he might have had to become human, that is, to be a human soul eligible for salvation. One might even see him as belonging among the apostate group of souls headed for perdition, because he abandoned the spirit.

Ap. John insists that Adam is more knowledgeable than his maker, Yalta-baoth. This, too, supports the idea that erect posture is an indicator of higher intelligence, of spirit-endowment. Nevertheless, Adam "falls," that is, be-comes dangerously like Yaltabaoth, and must be "reerected." Sophia accom-plishes this, and in the process raises up herself, as well as subsequent hu-manity. Yaltabaoth, however, is excluded. But *Ap. John*'s vacillation with regard to Yaltabaoth's theft—alternatively, legal acquisition—of the mother's power reveals an uncertainty about Yaltabaoth's position in the scheme of salvation. As I see it, *Ap. John* has trouble with the accommodation of the archontic principle, precisely because he signifies the *psuchē*. But even the *psuchē* that does not know to whom it belongs—and this *could* mean Yalta-baoth, too—will eventually be saved. Curiously sympathetic to the archon, *Ap. John* still dooms him to perdition. The inventor of the archontic system, Yaltabaoth, cannot be saved. He is the prisoner of the world he created, even though he did this on the pattern of the Pleromatic world.

A final note on Yaltabaoth's regret at having created the world: his repentance, unlike that of his mother, Sophia, does not seem to work. But then it was never expressly directed toward the Pleroma, as hers was. In fact, the text does not indicate whether the archon expressed his repentance to anyone. The theme may, simply, be a loyal reflection of the Genesis tradition without further elaboration.

Apart from Yaltabaoth—who, strictly speaking, *does* belong among Sophia's seed—the nonapostate offspring will be saved. In restoring herself to the aeon-world, Sophia redeems mankind. Christ, too, returns to the aeon after his third, final visit to the lower world. BG's reference to the Mother's raising up of the σπέρμα at the end indicates that the entire universe has been restored: Pleroma *and* humanity are brought back to the original state. Therefore, no distinction remains between earth and Pleroma. Still, the intervening story of how humanity obtained its Pleromatic element, the spirit, ironically includes sinful aeons and even the unsaved Yaltabaoth, who transmitted the spirit that was unavailable to himself.

The soteriology in *Ap. John* presents a comprehensive pattern of salvation for Sophia as well as for mankind, exemplified by Adam. The revealer in the account, Christ, announces that he will remain in the aeon after this last of his three visits. So his mission, too, has reached fulfilment. Thoroughly familiar by now, the pattern of initial harmony in the Pleroma, disrupted by an act of excess, and leading finally to a restoration of the equilibrium, has, at its center, the Sophia figure. In *Ap. John*, she both saves herself and is aided by powers above her. Thus, the text is ambivalent regarding the female's own, innate capacity.

A similar duality appears in *Exc. Thdot.*, where Wisdom represents soul vis-à-vis Christ's spiritual character. But here competition between the two is expressed in a manner different from that of *Ap. John*, in which the issue of androgyny looms large. For, in *Exc. Thdot.*, Sophia and Christ form a distinct pair. And yet, because pneuma and *psuchē* belong inextricably together, the text cannot avoid portraying the two as essentially one. Here, the "female" is potentially "male." This is spelled out in *Exc. Thdot.*'s salvation pattern, which posits a third level, beyond male and female.

CHAPTER 4

Females, Males, and Angels
in Clement of Alexandria's
Excerpta ex Theodoto

I n 1908 O. Dibelius declared the *Excerpta ex Theodoto (Exc. Thdot.)*—transmitted by Clement of Alexandria—to belong among the problem-children of early Christian literature.[1] This judgment might still be shared by the scholars who have translated and commented on this source. Writing in roughly the latter half of the second century, Clement gives no clue to the exact identity of Theodotus.[2] A second problem is the extent to which Clement's own voice may, at times, predominate in his rendering of *Exc. Thdot.* It is certain, however, that Clement's text presents an important source for Valentinian Gnosis and that it conveys highly esoteric and enigmatic speculations on the constitution of the human being, on the salvation of the members of the Valentinian church, and on the roles of Christ and Wisdom.

Intrigued by the uses of the terms "female," "male," and "angel" in passages of *Exc. Thdot.*, I set out to investigate these, presupposing a certain coherence in their use in the text. Consistency, however, is not generally attributed to *Exc. Thdot.*, and most scholars working with the text agree that it is a composite source.[3] Without taking a stand on this question regarding the text as a whole, I nevertheless propose the following theses with respect to the terms female, male, and angel in *Exc. Thdot.*:

A. The element *psuchē*, equated with the "calling" ($\dot{\eta}$ $\varkappa\lambda\tilde{\eta}\sigma\iota\varsigma$) and with the female, denotes the majority of the members of the Valentinian church. It is predominantly to this "psychic" group that *Exc. Thdot.* addresses itself.[4]
B. The element pneuma, equated with the "elect" ($\dot{\eta}$ $\dot{\varepsilon}\varkappa\lambda o\gamma\dot{\eta}$) and with the male, is superior to the *psuchē* in such a way that the lower, female *psuchē* element needs to acquire the nature of the male pneuma in or-

der to be eligible for salvation. The female becomes male in the wedding feast in the Ogdoad, the eighth realm situated immediately below the Limit (Horos), which is the threshold to the Lightworld, the Pleroma.

C. The united male and female entity, which has become completely male in the Ogdoad, merges with its male angel in another event, the bridal chamber in the Pleroma. Thus, only the fully male entity is eligible for unity with its angel. The three separate entities—female, male, and angel—are all portrayed in *Exc. Thdot.* both as groups of beings and as groups of elements. However, as far as the female *psuchē* and the male pneuma are concerned, it is important to understand these terms as designations of elements *in* people, not as *classes of* people.

D. The angels play a double role: they are guardian angels to the *psuchē* in the human being, and in the Pleroma they are male bridegrooms to the male bride (the entity that has transformed its female, psychic element into maleness).

E. Christ, a savior-figure, and Wisdom, a female creator-figure—both consisting of composite, even opposing, elements—relate to one another as pneuma to *psuchē*. Yet, these two figures are, essentially, *one*, at the same time that, as two, they compete with one another. This paradoxical relationship between Christ and Wisdom partly parallels that of the elements pneuma and *psuchē* in the human being, and it reflects the human being's relationship to its angel. Christ and Wisdom are compatible yet competing prototypes for the Valentinians.

THE ENVISIONED SALVATION OF THE "PSYCHICS"

Exc. Thdot. 21 is the first passage to be examined with respect to the terms female, male, and angel:

(1) The Valentinians say that the finest emanation of Wisdom is spoken of in "He created them in the image of God, male and female created he them." Now the males from this emanation are the "election" but the females are the "calling" and they call the male beings "angelic," and the females themselves the superior seed [τὸ διαφέρον πνεῦμα]. (2) So also in the case of Adam, the male remained in him but all the female seed was taken from him and became Eve, from whom the females are derived, as the males are from him. Therefore the males are drawn together with the Logos, but the females, becoming men, are united to

the angels and pass into the Pleroma. (3) Therefore the woman is said to be changed into a man, and the Church here on earth into angels. (Pp. 56–57)[5]

Wisdom—a "she" in *Exc. Thdot.*, notwithstanding the "he" of the Biblical reference—is responsible for the creation referred to in Gen. 1:27 (and in Gen. 2:21–22?). "Male" and "female" here do not, in my opinion, refer to gender, but to the "elect" and the "calling." Again, these designations concern elements, that is, constituents, in human beings, not classes of people. Calling the male beings "angelic," the Valentinians—the majority of whom are "females"—call themselves "τὸ διαφέρον πνεῦμα." Like R. P. Casey, F. Sagnard translates this term "superior seed,"[6] a choice that produces great difficulties in these scholars' further interpretation of *Exc. Thdot.*

Relying on E. Pagels,[7] I take τὸ διαφέρον πνεῦμα to mean not "superior seed," but "borne-apart" or, simply, "different" seed. Matters are further complicated by the fact that even though the expression is "τὸ διαφέρον πνεῦμα," Casey still translates "seed," not "pneuma,"[8] while Sagnard gives "τὸ διαφέρον σπέρμα," and translates accordingly.[9] The two scholars must have a reason to equate "superior" with "pneuma," an association unsubstantiated by the text.

Sagnard notes that Wisdom's emission has also been effected by Christ,[10] who, according to *Exc. Thdot.*, is whole, complete, and a perfect image of the Father.[11] Perceiving a balance between Wisdom and Christ, Sagnard seems to be saying that the male and female are equivalents as far as perfect parentage is concerned. Pagels, dissenting with Sagnard, sees τὸ διαφέρον πνεῦμα, the different seed, as inferior, because it has been emitted without the participation of Sophia's *syzygos*, Christ.[12] However, her attempt to separate Sophia's "complete" emission of the elect *together* with Christ, from Sophia's purportedly incomplete creation of the calling,[13] seems unconvincing.

Wisdom's emanation is the one in Gen. 1:27, and since it is called "the finest," one would expect it to be in harmony with Wisdom's consort, Christ. But syzygious creations are not central to *Exc. Thdot.*, and are not mentioned in paragraph 21. That Wisdom creates alone, should not be taken as a depreciation of her activity, for the text seems to applaud it.

Like Sagnard, Casey identifies the different seed—which he calls superior seed—with the elect.[14] J. F. McCue, on the other hand, agrees with Pagels's correction of Sagnard and Casey as regards the term "τὸ διαφέρον πνεῦμα," and he remarks on Clement's explicitness when he states that the Valentinians call themselves "females" and "the calling."[15] It is important to keep this statement in mind in the following, for one would perhaps expect Valentinians to refer to themselves as pneumatics (Casey's and Sagnard's assumption). Instead, these Gnostics outrightly state that they are in need of salvation.

Section 2 in *Exc. Thdot.* 21 elucidates the constitution of Adam. Here, Adam is categorized with "the finest emanation of Wisdom" of section 1. The male[16] remained in Adam, but his female seed (the rib) was taken out to become Eve. In some sense, then, Adam is the creator of Eve. She is the mediator of the female element, and subsequently produces more females, while males derive from Adam. Here, too, the gender designations refer to pneuma and *psuchē*: (2) does not speak of a different parentage for male and female human beings.

Section 3 "explains" the preceding section: the two kinds of elements, pneuma and *psuchē*, await different modes of salvation, it seems. The pneuma, Logos-like, is drawn together[17] with the Logos ("the like attracts the like"). The majority of Valentinians, however, who have not yet realized their pneuma but only their *psuchē*, must "become men," unite with their angels, and then pass on into the Pleroma. One may ask: What is the nature of this union? What is the gender of the angels? Why is maleness a prerequisite transformation for the females? *Exc. Thdot.* "explains" by way of offering a parallel: as the female changes into a male, so the earthly Church is transformed into angels. Here, one sees that the idea of transformation is connected with a corollary transition from the earthly to the heavenly level.

Casey says that "the salvation of [the calling, $\kappa\lambda\tilde{\eta}\sigma\iota\varsigma$] is dependent on the union with [the elect, $\dot{\epsilon}\kappa\lambda o\gamma\dot{\eta}$] so that both become part of the same male personality."[18] But this interpretation conflates the two modes of salvation for the males and the females, it seems to me. It is not the elect and the calling that are united,[19] according to *Exc. Thdot.*; rather, the females are affiliated to their angels while the males are "drawn to" the Logos. Moreover, it is important to note that the females must acquire male nature *before* they are united to their angels. Maleness denotes eligibility for unity with the angel, Logos. The "psychic" Valentinians, then, are not automatically fit for salvation; it is even questionable whether the few "pneumatics" are "naturally" saved. *Contra* Casey, the point is not that the elect pneuma is distributed among the Valentinians,[20] but that *all* Valentinians possess *psuchē* and, potentially, pneuma, which must be fully realized, made actual, so that the rising from female (psychic) to male (pneumatic) level may take place.

Arguing that both "pneumatics" and "psychics" make up the membership in the Valentinian church, Pagels counters Sagnard's view of "l'église, c'est à dire l'Assemblée idéale des élus" ("The church, that is to say: the ideal assembly of the elect").[21] But when Pagels says that Theodotus uses the name "Ecclesia" for Sophia to designate the figure's alienation from the savior, that is, her cosmos-aspect,[22] this judgment overly stresses the distance between the cosmos and the Pleroma. One should remember that Christ, too, possesses both a psychic and a pneumatic element, the former of which does not necessarily denote alienation. Both aspects are necessary for Wisdom as well as for Christ, and so both figures are, in their lower aspects, "female." In *Exc. Thdot.* 21.3, the Church is identified as female, which must become male in order to be saved. Neither Church (Sophia) nor Christ can be categorized as definitely "male" or "female" while they remain on earth. In parallel fashion, the human being cannot be defined as pneumatic or psychic but must, in the end, realize its pneumatic potential.[23]

Exc. Thdot. 22 includes the following:

(1) . . . the angels of whom we are portions were baptised for us. (2) But we are dead, who are deadened by this existence, but the males are alive who did not partake in this existence. . . . (3) Therefore we are raised up "equal to angels," and restored to unity with the males, member for member. (4) . . . "those who are baptised for us, the dead," are the angels who are baptised for us, in order that when we, too, have the Name, we may not be hindered and kept back by the Limit and the Cross from entering the Pleroma. (Pp. 56–59)

The "we" are the Valentinians on the psychic stage, those who are related to the angels with whom they seek unification. By undergoing baptism, the angels perform a preliminary, "vicarious" salvation for the Valentinians, providing a service for those "deadened by this existence."

Males and angels should not be equated here,[24] for the males are "pneumatics" who, like the angels, do not really partake of earthly life. Since the males are said to be angelic (N.B., *not* angels!), as in *Exc. Thdot.* 21, one might call them potential angels. The females, in their turn, are potential males, "pneumatics."[25] It is important to keep in mind that the restoration "to unity," in (3), is not that of one human being to another, but of one element, *psuchē*, to its corresponding pneuma, *within* the same human being.

Pagels, attempting to clarify the relationship between males and angels, draws attention to the Valentinian definition of "angel" in *Exc. Thdot.* 25.1: "a logos that has received a message from Him who is."[26] The elect, being potential angels, are drawn to the Logos in the end, as seen in *Exc. Thdot.* 21.3.[27] Sagnard interprets the text to mean that the male elements—which he equates with angels—will be reintegrated with the female seeds.[28] But this is not what baptism signifies. The point is that in this process, the female entities lost their femaleness, that is, the psychic element is superseded. If one may speak of any syzygy here, it is a male one, for the entity that enters the

Pleroma cannot be spoken of as incorporating the male and the female. Having become male, the saved Valentinian has "married" his male angel, his true, spiritual counterpart.[29]

The restoration requires the baptism ritual, which invokes "the Name," that of "the Son."[30] *Exc. Thdot.* 22.6–7 says: "Now the angels were baptised in the beginning in the redemption of the Name which descended upon Jesus in the dove and redeemed him. And redemption was necessary even for Jesus, in order that, approaching through Wisdom, he might not be detained by the Notion of Deficiency" (pp. 56–59). "Psychic" Jesus was redeemed; likewise, the Church will be lifted up to the higher level. The angels, who have been individually assigned to each "psychic," act as guardian angels to the psychic elements. The baptism—salvation—of these angels holds out hope for the redemption of every psychic element on earth. Wisdom, separated from "the Notion of Deficiency"—the Ennoia of Deficiency—signifies the higher image of the lower, deficient entity. Here, Wisdom corresponds to pneuma, the Ennoia of Deficiency to *psuchē*. Both Christ and Wisdom are split into two parts, *without necessarily being* two distinct personalities.

Casey, seeing *Exc. Thdot.* as mainly concerned with the elect, thinks that the baptism ritual deals with these. "In the case of the elect, the effect of the rite was not due ultimately to the angels, nor even to the Logos . . . but to the fact that through union with his angel the elect soul is baptized in the same 'Name' as the angels."[31] But the elect do not appear in this part of *Exc. Thdot.*: the males do not seem to need such a ritual of redemption. *Exc. Thdot.* 22 deals with the called, whose role vis-à-vis their guardian angels has already been spelled out, in 21. The males have no use for such angels, but for the Logos. Again, the modes of salvation for the two elements, the *psuchē* and the pneuma, are quite different, a point that Casey refuses to see.

On the next page, Casey, echoed by Sagnard, states that "in baptism the male angels and their counterparts are reunited in their original form and in the common possession of the 'Name.' "[32] The aim may indeed be the "re-establishment of harmony in the Pleroma,"[33] but the earthly ritual of baptism does not so much *effect* as *anticipate* this final restoration. The two parallel levels—the earthly and the Pleromatic—must be kept apart, for the "psychics" must be baptised while still on earth. Only on the Pleroma-stage does the final transformation into angelic-noetic life take place, and this happens *after* "the Lord's Day" (*Exc. Thdot.* 63.1; see below, p. 76), in the Ogdoad.

Exc. Thdot. 26.1–3 reads:

(1) The visible part of Jesus was Wisdom and the Church of the superior seeds [τῶν σπερμάτων τῶν διαφερόντων] and he put it on through the

flesh . . . but the Invisible part is the Name, which is the Only-Begotten Son. (2) Thus when he says, "I am the door," he means that you who are of the superior seed [τοῦ διαφέροντος σπέρματος], shall come up to the boundary where I am. (3) And when he enters in, the seed also enters with him into the Pleroma, brought together and brought in through the door. (Pp. 60–61)

Both Wisdom and the Church of the different seed are identified with the visible, psychic part of Jesus.[34] Casey, noting that Jesus identifies himself with Sophia and with the Church, is nevertheless puzzled by the fact that τὸ ὁρατὸν and τοῦ σαρκίου ("the visible" and "of the flesh") refer "to the same thing,"[35] to psychic Jesus. But why would visibility and flesh be incompatible? Maybe the trouble, for Casey, is that Sophia, the different seed, and psychic/fleshly Jesus are all identified as being in need of salvation because they are depicted on the lower, earthly level.

Jesus is also to be found elsewhere: at the Limit, Horos, which is the "door" to the Pleroma. Together, then, all three—Jesus, Wisdom, and the Church of the different seeds—enter into the upper region. It is the "Name," another part of Christ, that enables all three entities to ascend to the Pleroma. Just as the guardian angels in *Exc. Thdot.* 22 received baptism, so here, Jesus effects salvation both for himself and for Wisdom and the different seed.[36]

Next comes a long, allegorical exegesis of the Jewish ritual of the high priest in the Holy of Holies.[37] Sagnard notes that this exposition is related to that of Clement in his *Stromateis* 6,[38] but I see no reason to regard *Exc. Thdot.* 27 as non-Valentinian.[39] The text, in its entirety, is this:

(1) The priest on entering within the second veil removed the plate at the altar of incense, and entered himself in silence with the Name engraved upon his heart, indicating the laying aside of the body which has become pure like the golden plate and bright through purification . . . the putting away as it were of the soul's body on which was stamped the lustre of piety, by which he was recognized by the Principalities and Powers as having put on the Name. (2) Now he discards this body, the plate which had become light, within the second veil, that is, in the rational sphere the second complete veil of the universe, at the altar of incense, that is, with the angels who are the ministers of prayers carried aloft. (3) Now the soul, stripped by the power of him who has knowledge, as if it had become a body of the power, passes into the spiritual realm and becomes now truly rational and high priestly, so that it might now be animated, so to speak, directly by the Logos, just as the archangels became the high priests of the angels, and the First-Created the high priest of the archan-

gels [Clement's own comment follows in (4)]. (5) Thus, having transcended the angelic teaching and the Name taught in Scripture, it comes
to the knowledge and comprehension of the facts. It is no longer a bride
but has become a Logos and rests with the bridegroom together with the
First-Called and the First-Created, who are friends by love, sons by
instruction and obedience, and brothers by community of origin. (6) So
that it belonged to the dispensation to wear the plate and to continue the
pursuit of knowledge, but the work of power was that man becomes the
bearer of God, being controlled directly by the Lord and becoming, as it
were, his body. (Pp. 60–63)

Proceeding from the first veil area to the second, the priest, personifying
the soul, removes his body, the plate, and tacitly anticipates becoming "the
Name," his destination. Purification of the body is necessary for the ascension
and for the envisioned transformation of the *psuchē*. Piety and morality,
having until now brightened the "soul's body," are left behind. The plate
(body) is discarded within the second veil, that is, at the stage of the rational. It
belongs to the purified body to pray, and prayers are here carried upwards by
angels. At the next stage, however, only silent prayer is allowed. It seems that
the power of which the body is stripped is the demiurgic, psychic entity.
Passing on into the spiritual sphere, the soul now becomes truly rational, and at
this stage it will be inspired directly by the Logos. Finally, the ascending soul
becomes the Logos itself.

Suddenly, at this point (in [4]), Clement interjects a condemning note. The
church father has no taste for heretics who, without Scriptural consent, claim
to be able "to see God face to face." He goes on, however, to describe the
Valentinian exposition, which now expresses something important about the
evaluation of Scripture. For the soul has "transcended the angelic teaching and
the Name taught in Scripture," finding, instead, "the knowledge and comprehension of the facts." Evidently, the spiritual realm and the scriptural—even
angelic—teachings are incompatible with one another. What does this mean?
It means that as long as the Gnosis must be transmitted by way of dogmas and
written words, however "angelic," its real message cannot be conveyed.[40]
Unsymbolic, spiritual knowledge excludes written, conceptual Gnosis, which
remains on the psychic level.

Now the soul "is no longer a bride, but has become a Logos and rests
together with the bridegroom." This means that the *psuchē* has acquired the
nature of her mate, the Logos. The process by which the soul becomes
spiritual is rendered in sexual imagery, but it is an otherworldly "carnal" union
that is going on here, for a bride who becomes a (male) Logos leaves no place

for anything female, that is, psychic. The unification is not one of genders, but is a transcendental transformation to the completely male, the pneumatic. Here, female plus male equals male.

Finally, *Exc. Thdot.* 27 returns to the plate left within the second veil, the rational, "soul's body" sphere. "Dispensation," οἰκονομία, is contrasted with "the work of power" that makes the human being a "bearer of God." Moreover, the purified (discarded!) body becomes *truly* a body in the spiritual sense, the Lord's body. Of course, it is confusing to speak of "bodies" at this stage—due to the limits of human language—but the identification of the ascended, transformed soul with the Logos and the Lord demands this kind of image. The priestly action in the temple symbolizes this ascent of the soul from the earthly to the Pleroma realm.

Sagnard's insistence that *Exc. Thdot.* 27 must be attributed to Clement is based on his view that a *psuchē* cannot possibly ascend. In the study of Gnosticism it has become an axiom, unfortunately, that only pneuma, not *psuchē*, may go upwards; "se transformer en logoi" ("to be transformed into Logoi")[41] is unthinkable as regards the psychic element. Sagnard also expects the union to be syzygous, but that does not happen in *Exc. Thdot.* Instead, one finds a female—that is, a potential male—becoming fully male, helped by another male, the Logos.

O. Dibelius, too, assigns *Exc. Thdot.* 27 to Clement, but he is a little more detailed with respect to the puzzling lack of syzygy-imagery. Expecting such symbolism, Dibelius deems the bride-bridegroom language to belong to the (Orthodox) church. He attacks P. Ruben's old thesis, to the effect that λόγος γίνεϑαι (to become Logos) should be identified with ἀπηνόρῶσϑαι (to become male). This argument is, Dibelius says, "aus der Luft gegriffen" ("taken out of thin air"): "Denn hier [in *Exc. Thdot.* 27] handelt es sich um eine von der Logos beseelte, im Aufstieg am Ziele angelangte Seele, dort [in *Exc. Thdot.* 21] um die Vereinigung der Pneumatiker mit ihrem Syzygos; d.h. um die spezifische Valentinianische, auch in § 64 wiederkehrende Lehre" ("For here [in *Exc. Thdot.* 27] the issue is an ascending soul that—having been ensouled by the Logos—has arrived at its destination, while there [in *Exc. Thdot.* 21] the issue deals with the unification of the pneumatics with their *syzygos*, that is, the topic in the specifically Valentinian teaching, which also returns in § 64").[42]

In all three paragraphs—21, 27, and 64—I would argue, the goals and the way to those goals are consistent. The transition requires a movement from the female (psychic) to the realized male (pneumatic) nature. The three paragraphs (64 is to be treated later) agree with one another. But because the final Logos-identification is spoken of in bride-and-bridegroom language, scholars have felt compelled to see in the Valentinian adaptation of this language an (illegitimate) imitation of the symbolic imagery of the Orthodox church. Theodotus expands on the bridal imagery by transcending its usual connotations. A balanced, male and female, image of the syzygy does not occur anywhere in the *Exc. Thdot.* passages treated so far. Instead, the text presents salvation in terms of a different syzygy: the transformed female—now male—becomes united to its male counterpart which, again, is united to the male Logos.

CHRIST, ANGELS, AND THE BELIEVERS

Coming down from the Pleroma, Jesus brings with him the angels of the different seed (τοὺς ἀγγέλους τοῦ διαφέροντος), according to *Exc. Thdot.* 35.1. He does this so that the angels may aid the seeds in their redemption. However, this help is mutual, for the angels cannot reenter the Pleroma without bringing with them their psychic counterparts, the different seed. Unlike Jesus who "ha[s] the redemption in as much as he had proceeded from the Pleroma" (35.2), the angels do not possess the security of "automatic" salvation back into their home. As long as the psychic elements remain outside the Pleroma, so do the angels.

Furthermore, the Mother—another "psychic" as well as "pneumatic" emblem—also stays in the Kenoma ("emptiness," opposed to Pleroma),[43] for the time being. The full salvation for all, then, depends entirely on the psychic elements and their ultimate eligibility for the world above. Nothing "pneumatic" can ascend without its "psychic" companion: this holds for the Mother, for Jesus, and for the angels. Even if Jesus' salvation is guaranteed, he, too, awaits the perfection of the psychic elements for his own liberation.

J. Leipoldt and H.-M. Schenke correctly see the relationship between the angels and the seed as that of guardian angel and dependent, noting that "die Engel kümmern sich im eigenen Interesse um ihre Schutzbefohlenen. Denn sie dürfen nicht ohne sie in das Pleroma zurückkehren" ("the angels have their own interest in caring for those entrusted to them, for the angels cannot return to the Pleroma without them").[44] One might say that the angels have debased themselves for the benefit of the psychic element, and thus they are genuinely subjected to the rules of the Kenoma for as long as the psychic entity remains unsaved. Jesus, too, is a Pleroma-angel,[45] but unlike the guardian angels, he does not act as a helper for the individual "psychic."

Sagnard's interpretation of *Exc. Thdot.* 35 suffers from his consistent equation of "different seed" with the pneumatic element.[46] This means that, for him, the point of the temporarily suffering angels loses its weight, and he thinks that the angels' task is that of separating the psychic element from the "pneumatics."[47] When McCue writes that *Exc. Thdot.* 32–41, "like 21ff. . . . describ[e] the supracosmic angels, the imperfect angelic element temporarily embodied in this world,"[48] he, too, fails to discern the specific roles of the angels in paragraph 35. Angels appearing in this world do not automatically denote imperfection! These angels have been put into the world for the sake of the psychic element, and their stay here should not be negatively evaluated. (No Christian commentator on Jesus' incarnation would view the embodiment in decidedly negative terms.)

Pagels, referring to *Exc. Thdot.* 21.3, 35.1–2, and 41, stresses the different seed's affinity with Jesus and notes that they are not tied to the Logos (who is, as seen in paragraph 21, connected to the pneumatic element).[49] But *Exc. Thdot.* seems to me to be more concerned with the psychic entity's relationship to its guardian angel than with that to Jesus. The text goes on to describe the angels as "bound"; they "plead" on behalf of the different seed, are "restrained," and express a "zeal" to enter the Pleroma, "beg[ging] remission for" the different seed (35.3). Such behavior certainly shows that the angels are as eager as the psychic element to be allowed upwards. They may even surpass the psychic entity in eagerness, for no similar consciousness is portrayed with respect to the *psuchē*.

Further clarification of the difference between angels and the *psuchē* follows in *Exc. Thdot.* 36.1–2:

> Now they say that our Angels were put forth in unity, and are one, in that they came out from One. Now since we existed in separation, Jesus was baptised that the undivided should be divided until he should unite us with them in the Pleroma that we "the many" having become "one," might all be mingled in the One which was divided for our sakes. (Pp. 66–67)

Because the angels of the psychic elements are Pleromatic, they are not divided, but come from the Name, the One. The psychic elements, however, are surely divided, and it is for the sake of these that Jesus was baptised. One does well to note the tripartite schema: undivided—divided—undivided. Baptism represents the middle section, the division.[50] Division belongs to the Kenoma and undividedness to the Pleromatic world, which, prior to the creation, was kept in balanced wholeness, and which will, at the end, retrieve this wholeness. As long as the Dispensation rules, division reigns.[51]

Jesus seems to play a major role in this restoration. The psychic elements, however, do not unite with him but, through him, with their guardian angels. The life of the initiated is not, strictly, one in imitation of Jesus, as Quispel says,[52] but one striving to unite with one's guardian angel.[53]

Exc. Thdot. 39 speaks of the Mother who brings forth Christ in complete form (pp. 66–67). He then deserts her,[54] and the Mother's subsequent creations remain incomplete. Then: "Therefore, having produced the angelic elements of the 'called' she keeps them by herself, for the angelic elements of the elect had been put forth still earlier by the Male" (pp. 66–67). The passage that ties in with the beginning of this quotation presents difficulties acknowledged by both Sagnard and Casey, and the scholars' translations differ considerably.[55] Pagels's suggested reading may be helpful: "Therefore, having emitted also the angelic elements *of the topos of the called* . . . she kept them. . . ."[56] Referring to *Exc. Thdot.* 21, where Sophia bears the seed of both elect and called, Pagels puts these two passages in conjunction.[57]

One notes, however, that in *Exc. Thdot.* 39 a differentiation is made between the emission of the Mother and that of the Male, that is, Christ/Logos (or Adam, in *Exc. Thdot.* 21?). The "angelic elements of the 'called' " might be equated with the guardian angels of the "psychics" in paragraph 35. Kept outside the Pleroma—along with the Mother and with Jesus—these angels could thus be assigned to the Topos, that is, to the sphere of the Demiurge. The angelic elements of the elect, however, originate in the Logos and are, according to 21.3, drawn together with him at the end.

Sagnard suggests that the elements that the Mother keeps to herself are a kind of "semence pneumatique" ("pneumatic seed"), which is, nevertheless, " 'faible,' 'informe,' 'femelle' " (" 'feeble,' 'unformed,' 'female' "); but this does not fit with his equation of pneumatic with the male, angelic element.[58] Thus, his understanding of the two creations in *Exc. Thdot.* 39 becomes quite inconsistent.

Following Pagels, I cannot agree with McCue, who sees the angelic elements of the Topos as pneumatic elements.[59] *Exc. Thdot.* 39, as well as 35.1, seems to me to deal with the guardian angels of the psychic element, which are not to be confused with the pneumatic entity. It is important to note that paragraph 39 assigns angelic elements to *both* called and elect. This suggests that the angelic elements belonging to the called are, indeed, the guardian angels of *Exc. Thdot.* 35f., while the angelic elements of the elect equal the pleromatic Logos-counterparts of these elect.

Exc. Thdot. 40 follows: "Now those on the right were put forth by the Mother before the demand for the Light but the seeds of the Church after the demand for the Light, when the angelic elements of the seed had been put forth by the male" (pp. 68–69). "Those on the right" would seem to refer to the pneumatic element,[60] created by the Mother while Christ was still with her. Therefore, this creation is whole and complete, without lacking. After "the demand for the Light," that is, after Christ asked for Jesus to be sent down for the Mother's salvation, she puts forth the seeds of the Church, the psychic element.[61] Here, again, we find a reference to the creation by the Male, who emitted "the angelic elements of the seed." This emission now seems to have occurred at the same time as the Mother's second creation; it is not prior to her emission of the seeds of the Valentinian church (in contrast to *Exc. Thdot.* 39, above!).

The Male's creation here appears to be the same one that was in *Exc. Thdot.* 39, for I take the "angelic elements of the seed" to be those of the elect in the above passage. However, both 39 and 40 seem to contradict the creation account in *Exc. Thdot.* 21, particularly with respect to "the finest emanation of Wisdom" (see pp. 62–63, above). A certain competition between the Male and Wisdom begins to emerge. The author cannot quite decide who creates what. One notes, too, that the expected "those on the left"—supposedly opposed to "those on the right"—do not show up in this part of *Exc. Thdot.*[62]

Pagels seems to neglect the importance of the three emissions in *Exc. Thdot.* 40,[63] and she has no comments on the theme of competition between the Mother and the Male. McCue conflates the Male's creation—the angelic elements of the seed—with the guardian angels of the "psychics" when he makes the following triple equation: "It would seem that the angelic elements of the seed would be the same as the angels (masculine plural) of the dispersed seed of *Exc. Thdot.* 35.1, the same as the angelic, male, elect of 21ff. The angelic elements of the Topos would refer to the pneumatic elements present in this material order."[64] No: the angels of the different seed (35.1) and "the angelic elements of the 'called' " (39) both refer to the guardian angels of the psychic element. "The angelic, male, elect" of *Exc. Thdot.* 21 and "the angelic elements of the seed" (40) have to do with the elect and their Logos-nature.

Next:

41 (1) The superior seed [τα διαφέροντα], he says, came forth neither as passions, the seeds of which would have perished when they perished, nor as a creation, (2) but as offspring; since otherwise, when creation was being put together, the seeds would have been put together with it. Therefore, also it has an affinity with the Light, that is Jesus, whom the Christ, who besought the Aeons, first put forth. (Pp. 68–69)

That τα διαφέροντα are not passions, but offspring, ought to be taken at face value. If they had been passions, they would have become inextricably bound up with creation. Instead, they are ultimately eligible for redemption, due to their affinity with Jesus, the Light.

McCue notes the seed's relation to the Light, but he still, despite Theodotus's explicit statement, declares them to be passions. His judgment is based on the assumption that "the powers of the left [a term not found in *Exc. Thdot.* 40 or in 41], the first emission of the Mother, are formed by the Topos, not by the Light." He continues, "The elements on the right also come before the prayer for light. Both, therefore, are presumably brought forth like passions."[65]

Apart from the conjectural "powers of the left," there is no need to assume the Topos as a formator in *Exc. Thdot.* 40: Topos is not mentioned here. But most important, McCue seems dogmatically to connect the Mother and passion (that is, deficiency), even when the text goes against such a judgment.[66]

Exc. Thdot. 53.2, tells of Adam who unwittingly obtains the spiritual seed in his soul. Wisdom sows this seed in him, but it is the male angels who serve and take care of these seeds (53.3). Unbeknownst to Adam, he is "moved by Wisdom,"[67] just as the Demiurge is (53.4). According to 53.5, Adam's seed is "the 'bone,' the reasonable and heavenly soul [compare 21 and 27!] which is not empty but full of spiritual marrow" (pp. 76–77). Here is the evidence that the soul, *psuchē*, is potential pneuma, for the soul contains the spiritual essence to be fully realized as pneuma. Pagels aptly calls the bone psychic, its marrow pneumatic.[68] L. Schottroff draws attention to the extremely positive view of the soul in *Exc. Thdot.* 53.1,[69] and says that Adam receives the pneuma so that his bone should not be hollow. Schottroff also notes that Adam is "wesensgleich" ("of same nature") with Wisdom, Achamoth; by this she means that the human being, like Wisdom, finds itself outside of the Pleroma and thus in need of salvation.[70]

Further, Schottroff asserts, *psuchē* and pneuma connote essences that do not, strictly, exist independently as such.[71] These terms describe the human being in its relationship to salvation or perdition, to the two opposed poles of the dualism. It seems to me that Schottroff delivers a keen criticism against the claim that *psuchē* and pneuma are definite substances and, worse, that they refer to classes of human beings.[72] Schottroff feels that *Exc. Thdot.* wavers between a conception of classes and one of individual anthropology as regards these elements.[73] Possessing both *psuchē* and pneuma, the human being has the possibility to attain to its inner "marrow" encased in the "bone," to realize its pneumatic potential. As there is no bone without marrow, and vice versa, the *psuchē* and pneuma must be seen as companions in the Kenoma. Schottroff even goes so far as to deny "the pneumatic" an automatic salvation; like the *psuchē*, the pneuma, too, must decide whether it will tilt toward salvation or perdition.[74]

Schottroff's theories are supported in the immediately ensuing paragraphs of *Exc. Thdot.* Paragraph 54.2 states that Adam had the potential to balance all three natures—earthly, psychical, and spiritual—but because he did not succeed, subsequent humanity suffers his imbalance (56.2). Adam's two upper elements, *psuchē* and pneuma, are both divine[75]—both are "put forth through him but not by him" (55.2–3, pp. 76–77). Unfortunately, his earthly nature predominates.

McCue assigns all three elements to the "pneumatic" class of people, the two lower ones to the psychic class, and only the earthly element to material men.[76] But such a judgment hardly fits with the text, for all human beings possess all three entities. The question is whether one is able to realize the upper element, which lies present, perhaps dormant, in one's soul. Even Adam—not precisely a Valentinian ideal man—did possess the potential to realize his two upper elements, but failed. That he had these upper entities, however, was due to no virtue of his own.

Exc. Thdot. 58 speaks of Jesus bearing aloft and saving the Church, that is, the elect and the called (pp. 78–79). The former, those spiritually realized, are said to come from the Mother; the latter, "psychic" ones, from the Dispensation, "$\dot{\epsilon}\varkappa\ \tau\tilde{\eta}\varsigma\ o\dot{\iota}\varkappa o\nu o\mu\dot{\iota}\alpha\varsigma$" (58.1). In addition, Jesus saves the elements consubstantial with the elect and the called (58.2). This information is followed by an account, in paragraph 59, of Jesus wearing the "seed" as he went down to Space, Topos. This seed, which is from the Mother, he puts on, and it is "given form little by little through knowledge."[77] Undoubtedly, this is the seed mentioned in 58.2, and formation is the "growth pattern," so to speak, of the pneumatic element coming to its realization (compare 57.5). As he descends further, Jesus invests himself with psychic Christ, so that he may be compatible with the material world.

Exc. Thdot. 61 gives an exegesis of Jesus' crucifixion.[78] The effluences coming out from Jesus' side, for instance, signify the passions from which he is now liberated (61.3). One may recall Sophia, who, saved by Jesus, is also freed from *her* passions (*Exc. Thdot.* 45 and 67). In parallel manner, the soul anticipates its salvation when it will be restored to "the place [Pleroma] where [Jesus] is now leading the way" (61.5, pp. 80–81).[79] *Exc. Thdot.* explains that Jesus' spirit is now withdrawn, so that death may perform its task on him (61.6). Finally destroying death, the savior raises up the body freed of passion (61.7).[80] The paragraph concludes: "In this way, therefore, the psychic elements are raised and are saved, but the spiritual natures which believe receive a salvation superior to theirs, having received their souls as 'wedding garments' " (61.8).

Here, the text reveals that there are two different modes of salvation for the two elements. What is the significance of the *psuchē* acting as a wedding garment for the pneuma? The "clothing" with the garment seems to imply a separation *even as* the investiture hints at a unification.[81]

Exc. Thdot. 62 returns to the bone speculation, and to the separation of Christ's soul ("deposited in the Father's hands" [62.3]; compare with *Exc. Thdot.* 1.1!) from his spiritual nature, which "is not yet deposited but he keeps it" (ibid.). Sagnard translates the last element of 62.3, "$\dot{\alpha}\lambda\lambda$ ΄$\alpha\dot{\upsilon}\tau\grave{o}\varsigma$ $\sigma\tilde{\omega}\zeta\epsilon\iota$," as "c'est lui qui sauve" ("it is he who saves").[82] But J.-D. Kaestli disapproves of Sagnard's attempt to see a reflection of *Exc. Thdot.* 1.1 here, and instead suggests a separation of Italian (62.3) and Oriental (1.1) Christology.[83] And W. Foerster finds it incomprehensible that Jesus allegedly saves himself/his own pneumatic element.[84]

One may indeed wonder what such self-salvation means, especially in view of the statement that the savior's spiritual nature is not yet deposited. When will it be? I think *Exc. Thdot.* 63 answers the problem.

FROM OGDOAD TO PLEROMA

Exc. Thdot. 63 reads:

> (1) Now the repose of the spiritual elements on the Lord's Day, that is, in the Ogdoad, which is called the Lord's Day, is with the Mother who keeps their souls, the (wedding) garments, until the end; but the other faithful souls are with the Creator, but at the end they also go up in the Ogdoad. (2) Then comes the marriage feast, common to all who are saved, until all are equal and know one another. (Pp. 82–83)

Thematically, this links up with the end of *Exc. Thdot.* 61.8 as well as with the immediately preceding 62.3. It seems that the spiritual nature, the "bone," in 62.3 may be identified with the spiritual elements that will find their repose, $\dot{\alpha}\nu\alpha\pi\alpha\upsilon\sigma\iota\varsigma$, in the Ogdoad. Insofar as Jesus' spirit remains unsaved until the Lord's Day, such an identification appears legitimate. Sagnard interprets the Lord's Day to equal the Ogdoad, which itself equals the eighth day. This is the day of Jesus' own resurrection, the day after the Sabbath.[85]

The repose of the spiritual elements, however, remains connected with the Mother, who keeps these elements' counterparts, their souls, "until the end"— that is, until it is time to ascend from Ogdoad to Pleroma. That these souls function as wedding garments for the spiritual elements means that for each spiritual entity there is a corresponding soul-vestment.[86]

A second group of souls belongs to the Demiurge (63.2). These, too, apparently, will ascend *into the Ogdoad* when the spiritual entities are elevated further, into the Pleroma (34.2, pp. 64–65). The first group of souls and the spiritual elements stay together in the Ogdoad and partake in the marriage feast, the common salvation that equalizes them.[87] Suspense is maintained, however, for the "superior" salvation of the spiritual elements (61.8) has not yet been described.

Sagnard, echoing Irenaeus, *Adversus Haereses (AH)* 1.7.1, asserts that "rien de psychique ne peut entrer au Plerome" ("nothing psychic can enter into the Pleroma").[88] More recently, Pagels and McCue differ widely in their interpretation of *Exc. Thdot.* 63f. Arguing for the equalization of "psychics" and "pneumatics," Pagels does not quite discern the preliminary character of the Ogdoad wedding feast.[89] Nor does she sufficiently distinguish the two groups of souls treated in *Exc. Thdot.* 63.5.[90] The "other faithful souls" are not those described as wedding vestments for the spiritual elements, for these Demiurge-related souls do not ascend to the Ogdoad until the pneumatic elements have entered into the Pleroma (compare *Exc. Thdot.* 34.2, again). Suggesting that one should speak of pneumatic *elements* rather than pneumatic *persons*, Pagels asserts that "after the equalization 'psychics' and 'pneumatics' no longer exist as distinct species."[91]

This seems a most valuable insight. But when Pagels says that "both those who previously were psychics and pneumatics . . . have received 'souls' as 'garments' from the demiurge,"[92] she supports herself on *AH* 1.6.1. *Exc. Thdot.*, it seems to me, does not support such a thesis. Here, the pneumatic elements receive the Mother-guarded souls as wedding garments. The Demiurge's souls do not yet appear involved in the Ogdoad "wedding," the equalization. Also, why should the Demiurge's souls serve as garments to the first group of souls? This would seem redundant.

Exc. Thdot. 34.2 gives the solution to the puzzlement in paragraph 63, for when the Mother moves upwards, the Demiurge goes up to her previous place in the Ogdoad. A chain reaction takes place here: the redemption occurs in instalments. In this fashion, the saved souls and spirits move into the Pleroma, giving space to the Creator's souls ready for the Ogdoad.

Differing with Pagels, McCue basically agrees with Casey and Sagnard that there are two distinct stages of salvation: one for the "psychics," another for the "pneumatics."[93] McCue is puzzled by *Exc. Thdot.* 63.2, but he rightly calls the wedding feast a "penultimate stage" in the salvation.[94] He errs, however, in denying the "psychics" a pneumatic element.[95] Potentially carrying all three elements, the human being can never be certain that it will manage to realize the upper component, the pneuma. Schottroff's sober warnings with respect to anthropological models vs. "classes" should be heeded.[96] *Exc. Thdot.* admittedly vacillates between the two, but to speak of "psychics" as opposed to "pneumatics" makes sense only in so far as these designations express the *element's* present relationship "zu den Polen der Dualismus, zu Heil und Unheil" ("to the poles of the dualism, to salvation and perdition").[97]

Exc. Thdot. 64 describes the separation of the spiritual elements immediately after the wedding feast of equalization between soul- and spirit-entities in *Exc. Thdot.* 63.2:

> Henceforth, the spiritual elements having put off their souls, together with the Mother who leads the bridegroom, also lead bridegrooms, their angels, and pass into the bridal chamber within the Limit and attain to the vision of the Father,—having become intellectual Aeons—,in the intellectual and eternal marriages of the Syzyge. (Pp. 82–83)[98]

The wedding feast in the Ogdoad is now completed, and the spiritual elements divest themselves of their wedding garments. Imitating the Mother—who takes a surprisingly active role: she, not her bridegroom, is the "leader"—the now "naked" spirits lead their spouses, the angels. One may wonder whether these angels are the former guardian angels who have become Logos-figures. It seems that the two former angel roles have become conflated; there are, at this point, only "logoi," neither guardians nor souls.

The pneumatic entity enters the Pleroma with its bridegroom, the angel. Only at this stage, where bridal chamber equals Pleroma, is the vision of the Father possible, and only now are the spiritual entities transformed into noetic aeons. The bridal chamber, the "real" marriage event, accomplishes this change. The previous wedding feast in the Ogdoad produced a merged, male entity from a female and a male, the *psuchē* and the pneuma, and this step was the prerequisite for the completely male union in the bridal chamber, the merging of the male with his angel. Here, opposites no longer exist, and the imagery involving two distinct genders has no place. A truly pneumatic union is between male and male, between compatible entities.

The psychic, female entity has been saved into maleness: this is the significance of the events in the Ogdoad. The completed male pneuma further demonstrates its maleness when united with its male angel in the upper realm, in the bridal chamber. Together, these two compatible males constitute the Syzygy; thus, the Syzygy in *Exc. Thdot.* is not one of male and female, but of two males.

When the Mother enters the bridal chamber with her mate, the Savior, this event signifies her own full salvation. But has the Mother become male, too? One might almost surmise that she has, because she is united with Jesus. Thus, the argument of the essential identity between Wisdom and Jesus finds support in *Exc. Thdot.* 64. Unlike the psychic elements, however, the Mother does not seem to have acquired her maleness in the Ogdoad, for there her role was that of keeper of the wedding garments (63.1). Her salvation is foreshadowed in *Exc. Thdot.* 45: "the Saviour bestowed on her a form (μόρφωσιν)" (pp. 70–71), where the verb means to make eligible for maleness or, simply, to make male.[99]

Calling the Mother-Savior couple "premier et typique" ("primary and exemplary"),[100] Sagnard indicates the role model for the pneumatic entities in the bridal chamber. The primary couple, however, does not stay a couple in the gender sense. Aside from solving the gender distinction, the Mother's union with the Savior also, essentially, puts an end to the theme of competition between the two, for they are now one and the same.[101]

Leipoldt and Schenke find it interesting that "die untere Sophia" ("the lower Sophia"), as they call her, and her "children" meet their bridegrooms *before* they enter into the Pleroma.[102] (It seems unnecessary to hold on to the epithet "lower" for the Mother, for this adjective denotes devaluation and is not used in *Exc. Thdot.*[103]) The authors seem to expect the bridegrooms to appear *after* the Mother's and the offspring's entry into the Pleroma. Perhaps it is the active role of the Mother and of the spiritual elements that surprises the scholars, but they appear even more puzzled by the fact that the bridegrooms find themselves on the lower, Ogdoad level. The expectation of the waiting, higher, male element, anticipating its lower, female spouse, is dashed in *Exc. Thdot.*, for the envisioned union is not between male and female, but between compatible, pneumatic males.

Pagels, commenting on *Exc. Thdot.* 64, asserts that "the whole company of the redeemed now join with their syzygies, becoming 'noetic aeons,' go on to celebrate the consummation of the 'marriage' within the pleroma, rejoicing in the vision of the Father."[104] One need only emphasize that "the whole company" consists of entirely pneumatic elements and their angel bridegrooms. That the division "between psychics and pneumatics [is] not eternally sustained, . . . merely provisional . . . for the duration of the *oikonomia*,"[105] is, again, correct.

Paragraph 65 speaks of the "master of the feast" who stands outside the bridal chamber, listening joyfully to the voice of the bridegroom within (pp. 82–83). Himself ineligible for entry into the Pleroma, this figure can only be the Demiurge.[106]

In *Exc. Thdot.* 67 one finds speculations on flesh, birth, and form. "Flesh" is identified with "that weakness which was an offshoot of the Woman on high" (67.1, pp. 82–83). This refers to the Mother's creation of the unformed seed.[107] Next comes an explanation of the Savior's utterance to Salome in which he says that death will rule as long as women bear (67.2).[108] The text interprets this teaching in an unusually positive fashion: "he [the Savior] does not speak in reproach of birth since it is necessary for the salvation of the believers" (67.2). Birth and creation are not sins; they are necessities. The work of salvation depends on—and has as its point of departure—the material conditions brought about by the Woman's actions. Further, "this birth must be until the previously reckoned seed be put forth" (67.3). Which seed is this? Sagnard thinks that it is the pneumatic seed, which is distributed on earth in order to complete the number of the elect.[109] But it might, rather, refer to the seed emitted by the Male (*Exc. Thdot.* 39 and 40; see pp. 72–73, above).

Exc. Thdot. 67.4 elaborates on the creation by the Woman: her passions became creations when she put forth the formless beings. Because of her activities, "the Savior came down to drag us out from passion and to adopt us to himself" (67.4). Wisdom's salvation is, as Sagnard observes, the prototype of the redemption of the Valentinians.[110] But, *contra* Sagnard, Valentinians do not equal "pneumatics," for in the majority of these Gnostics it is the psychic element that predominates. Thus, the "psychics" need to be formed, that is, to acquire maleness. In parallel fashion, the Woman, Wisdom, becomes male when merged with her mate, the Savior, in the Pleroma.

Exc. Thdot. 68 reads: "For as long as we were children of the female only, as if of a base intercourse, incomplete and infants and senseless and weak and without form, brought forth like abortions, we were children of the woman, but when we have received form from the Saviour, we have become children of a husband and a bride chamber" (pp. 84–85).[111] I disagree with Sagnard when he identifies the female with the pneumatic element here.[112] On the contrary, it is the formless, psychic entity, born of the female *only*, that needs restitution and form, and this comes about when this entity becomes male. There is no possible balance in gender with respect to parentage in *Exc. Thdot.* 68, just as there is no equality of female and male in the ultimate salvation on high. The "we" in the quotation can have only one legitimate parent, for the Savior rescues the psychic element, as he redeems Wisdom herself. Both require maleness, form. Acquiring the Savior for a father means, for the *psuchē*, that it is no longer *psuchē* but pneuma.

The theme of competition between Wisdom and Savior has come up again: now they compete for parentage. But *Exc. Thdot.* has earlier said that Wisdom put forth both psychic and pneumatic elements (*Exc. Thdot.* 39 and 40; but these passages differ). Even so, rebirth is effected by the Savior, as the previous birth is due to Wisdom, the female. The temporariness of Wisdom's emission provides a clue, for creation is for the time being enmeshed in the Creator's schemes, subjected to his rules. Wisdom is a mediator, a temporary womb for the seed that should, ideally, *produce offspring directly from the male Savior*. Since this cannot be done, the solution to the dilemma is introduced by the Ogdoad-Pleroma speculations.

Thus, the theology of *Exc. Thdot.* turns out to be coherent with respect to the issues investigated here. The psychic element that merges with the pneumatic one in the Ogdoad wedding feast means that *female plus male equals male*. Because this entity still carries vestiges of femaleness, however, further "purification" is necessary. In the pleromatic bridal chamber the male entity and its angelic bridegroom unite, and here the equation becomes: *male plus male equals noetic male aeon*. To keep the two stages apart, and to realize their implication in the scheme of salvation qua salvation—that is, maleness—contributes to the solution of the disagreements between Pagels and McCue, it seems to me.

Finally, *Exc. Thdot.* 79 and 80 merit quotation:

> (79) So long, then, . . . as the seed is yet unformed, it is the offspring of the female, but when it was formed, it was changed to a man and becomes a son of the bridegroom. It is no longer weak and subject to the cosmic forces, both visible and invisible, but having been made masculine, it becomes a male fruit. (80.1) He whom the Mother generates, is led into death and into the world, but he whom Christ regenerates is transferred to life into the Ogdoad. (2) And they die to the world but live to God, that death be loosed by death and corruption by resurrection. (Pp. 88–89)

The "offspring of the female" recalls, in addition to *Exc. Thdot.* 68, *Exc. Thdot.* 21, where Eve is this female. Like 68, 79 speaks of the psychic, female element that must be transformed into maleness.[113] "Female" connotes the amorphous state, "male" the formed one. To be engendered in the bridal chamber, by the male Savior only, means to reach full maleness. The expression "a son of the bridegroom" stresses the maleness of both parent and offspring—any femaleness is now safely obliterated. In *Exc. Thdot.* 80 the first birth, by the Mother, is really death, yet the beginning of life envisioned above. As the life above becomes realized, death to this world follows.

"Death loosed by death and corruption by resurrection" aptly sums up the correlation between the transformatory stages explored in the text. To die to the world means to live up above. This life has two steps: the "public" wedding feast in the Ogdoad, and the "private" bridal chamber in the Pleroma, respectively. Leaving corruption behind, one is resurrected, as Jesus was, on the Lord's Day.

CONCLUSION

In the Pleromatic syzygial marriage, maleness denotes angelic wholeness; the female has been subjected and transformed into the male. Recalling *Exc. Thdot.* 21, where Adam's bone was extracted from him to make Eve, one might now say that Adam has retrieved his bone. He is restored to male, "angelic" completion. So, paradoxically, is Eve, who, as female, could never be a complete creature on her own. Her role is, essentially, to fill out the empty space in the male.

The story of the Kenoma and of the Valentinians in it comprises that of the temporary dispensation, that is, the basically artificial division of the sexes and of the genders. One recalls *Exc. Thdot.* 36.2, which deals with the significance of Jesus' baptism: the undivided should be divided in order to be reunited. Applied to *Exc. Thdot.* 79 (and to 21.2), this means that Adam was divided: his female bone was extracted and became an autonomous entity; at the final salvation, however, Adam regains his bone, becoming whole once more.

As noted, the bone consists of both *psuchē* and pneuma, of casing and marrow (*Exc. Thdot.* 53.5; and compare 51.2). Wisdom put the pneumatic seed into Adam but she also extracted the female element from him (21.2) and both were thereby continued in subsequent humanity. But it will not do to interpret Wisdom in negative terms, blaming her for the creation of the lower element. In *Exc. Thdot.* her identity is double: she is both the same as, and different from, the Savior, her spouse. United, the two become *one* male aeon, prototypes for the ascending Valentinians.

Schottroff's theory of pneuma and *psuchē* as relative determinations depending on the direction of the two entities[114] applies to Wisdom and Christ, too: both possess aspects that seem mutually exclusive. The paradox of simultaneous incarnation and transcendence, however, explains the boundary and gender-breaking capacities of both Wisdom and Christ. The two symbolize the human being in its constitution as at once material, "psychic," and "pneumatic."

The angels have a twofold role: as guardians for the psychic entity, and as *alter ego*[115] for the realized "pneumatic," the "bride" leading her bridegroom into the Pleroma. These functions are comparable to those of Wisdom and Christ, who in some respects, are also angels.

Just as the human being is twice united to its compatible companion—the *psuchē* to the pneuma, the male to the angel—so Wisdom and Eve, too, are finally merged with their respective spouses. Everything has come full circle, the origin has been restored, the saved Church has become angelic (*Exc. Thdot.* 21).[116] For all of these the solution implies that femaleness must be overcome in order for maleness to be fully restored, to become itself. Even in the Savior this pattern is clear: in his descending aspects, he is called Jesus and is clothed in the psychic, "female" element, in need of salvation; as ascending savior, he is pneumatic Christ, saving Wisdom, the Valentinians, and himself into maleness. That he keeps his marrow (*Exc. Thdot.* 62.3)[117] is eloquent evidence as to how seriously the text regards the salvation of the savior as well as that of the believers.

The merging of female and male into a male syzygy, which results in an angelic entity, is *Exc. Thdot.*'s way of contemplating the return to the origin, in which the divided becomes restored to unity. This kind of thinking emerges also in *Gos. Thom.*, where the association to Gen. 2 is more explicit: marking the position furthest away from Adam's pristine condition, the female signifies the last—third—stage of development. In my view, *Gos. Thom.*'s logion 114 calls for a backwards creation: the female must return to the male in order that this unified being might, once more, attain to the "living spirit" (Gen. 2:7's "living soul") stage *before* the first man was even put into Paradise, *before* the need for his division became apparent. How this understanding of Gen. 2 determines the solution of the female's salvation constitutes the central issue in the next chapter.

CHAPTER 5

An Interpretation
of Logion 114 in
The Gospel of Thomas

INTRODUCTION

During the last three decades or so the enigmatic *Gospel of Thomas* (*Gos. Thom.*) has received profuse scholarly attention. Debates over the gospel's origin, religious setting, and dependency on other segments of early Christian literature continue, and these debates find rapt audiences.[1] The sayings that constitute the gospel are generally acknowledged to possess a certain coherence, a "logic," despite their riddle-wrought language and imagery.

One of the most puzzling sayings of *Gos. Thom.* is the last one, logion 114:

Simon Peter said to them, "Let Mary leave us, for women are not worthy of Life!" Jesus said, "I myself shall lead her in order to make her male so that she may become a living spirit resembling you males. For every woman who will make herself male will enter the Kingdom of Heaven."[2]

In an attempt to give a fresh interpretation of this logion, I will relate it to other logia that may throw light on it. My investigation first devotes special attention to the language of transformation that turns up in several sayings. Next, logia that refer specifically to females, or women, are considered. After reviewing *Gos. Thom.*'s uses of the terms "image" and "bridal chamber," I turn to logion 61; it seems to me that this saying can be linked to logion 114, for both logia deal with a female disciple. Associating these two sayings, I argue that logion 114 speaks of an initiation ritual required for the female so that she may be restored to the lost unity of Adam in Gen. 2. The woman must first become male, then take the last step to the "living spirit" stage, which I take to be that of the "living soul" in Gen. 2.

LOGION 114

Peter's misogyny—directed specifically at Mary Magdalene—is well attested by other early Christian Gnostic sources such as *Gos. Mary* and *Pistis Sophia*.[3] Responding to Peter's utterance, Jesus defends Mary. His reply means, I think, that maleness is a prerequisite for becoming a "living spirit." This spiritual entity resembles the male disciples. Assuming that all of Jesus' followers are to become such spirits, one may infer that female followers will have to attain maleness *before* they may become "living spirits." Male disciples, then, appear to have to make only one step, from maleness to the spiritual level. Thus, the hierarchy of salvation here is: female ➔ male ➔ "living spirit."

That every woman taking the step into maleness will "enter the Kingdom of Heaven," implies an automatic salvation if the correct procedures are followed. Males, already "naturally" in the second category, may also become "living spirits." I suspect that the hierarchical order of female, male, and "living spirit" expresses that of Gen. 2; for the envisioned goal, as Jesus presents it, can be seen as a "backward" creation, from the female rib into the male Adam, back into the "living spirit" created by dust and God's breath (Gen. 2:7).[4] If this is a valid point of departure for an interpretation of logion 114, Jesus' directions to Mary imply that she must return via the male element to the spiritual being in Gen. 2:7.[5]

Both Ph. de Suarez and J.-É. Ménard understand the logion to hint at the primordial androgyny.[6] Ménard draws parallels with *Exc. Thdot.* and *The Pseudo-Clementine Homilies* that attest to the view that the Kingdom consists of males.[7] He also associates logion 114 with *Pistis Sophia* 113, where Mary Magdalene senses the interior man, Adam, in herself and thereby understands everything.[8]

B. Gärtner, too, draws parallels to other Gnostic texts, but he offers no direct exegesis of the logion.[9] R. M. Grant observes that "we might be tempted to take this notion [of the female becoming male] symbolically, were it not for the existence of Gnostic parallels."[10] Well, logion 114 might still be viewed "symbolically," as may "other Gnostic parallels." To adduce parallels does not preclude taking symbolism seriously!

A. F. J. Klijn thinks that the logion rejects marriage, and O. Cullmann calls it "frauenfeindlich" ("hostile to women"), but R. Kasser feels that Jesus elevates Mary.[11] Kasser stresses Mary's intelligence, noting that Jesus often addresses questions to her; she is more "spiritual" than the others. Showing a special affection for Mary, Jesus does not humiliate her but, instead, "accorde . . . à la femme une dignité supérieure à laquelle elle n'osait aspirer" ("gives . . . to the woman a superior dignity, to which she had not dared to aspire").[12]

It is noteworthy that Kasser never associates the Gen. 2 creation tradition with logion 114 (or with any other *Gos. Thom.* logion, for that matter). P. Perkins suggests that the logion may be hinting at a "community rule about the status of men and women."[13] E. Haenchen and J. Doresse both associate the saying to Gal. 3:28, "There is neither Jew nor Greek,"[14] but such a parallel does not seem helpful.

W. Meeks tries to link up Mary in logion 114 with Thecla (in the *Acts of Paul and Thecla*) who cut her hair and wore a man's clothing.[15] But dressing like a man and looking like one does not mean *becoming* a man. Imitation is not to be equated with full transformation. Moreover, the male[16] is not the final goal in logion 114, for the aim is to become a "living spirit." H.-C. Puech keenly observes that the envisioned spiritual state for the female is *beyond* male and female. Obtaining the same "title" ("living spirit") as the males, the female enters "une réalité neutre, indifférente à toute qualification ou distinction sexuelle" ("a nongenderized reality, indifferent to any sexual qualification or distinction").[17]

K. H. Rengstorf devotes a whole article to logion 114. Noting that the logion implies the abolishment of the female by the male—which is different from the way male and female are treated in some other *Gos. Thom.* sayings— he observes the differences in the logia's ways to salvation.[18] *Contra* Cullmann, Rengstorf does not judge logion 114 as misogynic. He connects the "live-giving spirit"—that is, the resurrected Christ ($\pi\nu\varepsilon\tilde{\upsilon}\mu\alpha$ $\zeta\omega\sigma\pi\sigma\iota\sigma\tilde{\upsilon}\nu$) of 1 Cor. 15:45—to Jesus' saying that he will make the female into a "living spirit" (ⲛⲟⲩⲡ̅ⲛ̅ⲁ̅ ⲉ϶ⲟⲛϩ̣). Effecting this transformation and salvation, the male Jesus makes the female first attain to perfection, to maleness.[19] But, again, maleness and perfection are not the same!

Rengstorf next adduces his key argument, that logion 114 can be understood in the light of Isis's lament, "I made myself into a man, even though I was a woman."[20] Isis, who conceives and gives birth to her son Horus after the death of her husband Osiris, can be said to have played the man's role. Rengstorf seeks a foundation for his Isis analogy by observing that in Egyptian religion the dead becomes Osiris, that is, male, and so the tension between female and male is broken.[21] Jesus is identified with Osiris, and thus the dead becomes Jesus. Rengstorf stresses the influence of traditional Egyptian religion on early Egyptian Christianity. He suggests that Christian (and Peter's) misogyny belongs to the Western, Roman tradition, whereas the positive view of the female in logion 114 can be attributed to the influence of Egyptian religion.[22]

But Isis making herself into a man does not, I think, parallel the "male-making" in logion 114. In the Egyptian material Isis makes *herself* male. In

Gos. Thom. it is initially Jesus who "will lead" Mary "in order to make her male"; in the next sentence, however, Jesus says, "every woman who *will make herself male will* enter"—so that *both* Mary and Jesus will effect the required maleness. Moreover, Isis is a goddess, Mary a human being. Also, Isis's activities are concentrated around the miraculous conception and birth of a son whose future role is to avenge Osiris's death at the hands of his brother Seth.[23] Isis is male only insofar as she plays the parts of both female and male in the act of conception. Her giving birth has nothing to do with "virginal birth,"[24] and Horus's true father is, indeed, Osiris. Such miraculous procreation and birth have no place in *Gos. Thom.*

The search for obscure parallels affords exciting entertainment, but is largely useless with respect to logion 114. Our goal should be, rather, to find out what the saying means in its context in *Gos. Thom.*—even if this aim appears at first impossible. Comparative endeavors—tantalizing though they may be—often lead astray, distracting us from the task at hand.

In *The Gnostic Gospels*, E. Pagels says that the logion "simply states what religious rhetoric assumes: that the men form the legitimate body of the community, while women are allowed to participate only when they assimilate themselves to men."[25] But further on in her book, Pagels has changed her mind and states that the saying "may be taken symbolically: what is merely human (therefore *female*) must be transformed into what is divine (the 'living spirit,' the male)."[26] Surely, the transition from the human to the divine level is essential, but Pagels is incorrect in identifying the "living spirit" with the male. These two are not the same; rather, the male is the condition for the "living spirit." In the same paragraph, Pagels sees a connection between Salome and Mary, noting that these women become Jesus' disciples when they transcend their human nature and so "become male." This is a valuable insight, though again, maleness does not denote full transcendence of the human nature.

IMAGERY OF TRANSFORMATION

Turning to other logia of *Gos. Thom.* in order to interpret logion 114, one may first concentrate on sayings characterized by transformation imagery.

Logion 11 is:

Jesus said, "This heaven will pass away, and the one above it will pass away. The dead are not alive, and the living will not die. In the days when you consumed what is dead, you made it what is live. When you come to dwell in the light, what will you do? On the day when you were one you became two. But when you become two, what will you do?" (P. 119)

After declaring the identical fate of the two heavens,[27] Jesus launches into utterances characterized by oppositions. The dead remain dead, but "the living will not die"; this last part may refer to the knowledgeable ones who will defy death. Stronger language follows, for Jesus tells his hearers that they are able to transform their aliment: they can turn dead matter into living substance. This indicates nothing less than a transformation from death to life *here on the earthly level.* Jesus is not speaking of events to come in an eschatological future, he is stressing the disciples' capacity in the present.

On the other hand, the disciples do not yet appear "to dwell in the light." Again, Jesus returns to past events, mentioning created Adam who was one, yet became separated. His separated state seems to be the crucial problem. How is he to get back to his original state of unity? It is worth noting that the logion does not explicitly advocate ascetic practices in order to achieve the primordial unity.

Ménard thinks that the eating of the dead hints at the demiurgic principle, which can be transformed by the human being.[28] When Kasser says, "dans le monde présent, pour vivre, on se nourrit de matière morte, mais dans le monde futur (la Lumière) ces procédés seront totalement inefficaces" ("in order to live, in the present world, one eats dead material, but in the future world [the Light] this procedure will be completely inefficacious"),[29] he seems to misrepresent the logion. For this part of the saying does not stress a future eschatology, but the disciples' present ability to transform dead into live matter.

Quite naturally, most scholars have interpreted the last part of the saying as referring to the Adamic state before the fall, the unity of Adam incorporating Eve.[30] The logion gives no answer, however; instead, it poses a challenging question to the hearers, which echoes the last part of the preceding sentence, "When you come to dwell in the light, what will you do?" Here, the light seems to refer to "Paradise regained."[31] Whether this event, dwelling in the light, will come about here on earth or in the beyond remains an open question. The saying has already spoken of miraculous, transformative powers in its audience; therefore, one should not automatically assume that "to dwell in the light" and the last question of logion 11 refer to the otherworldly future alone.

In logion 18 the disciples ask Jesus,

"Tell us how our end will be." Jesus said, "Have you discovered, then, the beginning, that you look for the end? For where the beginning is, there will the end be. Blessed is he who will take his place in the beginning; he will know the end and will not experience death." (P. 120)

Beginning and end are the same, according to Jesus. The disciples do not know this, and, in some sense, they may not yet really be disciples, not yet initiated into the secrets.[32] One notes that the latter half of the logion stresses the future: "will the end be," followed by three references to the one who *will* behave and know so that he gains salvation. As in logion 11, immortality is central to the regained position, the beginning.

Puech notes the preexistence of "le Spirituel" ("the spiritual one").[33] One may take this (conjectured) spiritual one to mean the person who has transcended the sexual divisions to the spiritual stage. But if the disciples are still males (most of them were so, according to the tradition), they may not yet be enlightened, that is, "spiritual." Concerning the "beginning and end" language, Ménard draws parallels to the Syrian *Liber Graduum*.[34] Unlike Adam, the one who is able to *reenter* Paradise will not die,[35] for the fall will not be reenacted. To become one, like original Adam, does not mean to imitate him in the fall, but to achieve his pre-Paradisial state, I would argue. It is not, therefore, a matter of "Paradise regained," as G. Quispel has it,[36] but of becoming Adam *before* he was put into Paradise. It was as a "living spirit" that he was placed in the garden that led to his subsequent division and misery.

One of the most quoted logia of *Gos. Thom.* is, undoubtedly, saying 22:

Jesus saw infants being suckled. He said to his disciples, "These infants being suckled are like those who enter the Kingdom." They said to Him, "Shall we, then, as children, enter the Kingdom?" Jesus said to them, "When you make the two one, and when you make the inside like the outside and the outside like the inside, and the above like the below, and when you make the male and the female one and the same, so that the male not be male nor the female female; and when you fashion eyes in place of an eye, and a hand in place of a hand, and a foot in place of a foot, and a likeness in place of a likeness, then will you enter [the Kingdom]." (P. 121)

The first part of this logion—the children being those eligible for the Kingdom—recalls logia 11 and 18.[37] Jesus' exegesis in saying 22 amplifies the language concerning the "one" and the "two" in logion 11. It is worth noting the different sorts of transformations required in saying 22. First, "to make the two one"[38] speaks of identification, merging. Second, "the inside" must be made *like*[39] "the outside," and conversely, as must "the above" and "the below." To be *like* something does not seem to imply full identification—

instead, the two entities are made interchangeable. No new creation takes place here, for the saying speaks of making something resemble its opposite.

Next, the logion returns to the "two," male and female, which must be made "one and the same." Note that it does *not* say that the female must become male (or vice versa). A totally new creation is demanded, not a reciprocal turning of something into its contrasting entity/element. Finally, a *fashioning* is required in the last part of logion 22: replacement of the former, earthly entity by a new eye, hand, foot, and likeness ($\varepsilon i\varkappa\acute{\omega}\nu$) ensures entry into the Kingdom.

Of these methods and languages of transformation and change, the one dealing with the "two" and the "one," "male" and "female," requires a creation that abolishes the pattern of opposites. The collapse of the two into one indicates a loss of dualistic relationships, a return to unity. On the other hand, the creation emphasizing the "like" does not require an elimination of the opposed terms. The word "like" (ⲚⲐⲈ) must be taken seriously, for the two entities seem to be allowed to remain two; neither entity becomes the other, but the two approximate one another and resemble each other. Curiously, the vice versa–format is lacking in the "above"-"below" sentence.

In the third type of transformation, to "fashion . . . in place of" means actively to replace one's current eye, hand, foot, and likeness with a new one fit for the Kingdom. Bodily members as such are not necessarily rejected—they have their use in the ordinary world—but a new, spiritual, imitative creation is demanded; even in the spiritual state eyes, hands, feet, and likenesses seem to be necessary. That the $\varepsilon i\varkappa\acute{\omega}\nu$ is included in the list suggests again the indispensability of the likeness. In this section on the "fashioning" it is essential to keep in mind the active role of the believer: new eyes, et cetera, will not *be given* to the devotee so that he may enter the Kingdom; instead, *the believer* must create these new elements. Such active creation as prerequisite for salvation must be understood as a mandatory procedure while the disciple is still on earth, that is, the substitution must come about before the bodily death. Logion 22 may even, in veiled fashion, be speaking of a ritual of such "spiritual" creation.

The three different changes in logion 22—the "two" made into "one," the opposites made to become interchangeable, and the substitution of spiritual elements for earthly ones—have not been sorted out by scholars commenting on the saying. B. Lincoln, arguing for the view that *Gos. Thom.* was written for initiates and noninitiates alike, discerns four groups of audiences.[40] He says of logion 22, "It seems likely that each of these terms [those describing the kinds of transformation] had a specific, technical meaning, referring to special ascetic rigors designed to produce the androgynous state."[41] If the methods of transformation can indeed be linked to the different levels of initiation, would these transformations be seen as sequential steps toward salvation? This remains unclear. I would like to emphasize, however, that *Gos. Thom.* nowhere hints at "ascetic rigors." Lincoln even goes so far as to suggest that self-castration may have been practiced, although he admits that this is "highly speculative."[42]

Gärtner does not think that "drastic methods are to be used to prevent the limbs from leading the way to sin"; instead, there must be a "substitution, so that the parts of the human body are not dominated by physical desire but by the man of light."[43] Stressing that "the final unity does not come about until man's heavenly soul is united with his 'angel' in heaven," Gärtner still allows for an "elect," pure status of the human being who has transcended earthly duality, becoming "a single one."[44]

Puech, listing parallels to logion 22 (e.g., in *The Gospel of the Egyptians*), notes that the man and the woman do not simply exchange their conditions; rather, the two cease to be separate entities.[45] Still, one should keep in mind that "becoming one" involves the female returning, as rib, into the male, who thereby becomes whole, and therefore autonomously male.

Meeks writes: "The emphasis on salvation by self-knowledge suggests that the terms 'male and female' are used metaphorically . . . to represent aspects of the individual personality. If so, then the process of 'making the two one' and 'making the female male' is a gnostic parallel to Philo's more philosophical use of the same metaphors."[46] This seems only partly accurate, for it is not a question of "aspects of the individual personality," but of the fateful division of the human being into male and female. Moreover, the two distinct terms, "making the two one" and "making the female male," should be kept strictly apart.

Both Rengstorf and P. Vielhauer have noted the importance of this distinction. Vielhauer judges both attitudes to be "genuin gnostisch" ("genuinely Gnostic"). But logion 22 contradicts logion 114, he says, for in 22, the sexual differentiation of the human being is "wesenlos" ("pointless").[47] Jesus' promise to make Mary male in logion 114 can be seen as a first step to the abolition of sexual divisions altogether. "Making the two one" does not occur at all in saying 114, but I take the "living spirit" stage to express the same goal. Thus, the "male" of 114 is on its way to becoming the "one" of logion 22.

Rengstorf argues that saying 22—which belongs rather with logion 11 than with 114—does not advocate the abolishment of the female as such. The tension between male and female is heightened and sustained in logion 22.

Even if both logia 22 and 114 speak of conquering the differentiation between male and female in order to reach the Kingdom, Rengstorf warns against using the two sayings to mutually interpret one another.[48]

In short, in logion 22 male and female are seen as an oppositional pair, a complementarity. On the other hand, where the male is invoked *without* being paired to the female—as in 114—it represents the step toward becoming a "living spirit." United, pre-Paradisial Adam is such a "living spirit," for he embodies both male and female, which are no longer separate entities and cannot be spoken of as pairs or opposites.

The expression "becoming like children" recurs in logion 37:

> His disciples said, "When will You become revealed to us and when shall we see You?" Jesus said, "When you disrobe without being ashamed and take up your garments and place them under your feet like little children and tread on them, then [will you see] the Son of the Living One and you will not be afraid." (P. 122)

To see Jesus as he really is can be equated to entering the Kingdom. Again, childlike innocence is required. J. Z. Smith, in his detailed study of logion 37, states: "While it is impossible and indeed illegitimate . . . to separate the 'realized' and the 'futuristic,' the 'anthropological' and the 'cosmological' aspects of the eschatology of *The Gospel of Thomas*, it is clear that to some degree the disciple, insofar as he is saved, is a New Adam and that the cosmos, insofar as it is redeemed, will be a New Eden."[49]

In the light of Smith's demonstration of the direct connection of logion 37 with the ancient Christian baptism liturgy, it seems possible to take this logion to mean that the disciples are not, strictly, yet saved.[50] They have not yet been baptised into the undivided, Adamic state.[51] There is no direct reference to baptism in the saying, but Jesus' answer may imply this ritual (or some similar kind of initiation), which will turn the disciples into *true* disciples.

A clear requirement for becoming a disciple is found in logion 55, where one reads: "Whoever does not hate his father and his mother cannot become a disciple to Me" (p. 124). Logion 101 repeats the expression, but adds—between "mother" and "cannot"—an amplification: "*as I do*" (p. 128; my emphasis). Jesus continues, however, in the same logion: "And whoever does [not] love his father and his mother as I do cannot become a [disciple] to Me. For My mother [gave me falsehood] but [My] true [Mother] gave me life" (p. 129). Here, the paradox returns: love and hate go together, or both must be repealed. The last sentence is admittedly garbled, but the two mothers appear to be diametrically opposed to one another. The true disciple must be able to imitate Jesus in his love/hate for his mother and father. If Jesus is speaking of only one pair of parents (and, perhaps, of only one Mother in the last sentence), the saying may demand the abolishment of either kind of attachment, whether it be love or hate. On the other hand, the distinction between the two pairs of parents (and Mothers) seems crucial.

Usually, logion 101 is interpreted as referring to Jesus' earthly parents, whom he hates, and to his spiritual ones, whom he loves.[52] Quispel and Puech both draw *Exc. Thdot.* 80.1 parallels.[53] Kasser thinks that the two sets of parents indicate, respectively, the archons—"il n'est plus guère question ici des parents selon la chair" ("it is no longer a question of parents according to the flesh")[54]—and God. It could even be that logion 101 again plays on the "two-one" imagery, for the disciples are told either to both love and hate, or to neither love nor hate. To give up positive as well as negative attachments may be another way of overcoming the dichotomies. But now, the "oneness" is not referring to the sexual division, but to the eschatological state of one's emotional life.

Logion 106 returns to the "two-one" language: "Jesus said, 'When you make the two one you will become the sons of man, and when you say, "Mountain, move away," it will move away'" (p. 129). The united human being—now a "son of man"—is capable of performing miracles;[55] or, as Ménard has it, of removing the passions.[56] The term "sons of man" has caused diverging scholarly interpretations. H. Koester states: "Whatever 'sons of man' means here, it is not used as a title for a specific figure." He feels that Gärtner's view of the expression—that "man" refers to the Savior, the immortal man—betrays "gnostic redeemer mythology."[57] Koester may be right that the term is no title, but the gospel is ambiguous, for in logion 86 one finds "Son of Man," capitalized, and here it obviously refers to Jesus.[58]

The plural "sons of man" indicates the disciples, who seek to become like Jesus—who is properly the "Son of Man." Puech says that to be a "son of man" means "partager avec Jésus un titre et une condition dont le privilège est, d'ordinaire, réservé à ce dernier" ("to partake, with Jesus, of a title and a condition whose privilege is ordinarily reserved for this latter one"). Keeping keen track of the distinction, however, Puech specifies that "'devenir fils de l'Homme' n'est pas à confondre avec 'être Fils de l'Homme'" ("'to become sons of Man' is not to be confused with 'to be Son of Man'").[59] Jesus ranks as the first among the "sons of man," and only he possesses the capitalized title "Son of Man."

Puech introduces another term, too: the "son of the male," which is, he says, a sort of synonym for "son of man."[60] It is possible to interpret Puech's view of the way of salvation in *Gos. Thom.* to include three stages: one must leave the "son of the woman" level in order to become a "son of the male," who, in turn, is born (or reborn) from the spirit.[61]

This schema is, essentially, the one I am arguing for with respect to logion 114: female ➤ male ➤ "living spirit." It is important to note, again, that the middle element, while referring to the male as opposed to female, *at the same time* indicates the male as a singular, autonomous term, as a stage between female and spirit. This unified, "male" (and yet *beyond* "male" and "female") Adam will, in turn, become a "living spirit." Males and "living spirits" resemble one another, as logion 114 states, but they are not identical. "Female" and "son of the woman" both point to the lower, female—that is, divided—stage, which must be left behind in order to achieve "maleness," "son of man" status.

THE USES OF FEMALE IMAGERY

It is time to turn to logia that deal specifically with images of the female. Logion 15 has Jesus say, "When you see one who was not born of woman, prostrate yourselves on your faces and worship him. That one is your Father" (p. 120).

Here, Jesus seems to talk about himself. However, his devotees, too, may have the potential to become like him, to be "not born of woman." If being reborn through the spirit includes obtaining a new set of parents, or a new (male) parent,[62] the disciples may escape the human condition. Like Jesus, they may acquire a spiritual origin.

But the last line of the logion indicates that it is Jesus who is the new parent of the disciples (who thereby become full-fledged devotees). Ménard sees the reference to the Father as indicating Jesus himself, not the invisible Father up above, and yet he also states that son and father are identified in this saying.[63] Other scholars have had more trouble with the passage. Kasser, for instance, decides that "your Father" is "Dieu."[64] Gärtner first judges likewise, then says that because Jesus is present among men, he "represents the Father" and therefore requires reverence.[65] And Grant draws Naassene parallels to the view that Jesus is not a son of a woman.[66]

In logion 46 Jesus returns to this issue:

Among those born of women, from Adam until John the Baptist, there is no one so superior to John the Baptist that his eyes should not be lowered (before him). Yet I have said, whichever one of you comes to be a child will be acquainted with the Kingdom and will become superior to John. (P. 123)

Lincoln observes that Adam was not born of a woman; however, *contra* Lincoln, I do see Adam as "included in the time span under discussion," and as belonging to this "category of people."[67] Because he "fell," that is, was separated, Adam is not positively evaluated in this saying—for, not being born of a woman, he instead gave birth to one, out of his side! That is Adam's primary trouble. I do not think, then, that Adam is "infinitely higher than John."[68]

At the present time, this logion teaches, it is suitable to lower one's eyes before John; but when one acquires the unity, one will be elevated above the Baptist. Having become a "living spirit," the disciple is no longer "born of woman." Ménard feels that *Gos. Thom.* heightens John's prestige, but Puech sees John as inferior to the disciples who are "fils de l'homme" ("sons of man"), no longer "born of women" (ᵉndjpo ᵉnᵉnhiome).[69] Obviously, Ménard and Puech hold diverging opinions with respect to the crucial question of realized vs. future eschatology.

At first glance, it appears strange that "those born of women" are opposed to the "children" who are to be acquainted with the Kingdom. As H. C. Kee observes, however, "there is no hint of a connection between becoming a child and a negative attitude toward sexuality," even though logion 46 disdains normal birth.[70] This insight supports the view that in *Gos. Thom.* as a whole, it is not necessary to see sexuality as the main target; instead, it is the separation of the human being into two that is the calamity. Ménard asserts that logia 46–50 are concerned with the return to the original unity, but the preoccupation with "the single one," the *monachos*,[71] does not (yet) include the implications of Syrian Christian asceticism.[72] It is worth keeping Ménard's judgment in mind, for I think it is important to discern the difference between male and female as *sexual beings* and as *one separated being*. In logion 46 *Gos. Thom.* appears unconcerned with the former, but keenly interested in the remedy for the latter.

Logion 79 can be viewed in relation to saying 46:

A woman from the crowd said to Him, "Blessed are the womb which bore You and the breasts which nourished You." He said to her, "Blessed are those who have heard the word of the Father and have truly kept it. For there will be days when you will say, 'Blessed are the womb which has not conceived and the breasts which have not given milk.'" (P. 127)

"The word of the Father," his "nourishment," is juxtaposed to the nourishment of the earthly mother. Earthly birth requires rebirth from the Father, which, in its turn, repeals the earthly one. At the end of the logion Jesus turns the woman's words into a negative statement; earthly conception and sustenance are devalued so that one almost expects the womb and the breasts to be cursed.

According to Gärtner, this logion expresses "negativism against marriage and the procreation of children."[73] But I think it is possible to see human procreation as a necessity, a prerequisite for salvation. Material, earthly birth makes spiritual birth possible. Earthly wombs and breasts will become unnecessary when the human being is unified. Jesus' last words may refer not to the present, but to the future—that is, he is not reproaching the woman. Ménard observes that material parentage is a part of the cosmic, created world.[74] But it seems incorrect to state that the logion presents no opposition between material and spiritual parentage; the division is implicit in the saying, which may be related to logion 101.

That saying 79 expresses community rules, as Perkins asserts, may be so.[75] However, the term "there will be days" points not to the present, but to a future time and insight of the saved. The last sentence may also oppose female to male birth, the latter being the spiritual rebirth. Such an interpretation would dovetail with the opposition between the carrying, nourishing woman and the Father, who feeds the devotees with his word.

Finally, as regards imagery of the female, one may adduce logion 105: "Jesus said, 'He who knows the father and the mother will be called the son of a harlot' " (p. 129). Jesus may be referring to anyone included in the time span "from Adam until John the Baptist,"[76] but he may also be speaking of himself. Ménard draws attention to the anti-Christian Jewish polemics against Jesus for being born out of wedlock.[77] Kasser wonders whether the copyist wrote "son of a harlot," *p'šere m'porne*, instead of "son of Man," *p'šere m'prôme*[78]—but this seems unlikely, because the parents are treated as a pair, in ambivalent terms. Earthly parentage implies "illegitimate" birth for the human being.

One may compare logion 105 to logia 55 and 101, which deal with the ambiguities of parentage.[79] Logion 105 also connects with the following one, 106, where those who make the two one, will become the "sons of man."[80] Losing the "mother," the harlot, the devotee acquires a "father" only. Logion 105 may not even be referring to *one* parent (as opposed to two), but to earthly *vs.* heavenly parentage. "Son of a harlot" stresses the earthly, material parentage, and here the emphasis rests on the female. When one becomes "son of man," however, one loses not only one's material parents, but the association with the female altogether. Having only a father for a parent means that no female counterpart is required for this male parent.

"IMAGES"

Logia 83–84 deal with the problem of one's perception of the Father and with the "images." The first logion is:

Jesus said, "The images are manifest to man, but the light in them remains concealed in the image of the light of the Father. He will become manifest, but his image will remain concealed by his light."

And logion 84:

Jesus said, "When you see your likeness, you rejoice. But when you see your images which came into being before you, and which neither die nor become manifest, how much you will have to bear!" (P. 127)

At first, saying 83 seems to contradict itself, for Jesus says that "the images are manifest to man," and then that the Father's image "will remain concealed." To further complicate matters, the next logion speaks of "your images . . . which neither die nor become manifest." In order to sort this out one may, first, assume that Jesus speaks about himself when he invokes "the Father." In that case, "the image of the light of the Father" refers to God himself, who cannot be revealed. Jesus "will become manifest," but his image will remain hidden.[81] This is so because the light in the image prevents it from being seen. Strangely, light conceals, it does not reveal. This highest image, which the light hides, is the ultimate reality.[82]

The images—note the plural—"manifest to man" may be seen in opposition to the utterance in logion 84, where the disciples' own, preexistent images are said to "neither die nor become manifest." However, there may be no real division between the images in 83 and 84, because the manifest ones are those reflected into the earthly world. The images in their heavenly ineffability cannot be understood as long as the disciples remain unenlightened, uninitiated into the mystery of reuniting with these images. Full manifestation will come about when the state of unity between disciple and his upper image is effected.

In logion 84, the "likeness" must be distinguished from the "image." The former seems simply to refer to one's mirror-image, or perhaps to one's spouse. Klijn observes the differences in reaction to likeness and to image: one causes rejoicing, the other, apparently, suffering. Redemption—that is, meeting with one's image—produces suffering.[83] Puech distinguishes between the two, *eikōn* and *eine*. The latter refers to exterior, bodily appearance,[84] while the preexistent images[85] are not subject to manifestation, and cannot be revealed in this world. *Eikōn* is that which each spiritual person was before he appeared in the earthly form and world, says Puech.[86]

Gärtner mixes up *eikōn* and *eine*, thinking that "likeness" is the inherent property of the enlightened one. He fails to discern the juxtaposition of likeness and image, relegating the images totally to the heavenly world.[87] Ménard argues that the revealed images in logion 83 do not preclude the concealment of the real image by the light of the Father; only those possessing Gnosis may see the light which, for the unenlightened, obscures the image.[88] That the final identification of *eikōn* and *eine* symbolizes a *hieros gamos*,[89] seems doubtful. For *Gos. Thom.* draws no salvific connection between these entities; the unification of *eikōn* and *eine* is never an issue.

Grant states, "To see the image is to see Christ, which means to see the Kingdom and, indeed, the inner man. This true image neither dies nor is openly manifest. . . . Saying 83 explains why the image cannot be fully seen now."[90] And Quispel puts it this way: "Man is pleased when he looks at his outward appearance as reflected in a mirror. But when he sees his image, eikon, or guardian angel which is now in heaven beholding the face of God ever since the world was created, will he be able to support this encounter with his real self?"[91]

One may attempt to solve the problematic differences between likeness, earthly image, and heavenly image by saying that there are, for practical purposes, three entities. There is the material, mirror-reflected likeness (which can also be interpreted as one's spouse, it seems); then a lower, earthly, manifested image visible to everyone (for instance, Jesus in his human form, the disciples in theirs); and third, the upper, unmanifest "self" revealed only to the enlightened ones. The two images are connected, but there is no envisioned merging between upper image and likeness (*contra* Ménard).[92] Vitally connected, the two images—the upper and the lower one—are, in reality, one and the same. It is up to the disciples to effect the unification of the two. The earthly and the heavenly images appear, to the unenlightened, as two distinct entities, but they are indeed identical.[93]

The tripartition may be paralleled to the one in logion 114: the female is Adam's "likeness," being born out of him; earthly Adam is a lower reflection of his upper self; his heavenly image may be traced back to pre-Paradisial Adam, the "living spirit" (it is this level, of course, that is the goal of logion 114). This parallelism means that the separation occurs on two levels: between Eve ("likeness") and Adam (lower image), and between this Adam and his "living spirit" self. This autonomous Adam is not thought of in terms of "male" as opposed to "female," but is wholly self-contained, not yet in need of a "helper" (Gen. 2:18), not yet conceived as a potentially divided being.

Logion 85 is a comment on this interpretation, for here Jesus says, "Adam came into being from a great power and a great wealth, but he did not become worthy of you. For had he been worthy, [he would] not [have experienced] death" (p. 127). How could Adam, who lived before the disciples, not "have *become* worthy" of them? Obviously, the logion is referring to the preexistent, archetypal images of the disciples. Adam lost his chance of immortality: he allowed himself to be divided, and this separation meant his death.

Gärtner interprets the "great wealth" to mean "the heavenly part of Adam,"[94] and this seems correct. Ménard, curiously, mistranslates the passage, saying that "Adam vint d'une grande puissance et d'une grande *chute*" ("Adam came from a great power and from a great *fall*").[95] Is it because Adam's demise is emphasized in logion 85 that Ménard says "fall"? In any case, it has nothing to do with the text. Adam's mortality is, still, a consequence of his division, or, rather, it *is* this division. The question is: how can he be reunited to himself?

THE "BRIDAL CHAMBER" AND SALOME

The two logia dealing with the "bridal chamber" seem to me to connect with Adam's reuniting. These logia are also important with respect to logion 114 and its interpretation. First, in saying 75 Jesus says, "Many are standing at the door, but it is the solitary one who will enter the bridal chamber" (p. 126).

Who is this solitary, *monachos*?[96] And who is his bridegroom? I suggest that the solitary is the prototype of Adam who needs to be reunited to himself. In fact, this "single one" may already be incorporating the two genders in himself, and he now requires the last step, the "living spirit" stage. Going into the bridal chamber, he (or, as the case may be, she) is imaged as bride. The bridegroom is Jesus.

Quispel draws the parallel to the Matthew parable of the wise and the foolish virgins. *Monachos*, then, means *parthenos*. The *monachos* is the unified human being, Quispel says.[97] But the logion speaks of the ritual required for this unification *into the "living spirit" stage*, I think. In the bridal chamber the *monachos* becomes truly unified, with Jesus as the bridegroom, the mystagogue. Again, it is useful to remember Ménard's observation that the *monachos* may not imply an ideal of asceticism.[98] The initiate in the bridal chamber—whether "male" or "female" *monachos*—is no longer characterized by gender. Already an avowed solitary, the candidate now seeks full "living spirit" status.

Logion 104 is:

> They said [to Jesus], "Come let us pray today and let us fast." Jesus said, "What is the sin I have committed, or wherein have I been defeated? But when the bridegroom leaves the bridal chamber, then let them fast and pray." (P. 129)

Here, Jesus sees himself as sinless, and this should also be the state of the disciples. As long as Jesus is around, that is, as long as he can act as an initiator in the bridal chamber ritual, there is no need for fasting and praying. Sinlessness seems the prerequisite for entrance into the ceremony. Religious rules may again come into force when Jesus leaves the disciples and the world.

Ménard says that because the true Gnostic never leaves the bridal chamber, the traditional religious prescriptions need not be followed.[99] Such an interpretation appears ill-chosen, however, for both disciples and Jesus may leave the chamber. In fact, most of the disciples have not yet entered, and Jesus warns that he will soon be gone. Perkins, following Ménard, insists that "the Gnostic rejects fasting permanently" because neither disciple nor Jesus ever leaves the bridal chamber.[100]

However, salvation is never secured—indeed, it has barely begun. I think logion 61 expresses, in veiled language, the ritual of the bridal chamber:

> Jesus said, "Two will rest on a bed: the one will die, and the other will live." Salome said, "Who are You, man, that You, as though from the One, (or: as <whose son>, that You) have come up on my couch and eaten from my table?" Jesus said to her, "I am He who exists from the Undivided. I was given some of the things of My Father." <Salome said>, "I am Your disciple." <Jesus said to her>, "Therefore I say, if he is <undivided>, he will be filled with light, but if he is divided, he will be filled with darkness." (Pp. 124–25)

Jesus' first sentence seems to fit better with the preceding logion, 60, than with 61, notwithstanding the reference to the "bed," ϭⲗⲟϭ, both in this sentence and in Salome's question. Understandably, scholars have had great difficulties precisely with this "bed." Quispel, for instance, uses "Speiselager" ("Larder") for "couch," and A. Guillaumont et al. have "bench," as does Gärtner.[101] There seems to be some resistance to the image of Jesus and Salome possibly sharing a bed, or couch. Both eating and sharing a couch connote intimacy. I think that the sacred meal and the couch may refer to an initiation ritual in which Salome, a solitary, has been made a true disciple, a united "living spirit." It is significant that she states "I am Your disciple" immediately *after* she has received Jesus' revelation of who he is. Also, the activities regarding the food and the bed have already taken place, that is, only now is Salome fully cognizant of Jesus'—as well as her own—identity.

It is Jesus' self-proclamation that produces Salome's statement of fidelity to him, perhaps even *identity* with him. Jesus is "from the Undivided," and so is the initiate after the completion of the ritual in the bridal chamber. Unity entails light, division darkness; again, I see this as a reference to Adam's state. Jesus has made Salome his "bride," he has restored her to the pre-Paradisial Adamic condition. She is no longer "female," but a "living spirit."

However—keeping logion 114 in mind—one might say that Salome has gone through an intermediary stage, the "male" one.[102] Whether this has happened to her in the bridal chamber, or whether it is part of being a "solitary," remains uncertain. In any case, she is now, like Jesus, whole and undivided. Again, she is the only disciple in this gospel who says of herself that she is Jesus' disciple,[103] and I take this to mean that she is the only one, so far, who has been initiated into Jesus' mysteries. One should note, too, that in the next logion, 62, Jesus immediately says that it is to the worthy ones that he has revealed his mysteries; Salome, clearly, must be such a worthy recipient.

Koester notes that Jesus' identification formula in logion 61, "I am He who exists from the Undivided," belongs to the category of revelatory language. Here, the divine qualities of the speaker are unmistakable.[104] Salome's part in the logion has been less interesting to scholars, but Ménard notes that she is "étonnée" ("astonished"), although the commentator forgets himself and writes "Marie" instead of "Salome"[105] (perhaps Ménard expects Mary Magdalene, and not Salome). Kasser interprets Salome's reaction as an act of submission,[106] but that seems too strong a statement. Puech, stating that the goal for the disciples is to become one with Jesus, does not apply this insight in Salome's case.[107]

R. Schippers draws a parallel to the thwarted bridal scene in *The Acts of Thomas*, where Jesus appears, convincing the bridal couple to abstain from the carnal part of married life.[108] But such an association detracts from the (possible) sexual innuendo in logion 61, and it raises, once more, the spectre of asceticism. De Suarez notes that Jesus has given Salome what she lacked so that she, previously " 'déserte' sera remplie de lumière" (" 'empty,' will be filled with light") and will realize her unity. He also speaks, loftily, of a "fusion momentanée de l'amour" ("momentary fusion of love"), but does not press the language with respect to the logion. However, de Suarez admits the ambiguity of the imagery regarding the couch.[109]

JESUS, SALOME, AND MARY MAGDALENE

Jesus' interaction with Salome in logion 61 may be compared to his words about Mary in logion 114. In logion 61 he is initiating Salome; in logion 114 he is promising Mary that she, like Salome, will become a "living spirit." Mary, too, will be able to say "I am Your disciple," that is, "I have become like you." Jesus puts himself in an active role vis-à-vis Mary, saying that he will "lead her." But at the same time, he states that she will have to "make herself male." This indicates the mutual responsibility in the ritual, for the acquisition of unity requires active participation of both mystagogue and initiate.

One question is whether Salome and Mary, being women, need to be solitaries *before* they enter the bridal chamber ritual. If they are solitaries, they already include the male within them, that is, they have become "male." Only in the ritual do they then turn into "living spirits." Male disciples, who already are "natural" males, must vow "solitariness," and then they will be eligible for "living spirit" status. If these disciples are to become such spirits, they do not have to "become female," because no such requirement is mentioned in the gospel. As solitaries, they may already incorporate the "female" part of themselves. It is significant that no male disciples are portrayed in the same situation as Salome, or as Mary. One should recall, again, that the males "resemble" "living spirits," but they are not equated with these spirits.

It seems that those who enter the bridal chamber have already "made the two one," because they are solitaries. Solitariness does not automatically imply asceticism, however. On the whole, *Gos. Thom.* seems quite uninterested in asceticism; it may even be a "pre-ascetic" document, if one may use such a term. Sexual abstinence, the prohibition of procreation and marriage, is never mentioned in the gospel. What the text demands is no less than the unification of the separated sexes. Paradoxically, "to make the two one" explicitly invites interpretation along "sexual" lines.

The fact that Jesus deals with two female disciples strengthens the suspicion that there may be sexual overtones to what takes place in the bridal chamber. "To be made male" might imply, for Salome and Mary, to become like Jesus, as a male man. Here may be the distinction, in fact, between what "solitary" means for male and for female disciples. For, following Jesus' words about Mary in logion 114, it could be that both steps—becoming "male" and becoming "a living spirit"—happen to female disciples in the bridal chamber. But for the male disciples, who do not need to "become female," their solitariness may imply the necessity of only one step, because they already resemble "living spirits."

In logion 114, then, Jesus promises to take Mary back to the undivided state of pre-Paradisial Adam in Gen. 2. Adam not only regains his rib, he goes even further and becomes again a "living spirit," fresh from God's hand. For Adam's male characteristic is a secondary one; the "living spirit" denotes his pristine status, which does not yet include hints of division. Only Jesus can re-create Adam in his disciples, he is the initiator into the mystery of regaining this state. Because female disciples are "twice removed" from the "living spirit" condition, they need to become males before they may acquire this final status.

Taking the sequence of Gen. 2 seriously, one notices that Adam is never called "living soul" ("living spirit," in *Gos. Thom.*'s term) after he becomes "male"—that is, after he turns out to need a "helper," which, significantly, he himself incorporates. Further, the Kingdom of Heaven is pre-Paradisial in *Gos. Thom.*, because Paradise possesses all the connotations of the division and the "fall." The "living soul" Adam was not created *in* Paradise, one notes.

Klijn observes that the Coptic translator of *Gos. Thom.* does not know the "single one," or simply "one," as a technical term.[110] Even when *monachos* is used I am not sure that the term should be taken to connote asceticism. One needs to be cautious in imputing ascetic tendencies to such logia as, for example, 16, 49, and 75.[111] *Gos. Thom.* does not refer to ascetic community rules, to abstention techniques, or the like, but instead deals cryptically with the mystery involved in acquiring the "living spirit" stage. This is equated with "entering the Kingdom." Earthly males and females cannot enter this Kingdom; only those who can re-create the pre-Paradisial Adam are eligible for entry. The bridal chamber effectuates this transformation. Female disciples must, as a first step, become male. I think that male, "solitary" devotees are already seen to possess the incorporated "male-and-female," Paradisial Adam in themselves. The women, on the other hand, must be *made* solitaries, that is, "male," before they may enter the final stage of the "living spirit."

Gos. Thom. logia 114 and 61 are concerned with the salvation of the female disciples, as I see it. There is no outspoken concern with the male followers of Jesus. Logion 114 reveals that males, ideally, already are "one," but women are "two." It was a woman who, so to speak, "made" Adam "two." Therefore, the woman's salvation is more complicated than that of the male devotee.

The relationship between Jesus and Mary Magdalene not only reflects the specific ties between mystagogue and initiate, but also (perhaps inadvertently) brings up the issue of a female partner, a *syzygos*, for Jesus. *Gos. Phil.* testifies explicitly to the initiator-initiate relationship but, in contrast to *Gos. Thom.*, emphasizes it as one between "spiritual spouses." A central theme in *Gos.*

Phil., the required equality and balance between male and female expresses a spiritual goal different from that in *Gos. Thom.* Personifying Jesus' *syzygos*, Mary represents the female partner whose presence is necessary for the production of "spiritual" offspring. She also connotes the female, Pleromatic entity, a figure absent from *Gos. Thom.*, for that gospel acknowledges no higher, female principle.

CHAPTER 6

"The Holy Spirit" Is a Double Name

INTRODUCTION

The *Gospel of Philip* (*Gos. Phil.*) 60.10–20[1] explicitly attests to the doubleness of the Sophia-figure—a doubleness that may be discerned in other parts of the text as well. The immediately preceding passage, 60.5–10, invokes another female entity, the Holy Spirit, who also possesses a double character. A third female is Mary, of whom there are three, according to *Gos. Phil.* 59.5–10 (pp. 135–36); the three Marys comprise Jesus' mother, Mary Magdalene, and Jesus' mother's sister, but the three sometimes blur into interchangeable personalities. Functioning as *Gos. Phil.*'s primary female metaphors,[2] the elusive Mary, the Holy Spirit, and the double Sophia seem to play similar parts and often appear outrightly identified with one another.

G. S. Gasparro, Y. Janssens, and B. Barc have observed—and ably argued for—such identification.[3] Many male scholars have been less attuned to this viewpoint, though they may hint at it.[4] For example, H.-M. Schenke suggests that the Holy Spirit can be seen as Christ's Pleromatic *syzygos*, Sophia as the partner of the Soter in the Ogdoad, and Mary Magdalene (alternatively, Jesus' mother Mary) as the companion of earthly Jesus.[5] But such a tripartite division runs the risk of preventing the notion of an identification of the three females.

Moreover, one will note that *Gos. Phil.* insists on interaction between the realms (whether three or two) in spite of the divisions they represent. To provide an example: Truth is said to bring "names into existence into the world because it is not possible to teach it without names. Truth is one thing and it is also many things for our sakes" (54.10–20, p. 133). Preexistent, Truth "is sown everywhere. And many see it as it is sown but few are they who see it as it is reaped" (55.20–25, p. 133). The only way to receive Truth—which "did not come into the world naked"—is via "types and images" (67.5–15, p. 140). The gospel underlines that one may apprehend Truth exclusively through symbols, never directly.[6]

At one point *Gos. Phil.* identifies Truth with the Mother (77.15, p. 146), an entity I would equate with the Holy Spirit. The Mother, as Truth, can be seen as a higher image of the Spirit—who may reveal herself as Holy Spirit or as "spirit of the world" (77.10–15, p. 146). I would argue that the varied appearances of Truth and the doubleness of the Holy Spirit, of Sophia, and of the Mary-figure can all be correlated to each other. In addition, when the Holy Spirit, Sophia, and Mary appear as the female *syzygos* of Christ/Jesus, they may, by extension, symbolize the spiritual as well as the earthly partner for the (male) human being.

Seeking to avoid any impression of a static, strict separation into realms—à la Schenke, above—I suggest a collapse of tripartite as well as dualistic models into a synthetic view. To my mind, it is in the ritual of the bridal chamber[7] that such a collapse is actively sought and made possible. This most important sacrament in *Gos. Phil.* achieves the unity of male and female *in this life*, thereby creating the transcendent Pleroma here and now. The bridal chamber aims at such "pre-Paradisial"[8] unification by providing spiritual rebirth for the partakers; one's "original nature" (53.20–25, p. 132) is regained, and immortality is ensured.

For the Holy Spirit, Sophia, and Mary, the bridal chamber means resolution of their double roles. The human beings in the bridal chamber effect the dissolution of this female's double nature precisely by embodying her envisioned state. Thus reflecting the goal of the female entity, the human being works to heal both itself—as split into male and female, Adam and Eve—and the divided Spirit. There are two interdependent integrations: that of the human being, male with female, and that of the split female entity, Holy Spirit–Sophia–Mary, who rejoins her lower to her upper self. In the enactment of the bridal chamber "the world has become the aeon" (86.10–15, p. 151)— that is, the world with its divisions has been abolished.

I take *Gos. Phil.*'s utterance " 'The Holy Spirit' is a double name" (59.10– 15, p. 136) to refer to the Holy Spirit's division into a lower, Kenomatic and a higher, Pleromatic condition: a "worldly" and a "Holy" Spirit. Beyond her separation, the figure is in reality *one*, and if she again becomes simply "Spirit" the epithets "Holy" and "of the world" will disappear and the dualism dissolve. For "the Holy Spirit" may well belong among the names that "are in the world to deceive. . . . They have an end in the aeon" (53.35–54.1, p. 133).

I will first examine *Gos. Phil.*'s treatment of Mary and her relationship(s) with Jesus. His interactions with her may allude to the goal, the bridal chamber. Second, I will concentrate on the metaphors "wind" and "breath" for the Spirit. Parallels and differences between Adam's and Jesus' births will be treated here. Jesus' baptism-rebirth—essentially a bridal chamber event—may signify the awaited rebirth for his followers. Next, I will treat specifically the gospel's portrayal of the doubleness of the Holy Spirit and of Sophia. This section also deals with the prayer by Jesus at the Thanksgiving (58.10–15, p. 135) and with the apostles' petition for Sophia (59.25–30, p. 136); I think both prayers express the quest for the *syzygos*. Finally, I will argue that the earthly marriage should be seen as a symbol and a prerequisite for the bridal chamber sacrament. In this regard, the earthly marriage warrants a positive evaluation. My conclusion will be tied in with the resolution of the female entity's doubleness. It is the human being that plays the main part in effecting this resolution, for the bridal chamber activity momentarily resolves the plight of the split hypostasis. This is so because the ritual affects not only the actual, human partakers, but also Sophia, "the virgin who came down" (71.5–10, p. 143).

MARY'S ROLES

Right after the statement concerning Truth, which is seen by few "as it is reaped,"[9] comes the passage:

> Some said, "Mary conceived by the Holy Spirit." They are in error. They do not know what they are saying. When did a woman ever conceive by a woman? Mary is the virgin whom no power defiled. She is a great anathema to the Hebrews, who are the apostles and [the] apostolic men. (55.20–30, p. 134)

Here, one recognizes the Syrian Christian notion of the Holy Spirit as female. "The virgin whom no power defiled" recalls the Spirit-figure in other Gnostic texts.[10] While *Gos. Phil.* disavows *one* particular kind of connection between Mary and the Holy Spirit, it establishes another tie by associating Jesus' mother with the virgin, the Spirit.

Is it her elevated, spiritual status that makes Mary an anathema to the Hebrews? It is worth noting Giversen's rendering of this part of the passage: "She is lord over those who belong to the multitudes of the Hebrews, that is the apostles."[11] W. W. Isenberg's translation seems to stress the rivalry for authority between Mary and the apostles, while S. Giversen's interpretation clearly sets Mary above them. Mary may be an anathema precisely because of her special claim to power.

The equation "Hebrews = apostles" is noteworthy, especially in comparison with another *Gos. Phil.* passage: "When we were Hebrews we were orphans and had only our mother, but when we became Christians we had both father and mother" (52.20–25, p. 132).[12] In light of *Gos. Phil.* 55 one might say that those who do not appreciate Mary as the spiritual woman, remain Hebrews. She is the mother, and Jesus the father, of true Christians. Among the apostles, only those who recognize Mary's position are real Christians and real apostles; the rest, the skeptical ones, remain among those who have not yet "received the Lord" (62.5–10, p. 137).

Schenke sees Mary here as an incarnation of Adam's (or Seth's) spiritual wife.[13] J.-É. Ménard thinks that the gospel rejects the Holy Spirit's impregnation of Mary because Mary already has a husband, Joseph,[14] but this view skirts the issue of "male" vs. "female" impregnation, for the point is the Holy Spirit's femaleness. Janssens interprets the passage as expressing a view of female inferiority, for "l'Esprit n'est donc pas Dieu" ("the Spirit, however, is not God").[15] But I do not think the Holy Spirit lacks in holiness in *Gos. Phil.*, and therefore the inferiority thesis does not convince me.

Gos. Phil. 55 is "usually put forward as a theological joke," observes J. Lagrand, who attributes the formulation to a possible "Christian reaction against the error of assuming that Mary had sexual intercourse with the Deity."[16] And B. McNeil draws on a late Christian Arabic Sibylline prophetic text that predicts the birth of Antichrist when a woman conceives by another woman. He differentiates between public and private revelations of the apostles, and revelations given to episcopal and initiated successors, respectively.[17] But the text testifies to no such double roles of the apostles. In any case, McNeil feels that *Gos. Phil.* elevates Mary above any apostolic position.[18]

Gos. Phil.'s section on the three Marys is: "There were three who always walked with the Lord. Mary his mother and her sister and Magdalene, the one who was called his companion. His sister and his mother and his companion were each a Mary" (59.5–15, pp. 135–36). The adverb "always" suggests that the women may have been closer to, and more ardent followers of, Jesus than were the other (male) disciples. Inconsistently, the second Mary is called Jesus' mother's sister, and then *his* sister, but this might be a scribal error. According to Ménard, she is Mary-Salome, of Matt. 28:56, an important Gnostic figure.[19] The term "companion," ϩⲱⲧⲣⲉ, for Mary Magadelene, can mean "spouse" or "wife."[20] I think the last sentence can be interpreted as an identification of the three Marys; they mark an integration of Jesus' *syzygos*.[21]

Ménard observes that the blurring of Mary the mother and Mary Magdalene can be found in the work of the Syrian Ephrem. He makes Mary the mother the resurrection witness and the recipient of the prohibition to touch the risen Christ in John 20:17![22] Such an identification of the two females serves to deliberately weaken Mary Magdalene's position as Jesus' possible spouse, for "by the end of the second century Mary Magdalene had become identified with

Mary sister of Lazarus and the woman in Luke 7:36–50," informs R. M. Grant.[23]

The theologically threatening position of Mary Magdalene is further amplified in one of the most perplexing sections of the gospel—an admittedly badly broken part of it:

> And the companion of the [Savior is] Mary Magdalene. [But Christ loved] her more than [all] the disciples [and used to] kiss her [often] on her [mouth]. The rest of [the disciples were offended] by it [and expressed disapproval]. They said to him, "Why do you love her more than all of us?" The Savior answered and said to them, "Why do I not love you like her?" (63.30–64.10, p. 138)[24]

"Companion," κοινωνός, naturally hints at sexual intercourse.[25] *Gos. Thom.*, *The Gospel of Mary* and *Pistis Sophia* also attest to rivalry between Mary Magdalene and the male disciples.[26] In contrast to the two latter writings, *Gos. Phil.* does not present the competition as concerning prowess in interpreting revelations. In *Gos. Phil.*, the disciples feel left out of the Savior's love. Jesus' kissing Mary occurs in the disciples' presence; the kiss is not a private, ritual act belonging in a secluded cultic context.

But the kiss may not express any sexual love for Mary, although the disciples appear to interpret it that way. Do they wish to be kissed as Mary is? One notes that their disappointed question meets with no real answer—a tactic known from *Gos. Thom.*, for instance, where Jesus often answers by nearly echoing the inquiry. *Gos. Phil.* asserts that Jesus indeed loves Mary more than he loves the disciples, whose perception thus seems correct. If Mary is Jesus' *syzygos* and if his love for her is that of a man toward a woman, then one may assume that this love differs from his feelings toward his disciples. On the other hand, Jesus' near-mocking reply may indicate that the disciples fail to understand the meaning of the kissing. I think the kissing hints at the non-public activities in the bridal chamber sacrament.

Schenke thinks the kiss forms the nucleus of this sacrament: it is a holy kiss given by mystagogue to initiate.[27] But why does *Gos. Phil.* not refer to the bridal chamber in this context, then? Both W. Meeks and Janssens see the kiss as an act of conception, and J.-M. Sevrin shrewdly observes the disciples' archontic role here.[28] Sevrin's insight supports my suspicion that the disciples fail to understand the kiss between the Savior and Mary; therefore they are not yet perfect Christians, are perhaps still in the "Hebrew" stage!

Sevrin wavers on the issue of whether the kiss belongs in the bridal chamber context. To make Mary "concevoir des semences spirituelles" ("conceive spiritual seeds"), says Sevrin, accords with another *Gos. Phil.* section,

namely, 58–59, which speaks of conception and giving birth.[29] This passage
occurs just before the information about the three Marys. Full of lacunae in the
beginning, it reads:

> . . . [place . . .] from the mouth, [because if] the word has gone out from
> that place it would be nourished from the mouth and it would become
> perfect. For it is by a kiss that the perfect conceive and give birth. For this
> reason we also kiss one another. We receive conception from the grace
> which is in each other. (58.30–59.10, p. 135)

Furnishing a possible emendation to the first part, I supply Ménard's translation: "[Celui qui se nourrirait] de la bouche [et si] le Logos (λόγος) en sortait,
il nourrirait par la bouche et deviendrait parfait (τέλειος)" ("[The one who will
nourish himself] from the mouth [and if] the Logos . . . emerges from it, he
will nourish by the mouth and will become perfect").[30]

The writer includes himself among the "we," the perfect who are able to
conceive and beget spiritually. Ménard's hypostasized "Logos" makes this
interpretation possible, for the perfect are fed from the mouth of the Logos
who provides himself as nourishment. It is in this context that Jesus' kissing
Mary ought to be understood. The Logos lives in those whom he has kissed,
hence the disciples' jealousy, for they are not yet worthy of the kiss. Because
Jesus is not directly available in *Gos. Phil.* 58–59—in contrast to 63–64—the
perfect receive his substance, *charis*, from one another.

Neither the kisses between the perfect nor the kissing of Jesus and Mary
Magdalene appear to belong in any secluded context; both seem public occurrences. And the perfect in *Gos. Phil.* 58–59 are probably both male and
female, even though sexual differences have ceased to matter, for spiritual
conception and birth hardly depend on two opposed genders. In short, the
kisses in 58–59 do not carry explicit sexual connotations. However, the kissing activity between Jesus and Mary *does* appear in a different light, because
the sexual associations are still strongly present here. I think Jesus deliberately
provokes the male disciples' jealousy in order to demonstrate that they do not
understand the kiss. Unenlightened, the disciples merely prove their inferior
status as compared to Mary. From their point of view the kiss seems a sexual
act, and the spiritual love expressed in the kisses to Mary plays on the sexual
connotations. Jesus is making Mary "spiritually" pregnant; if she had not been
female, one might more comfortably compare the kisses she receives with
those exchanged between the perfect in 58–59.

Kissing transmits nourishment; the Logos gives the spiritual seed necessary
for spiritual offspring. Mary, too, will probably bear spiritual, not material,

children. But in her case there remains the inescapable parallel to the less spiritual parts of the body, which would receive material seed; thus, Jesus' kissing Mary does not completely lose its more realistic sexual reference.

With varying results, scholars have attempted to make sense of the spiritual "sex-life" depicted in these passages. H.-G. Gaffron wonders what the "spiritual birth" in *Gos. Phil.* 58–59 would mean, noting that the kiss here is collective.[31] Meeks takes issue with Gaffron's reactions, especially the latter's notion that the kiss has nothing to do with the bridal chamber sacrament.[32] However, if the perfects' kissing is public—a kind of greeting, perhaps—I suspect their action alludes to, but does not itself constitute, the bridal chamber ritual. It seems reasonable to interpret the perfect as imitating Jesus and Mary.

Like Gaffron, Sevrin characterizes the kissing in *Gos. Phil.* 58–59 as collective and "communaire" ("communal"), but he perceptively distinguishes this action from that of 63–64, which he deems "sexuelle et binaire" ("sexual and binary").[33] Whether seen from a nonenlightened or a spiritual viewpoint, the kissing preserves both sexual and spiritual dimensions, particularly in 63–64. For Jesus' kissing Mary is a deliberately paradoxical action, which gives rise to opposed interpretations by different audiences.

According to the traditions echoed in *Gos. Phil.*, Jesus himself has a double nature and is the product of a double birth. Therefore, the pointedly two-tiered character of his actions should not be underestimated. As Logos, Jesus feeds the perfect with the seed for their own rebirth, and he impregnates Mary with spiritual substance. It is now pertinent to investigate *Gos. Phil.*'s thoughts on two particular spirit-symbols: wind and breath.

SPIRIT AS WIND AND BREATH. JESUS' BAPTISM

Distinguishing between "the spirit of the world" and the Holy Spirit, *Gos. Phil.* 77.10–20 states that when the former "blows, it brings the winter. When the Holy Spirit breathes, the summer comes" (p. 146).[34] Elsewhere, summer and winter are identified as the aeon and the world, respectively (52.25–30, p. 132).[35] Here the text informs us, "Those who sow in winter reap in summer." The believers are exhorted to behave in this fashion, for summer follows winter, the world gives way to the aeon. Another passage states that for the human being in the bridal chamber sacrament, "the world has become the aeon" (86.10–15, p. 151).[36] This bears directly on the imagery of the seasons, for in the bridal chamber the partakers actively accomplish the abolishment of the world, the winter. To put it another way, the spirit of the world gives way to the Holy Spirit. One should note, however, that both spirits are rendered by the term *pneuma*, and that both create their kind of life in their respective seasons.

Gos. Phil. testifies to an explicit doubleness in the Spirit's action: "Those . . . whom the Spirit (itself) begets, usually go astray also because of the Spirit. Thus, by this one and the same breath the fire blazes and is put out" (60.5–10, p. 136).[37] Lacking the epithets "Holy" or "of the world," the Spirit has a twofold, contradictory task: it gives life and destroys it. Furthermore, to be spiritually begotten does not guarantee salvation, for the life-giver's ways are unpredictable.

The fire is the constitutive element kindled in the earthly marriage as well as in the bridal chamber (85.30–86.5, p. 151). Both the worldly and the Holy Spirit in *Gos. Phil.* 77 denote the *one* Spirit that ushers in winter or summer, world (the place of material marriages) or aeon (the bridal chamber realm). The life, "fire," of both kinds of marriages is attributed to the Spirit, working in opposed ways.

In view of *Gos. Phil.* 85–86, one may say that the human being in the bridal chamber inaugurates the aeon. This is due to the Spirit's workings. One may read *Gos. Phil.* 60 as a warning both against the assumption that there are *two* diametrically opposed Spirits—one working to save, the other to destroy—and against too smug a feeling of spiritual accomplishment. Perhaps only the bridal chamber finally secures the reborn into the safety of the aeon, in which the Spirit no longer acts in a worldly way. The gospel's statement, "Love is the wind through which we grow" (79.25–30, p. 147),[38] would suit the bridal chamber context.

Water and fire give rise to the soul and the spirit, says *Gos. Phil.* 67 (p. 140). These two generative principles (plus light, here equated with fire) enable one to become a "son of the bridal chamber." The text distinguishes between the formless fire and the white, "bright and beautiful" one. In light of *Gos. Phil.* 85–86, the first fire may belong to the earthly marriage, the second to the bridal chamber. The first, night-and-winter fire would then be due for extinction, while the second would persist in the day, the aeon. So, the *one* fire of *Gos. Phil.* 60 has here, in 85–86, been separated into two, each appointed to its realm.

Janssens compares these two fires to "une double action de l'Esprit Saint . . . et une double aspect de Sophia Achamoth . . ." ("a double action by the Holy Spirit . . . and a double aspect of Sophia Achamoth").[39] Thus, she refuses to radically divide the fires into two. More inclined to a traditional, dualistic standpoint, Ménard designates the material fire a creation by Achamoth and the archons.[40]

It may now be time to present the most succinctly antidualistic statement of *Gos. Phil.*:

> Light and darkness, life and death, right and left are brothers of one another. They are inseparable. Because of this neither are the good good, nor the evil evil, nor is life life, nor death death. For this reason each one will dissolve into its original nature. But those who are exalted above the world are indissoluble, eternal. (53.10–25, p. 132)[41]

Dichotomies are illusory and will disappear for those who are able to transcend oppositions by freeing themselves from the dualism of the world. Opposites are makeshifts; names, too, deceive, according to the ensuing section in *Gos. Phil.* 67. Diverting from Truth, names belong to the world, not to the aeon (53.10–25, pp. 132–33).[42] Truth and names relate to one another as do the "exalted" to the dichotomies destined for obliteration.

Fire occurs again in *Gos. Phil.* 63:

> Glass decanters and earthenware jugs are both made by means of fire. But if glass decanters break they are done over, for they came into being through breath. If earthenware jugs break, however, they are destroyed, for they came into being without breath. (63.5–15, p. 138)[43]

Perhaps earthenware jugs are demiurgic creations, as suggests Janssens.[44] Pottery stands no chance of rebirth, but glassware, already once infused with Spirit, may be redone. In view of *Gos. Phil.* 60, one may speculate whether the same Spirit (breath) that gave the glass vessel life might also ruin it.

The most pertinent example of a breath-born being is, of course, Adam. He "broke," fell, because of his spouse (= Spirit), but was also reborn through her. *Gos. Phil.* 70 reads, in part:

> The soul of Adam came into being by means of a breath, which is a synonym for [spirit]. The spirit given him is his mother. His soul was replaced by a [spirit]. When he was united (to the spirit), [he spoke] words incomprehensible to the powers. They envied him. . . . (70.20–30, p. 142)

Ménard gives "Son *compagnon* est l'[ésprit ($\pi\nu\varepsilon\tilde{\upsilon}\mu\alpha$)]" ("his *companion* is the [spirit . . .]"),[45] instead of "which is a synonym for [spirit]." According to Gen. 2:7, Adam is made of spirit and earth; he possesses a double nature. As a glass vessel, however, he can be re-created. Indeed, Adam appears to have needed immediate repair. The Spirit who replaced his soul is both mother and spouse. Recall Mary's double roles vis-à-vis Jesus in *Gos. Phil.* 59![46] Adam's lost soul is Eve who, by breaking away, "broke" her husband, and his true companion is now the spirit. "If the woman had not separated from the man she would not die with the man. His separation became the beginning of death," says the text in an adjoining passage (70.5–15, p. 142). But one may suspect that Adam's new spirit-spouse can help him escape the death-sentence by re-creating him into a spiritual entity.

"They envied him" startlingly recalls the jealous disciples' reaction to Jesus kissing Mary Magdalene in *Gos. Phil.* 63–64. Like the disciples there, the powers here realize that something important, but incomprehensible, is happening.

With regard to *Gos. Phil.* 70, one should keep in mind that Eve, though now autonomous, is still a breath-born soul,[47] for she was in Adam at his creation. Consequently she, as well as Adam, relates to the spirit. Here I think we can begin to see the twofold speculations on the syzygy in *Gos. Phil.*: on the one hand, there is the expected male-female syzygy, Adam and the spirit, Jesus and Mary Magdalene; on the other hand, the text attests to a same-gender "pair" constituted by a lower and a higher image for the same being.[48] Eve as soul is still connected to the spirit who forms Eve's higher self. This self is no other than Adam's new spouse. Paradoxically, Adam has both lost and gained a wife, the *same* wife.

Gos. Phil. instructs, "Adam came into being from two virgins, from the Spirit and from the virgin earth" (71.15–20, p. 143).[49] Spirit and earth connote the double birth expressed in the glass/earth imagery. The passage continues, "Christ, therefore, was born from a virgin to rectify the fall which occurred in the beginning" (15–25). Wishing to stress the difference between Adam and Christ, the text also furnishes the link, virgin birth, between the two.

Referring to P. Krüger, Ménard observes that "dans la mariologie syriaque Marie est la terre vivante" ("in Syriac Mariology, Mary is the living earth"),[50] which further emphasizes the parallel between Adam and Christ. Remembering *Gos. Phil.*'s denunciation of Mary's pregnancy by the Holy Spirit, in 55, one now sees that 71 wishes to guard against the suspicion that Christ, too, may have had two virgin mothers.

In *Gos. Phil.* 70.5–71.25 the two Adam-passages are interwoven with an account of Jesus' conception and baptism: "Jesus revealed [himself at the] Jordan; it was the [fullness of the kingdom] of heaven. He who [was begotten] before everything was begotten anew" (70.30–71.1, p. 142). Jesus' baptism seems to be his second, spiritual birth. "Fullness" is Pleroma (the text's term), which here seems equated with the Jordan. Thus, the Jordan has shown itself in its capacity as Pleroma.[51]

The next paragraph is:

Is it permitted to utter a mystery? The Father of everything united with the virgin who came down, and a fire shone for him on that day. He appeared in the great bridal chamber. Therefore, his body came into being on that very day. It left the bridal chamber as one who came into being from the bridegroom and the bride. So Jesus established everything in it through these. It is fitting for each of the disciples to enter into this rest. (71.1–20, p. 143)[52]

Generally, this section is taken to refer to Jesus' baptism. His two parents give Jesus a pneumatic body (one assumes he already possesses a material one[53]). "The virgin who came down" can be equated to the Spirit, Sophia. After appearing (= being spiritually born)—as fire?—Jesus leaves the bridal chamber, presumably in order to teach others about it. For the disciples' goal is to enter the chamber,[54] which means both to be spiritually joined, as the Father and the virgin were, and to be reborn as spiritual entities. Jesus is the paradigmatic "son of the bridal chamber."

At his baptism Jesus had an effect on the water: "By perfecting the water of baptism, Jesus emptied it of death. Thus we go down into the water, but we do not go down into death in order that we may not be poured out into the spirit of the world. When that spirit blows . . ." (77.5–15, p. 146).[55] Perfection entails immortality. If death resided in the water, the baptized would emerge covered with the correlate "spirit of the world," the destructive aspect of the Spirit. Elsewhere, the gospel says that "the living water is a body," and this water is likened to "the living man" (75.20–25, p. 145). A "Christ"-body to be put on, the water is a pneumatic element precisely because of Jesus' perfection of it.

I think Janssens is mistaken when she judges water-baptism to stem from the demiurge, for the text does not depreciate water. Even if it contained both life and death *before* Jesus' action, the water need not necessarily have been evaluated negatively. Janssens notes that the section on Jesus' perfecting the water follows logically from a passage arguing for the complete holiness of the priest, even of his body.[56] By consecrating the bread and the cup, the priest consecrates himself, the text maintains (77.1–10, p. 146). Thus, the Savior's perfecting of the water in *Gos. Phil.* 77 is parallelled in the priest's consecrating actions. There are echoes here of the gospel's consistent argument concerning the perfection of the true Christians—those who, in fact, are no longer Christians, but have become Christ (61.30–35, p. 137; 67.25–30, p. 140).

Another passage deals with the Holy Spirit's role in begetting: "Through the Holy Spirit we are indeed begotten again, but we are begotten through Christ

in the two. We are anointed through the Spirit. When we were begotten we
were united" (69.1–10, p. 141). The phrase "in the two" has been understood
in different ways. R. McL. Wilson gives, "through Christ. In the two we are
anointed," which seems preferable to Isenberg's translation. But Wilson interprets "in the two" to mean the two periods of "natural and spiritual" birth,
though he notes that "in the two" appears again, in lines 10–15 of the passage,
where it clearly refers to the elements water and light. These would parallel
Spirit and Christ.[57]

I venture that one may also relate "the two" to the parents in *Gos. Phil.* 52.[58]
The mother—whose children are (Hebrew) orphans—can be equated to the
Spirit. When the Spirit acquires a male partner, her offspring become Christians. Eve, as Adam's soul, aspires to the same goal; this is the uniting through
begetting. As Jesus was engendered in baptism by the virgin and the Father,
his followers must be begotten by Spirit and Logos.

To recapitulate the beginning of this section: Spirit emerges in both a
positive and a negative aspect. As kindler and as extinguisher of the life-fire,
the Spirit creates both life and death; one recalls that this is one of the
deceptive pairs of opposites in *Gos. Phil.* 53![59] Beyond the Spirit's divisive
attributes, the entity is in reality *one*, a nonconceptual force. I will deal with
passages testifying to this character's doubleness, and then with the decidedly
positive aspect of the Spirit, namely, in the eucharist. The emphasis on the
paradoxical qualities of the Spirit will yield to the definitely positive ones that
are, understandably, quite at home in the sacramental context.

THE AMBIGUOUS SPIRIT. THE EUCHARIST

The statement, "And the companion of the [Savior is] Mary Magdalene,"[60] is
immediately preceded by, "As for the Wisdom who is called 'the barren,' she is
the mother [of the] angels." The text here appears to correlate the two figures
Mary Magdalene and Wisdom. "Barren" Wisdom paradoxically has angel-
children, putatively the envisioned product of Jesus' spiritual impregnation of
Mary.[61]

That Sophia's sterility can be explained—"weil sie von sich aus nichts
Pneumatisches gestalten kann" ("because she, by herself, cannot create anything pneumatic"), as Gaffron has it[62]—seems a misguided judgment that
misses the paradox. One must assume that both mother and angels are pneumatic beings. However, on the previous page, Gaffron has decided that Sophia's angel-offspring are the archons. Such a conclusion makes little sense in
this context, or in *Gos. Phil.* on the whole. Gaffron evidently assumes that

only Soter, Sophia's *syzygos*, qualifies as pneumatic, and because he is not invoked here, Sophia's creations must by necessity be inferior.
Sophia also appears in this passage:

> The apostles said to the disciples, "May our whole offering obtain salt." They called [Sophia] "salt." Without it no offering [is] acceptable. But Sophia is barren, [without] child. For this reason she is called "a trace of salt." [But] where they will be in their own way, the Holy Spirit [will (also) be, and] her children are many. (59.25–60.5, p. 136)

One recalls that neither apostles nor disciples receive a completely positive evaluation in *Gos. Phil.*[63] Petitioning for their *syzygos*, Sophia, the apostles ask for their own salvation through a sacrament, the bridal chamber. "Offering" refers to the apostles themselves, I think, and they are expressing their hope—to the disciples—that they may be united to the *syzygos*. Only in that way will they become "acceptable" offerings. The last part of the section hints at the pneumatic entities, the "many children" to be produced in the syzygial union. In the world, the "winter," Sophia remains barren, childless. But when she becomes fully Spirit, in the aeonic bridal chamber, the "summer," she will produce spiritual offspring. "Where they will be in their own way. . ." alludes to the bridal chamber where the apostles will fully come into their own. As long as they remain in the world, both they and their partner(s) stay in a defective state.

Gasparro notes the ambivalent symbolism of salt. Salt denotes death, but also "la semenza spirituale prodotta dalla Madre e a lei consustanziale" ("the Spiritual seed produced by the Mother and consubstantial with her").[64] Ménard renders the first sentence, "Mais (δέ) la Sophia (σοφία) est stérile (στεῖρα) [sans le] Fils" ("But (. . .) Sophia (. . .) is sterile (. . .) [without the] Son").[65] According to this translation, Sophia stays sterile as long as she has no access to Soter. Referring to the "mother of angels" passage, *Gos. Phil.* 63, in which he deems Sophia "psychique" ("psychic"), Ménard states that in 60, Sophia "n'engendre que des avortons" ("engenders nothing but abortions").[66] But I doubt whether the text supports such an interpretation, for barrenness and abortions should not be equated here.

Further on in 60, *Gos. Phil.* reveals: "Echamoth is one thing and Echmoth another. Echamoth is Wisdom simply, but Echmoth is the Wisdom of death which is . . . the one who knows death which is called 'the little Wisdom' " (60.10–20, p. 136).[67] Echamoth corresponds to the more common name for Wisdom, Achamoth. "One thing" and "another" are both rendered by ⲕⲉⲟⲩⲁ, which may make it possible to doubt whether the passage really makes a distinction between two separate entities; rather, the lacking "a" in Echmoth may indicate that "the little Wisdom" forms an aspect of Echamoth.[68] Recall, again, the Holy Spirit vs. the worldly one, both of which refer to the same, transcendent Spirit entity. Insofar as death can be equated with world, a convincing parallel emerges between Echamoth/Sophia/Holy Spirit and Echmoth/"the little Wisdom"/spirit of the world. It is also worth noting that *Gos. Phil.* 60.10–20 follows as a logical continuation of the (previously treated) sentence, "Thus, by this one and the same breath, the fire blazes and is put out." I am therefore inclined to see the Echamoth/Echmoth passage as parallel with "this one and the same breath."

Janssens draws the connection to the doubleness of Sophia and the Holy Spirit in *Gos. Phil.* 59–60, and Gasparro maintains that it is Sophia/Achamoth who reveals herself on two different levels, as Echamoth and Echmoth.[69] Wilson, however, adheres to the view of a decidedly split Sophia.[70] Sevrin suggests an identification of "the little Wisdom" with the sterile Sophia in 59, and he connects "Achamoth" (Echamoth/Echmoth) with Mary Magdalene, who gives birth to pneumatic seeds.[71]

In the next paragraph the "perfect man" is portrayed as harnessing the powers, here seen as domestic animals. Acting similarly,

The Holy Spirit shepherds every one and rules [all] the powers, the "tame" ones and the "wild" ones, as well as those which are unique. For indeed he [gathers them (and)] shuts them in, in order that [these, even if they] wish, will not be able [to escape]. (60.25–35, p. 136)[72]

Separated into three categories, the powers are all subjected to the Holy Spirit. The three-part schema recalls the previously treated dichotomies to which were added the "indissoluble, eternal" ones (*Gos. Phil.* 53);[73] these would correspond to the "unique" ones beyond the contrasted "tame" and "wild." Acting as a guard or judge, the Holy Spirit—whom Isenberg calls "he," the entity's female nature notwithstanding—decides the fate of all three groups.[74]

Gos. Phil. 55, too, mentions the Holy Spirit's relationship to the powers. Thinking that they act autonomously, the powers are in fact subject to remote control, for "the Holy Spirit in secret was accomplishing everything through them as it wished" (55.15–20, p. 133). Furthermore,

The saints are served by evil powers for they are blinded by the Holy Spirit into thinking that they are serving an (ordinary) man whenever they do (something) for the saints. Because of this a disciple asked the Lord one day for something of this world. He said to him, "Ask your mother and she will give you of the things that are another's." (59.15-30, p. 136)

Here, *Gos. Phil.* introduces another division, that between saints and (ordinary) men. By the Holy Spirit's deception, the powers—now designated "evil"—unwittingly serve the saints. The explanative "(b)ecause of this" overtly parallels the preceding information with the disciple's unenlightened request for a worldly favor. And, in line with the section about Jesus' kissing Mary Magdalene, the disciple is here cast in an archontic role. The Lord's cryptic reply indicates that he will obtain an unexpected gift, ἀλλότριον, which would be better translated as "something alien," that is, something not of this world.[75] The disciple's problem is that he does not know his real mother, the Holy Spirit, who gives otherworldly boons.[76]

Moreover, the disciple's request reflects the petition by the apostles (to the disciples!) for salt in *Gos. Phil.* 59. This quest for the *syzygos* emerges most clearly in Jesus' prayer: "He said on that day in the Thanksgiving, 'You who have joined the perfect, the light, with the Holy Spirit, unite the angels with us also, the images" (58.10–15, p. 135). Jesus may be speaking to the Father,[77] or to his own higher aspect, Soter. It seems that the lower, "image" Jesus includes himself among the "us" asking for salvation.[78] The first set of syzygies in the passage is the perfect and their spouse, the Holy Spirit;[79] the second pair, images and angels, has not yet been united. In light of *Gos. Phil.* 63, the angels can be seen as the children of Wisdom, the Holy Spirit.[80] It seems safe to say that the eucharist here is connected to the bridal chamber ritual,[81] and I suggest that the former may be a prerequisite for the latter.

Gos. Phil. 56–57 contains a long argument concerning the resurrection of the flesh. Only the perfected, not the material, flesh is capable of resurrection. Perfected flesh "belongs to Jesus and his blood. Because of this he said, 'He who shall not eat my flesh and drink my blood has not life in him' (John 6:53). What is it? His flesh is the word, and his blood is the Holy Spirit" (57.1–10, p. 134).[82] In an earlier context the believers have been fed with the word of Jesus.[83] Such feeding allegedly led to conception and the birth of spiritual offspring. But in *Gos. Phil.* 57, the flesh (word) and blood (Holy Spirit) refer to the eucharist context. The life provided by the eucharist still seems to entail the begetting through Christ and Holy Spirit in 69.[84]

Elsewhere the cup is said to be "full of the Holy Spirit, and it belongs to the wholly perfect man" (75.15–20, p. 145). Evidently, the cup does not require perfection in advance, for the cup ensures *reception* of the perfect man, according to the following sentence. In van Eijk's words, "he who receives the Eucharist, receives, or rather, becomes the Logos, the Pneuma, the Perfect Man."[85] Comparing *Gos. Phil.* 75 with other passages that invoke the perfect man, one may conclude that the eucharist is a precondition for knowing how to harness the powers (*Gos. Phil.* 60), and for the begetting of spiritual children with the help of transmitted grace (*Gos. Phil.* 58–59).[86] Containing in themselves Christ and the Holy Spirit, the perfect have achieved syzygial status; they are "unique" (*Gos. Phil.* 60), "indissoluble, eternal" (53), "saints" (59).[87] In these beings, the primordial split between Adam and Eve has been overcome, death vanquished.

THE EARTHLY MARRIAGE AND THE
BRIDAL CHAMBER SACRAMENT

With respect to *Gos. Phil.* 57—and referring to 58 and 75—Ménard notes, "L'Eucharistie est une sacrement semblable à celui de mariage: le Logos et l'Esprit Saint engendrent l'enfant spirituel" ("The eucharist is a sacrament similar to that of marriage: the Logos and the Holy Spirit engender the spiritual child").[88] The imagery in 58 particularly evokes associations with marriage, for this is where Jesus asks for "us" to be joined to the angels, in imitation of the union between the perfect and the Holy Spirit. Van Eijk is puzzled by this passage, because the gospel "nowhere else talks about the eschatological marriage as the union between the angel and its εἰκών."[89] However, angel and image, εἰκών, quite clearly form the eschatological correlate to husband and wife in the earthly union.[90]

The gospel's treatment and evaluation of earthly marriage have caused diverging scholarly interpretations. Some scholars incline toward outright denigration of material marriage as portrayed in *Gos. Phil.*,[91] perhaps on the basis of the following passage:

> Indeed marriage in the world is a mystery for those who have taken a wife. If there is a hidden quality to the marriage of defilement, how much more is the undefiled marriage a true mystery! It is not fleshly but pure. . . . It belongs not to the darkness or the night but to the day and the light. (82.1–15, p. 149)[92]

However, a careful reading of this does not warrant a totally negative view of earthly marriage. To those engaged in such a union, their situation seems a "mystery." This term is usually reserved for aeonic, transcendent activities and qualities, but here it appears equivalent to the "hidden quality" of "the marriage of defilement." The veiled connection between the two types of union is that they are both mysteries, though only one is the "true mystery." In the last sentence one recognizes the proper imagery for the world, "darkness" and "night," and for the aeon, "day" and "light." These contrasts do not, in my opinion, represent a rejection of earthly marriage; instead, this union forms the condition necessary for eligibility for the bridal chamber marriage. Ménard correctly states that the earthly marriage is a sacrament, a symbol, and Grant sees "salvation as equivalent to marriage," which is an "archetype of salvation."[93]

The earthly marriage is described as a "mirrored ($εἰκονικός$) bridal chamber" (65.10–15, p. 139). From this union, one receives the powers to combat the unclean spirits. Men may be attacked by female unclean spirits, women by male ones. Obviously, the single state presents dangers, leaving a person vulnerable to the unclean spirits, for only the mirrored bridal chamber ensures against their advances (65.20–30). Above, in 58, the image and the angel appeared in an eschatological context, but in 65, the earthly partners carry "image" and "angel" designations and thus seem commensurate with the bridal chamber partakers.

In *Gos. Phil.* 66.1–5 the text explicitly informs us that the presence of the Holy Spirit protects against unclean spirits. One may therefore see the powers in 65 as impersonators of the Holy Spirit, for this entity constitutes the male power in the female and vice versa. So, it is the Holy Spirit who is one's true spouse. This state of things of course recalls the Spirit as Adam's partner.

Gaffron, perceiving that "die himmlische Syzygienwelt . . . bildet sich . . . in der irdischen Ehen ab" ("the heavenly world of syzygies . . . reflects itself . . . in the earthly marriages"), thinks that these earthly marriages keep their syzygial connections even when under attack by the unclean spirits.[94] Matters can be put even more strongly, for according to *Gos. Phil.* 66, the acquired ("male" or "female") Holy Spirit power renders the married pair immune to such attacks.

Gos. Phil. claims that "the image must rise again through the image. The <bridegroom> and the image must enter through the image into the truth: this is the restoration" (67.15–20, p. 140).[95] Here, "image" has two referents: it refers, first and third, to the earthly spouse, and second and fourth, to the mirrored bridal chamber. But he, the bridegroom, can now be seen not only as the earthly husband, but also as the Holy Spirit male power protecting his wife.

Those who enter the truth "shall go in there by means of lowly types and forms of weakness" (85.20–30, p. 150). These "means" refer to the earthly marriage and probably also to the spouse(s). Even if characterized by "weakness," the earthly marriage remains unrepudiated, a required state for advancement to the bridal chamber. "Weakness" appears again: "Whereas in this world the union is one of husband with wife—a case of strength complemented by weakness—in the aeon the form of the union is different, although we refer to them by the same names" (76.5–10, p. 145). Isenberg's translation differs from that of W. Till, who says, "Während die Vereinigung in dieser Welt (*κόσμος*) Mann und Frau ist, der Ort für die Kraft und die Schwäche, ist im Äon . . ." ("While the union in this world [. . .] is man and wife, the place of strength and weakness, in the aeon . . .").[96] This rendering seems to establish the *world* as the place for strength and weakness; it is therefore not necessary to interpret these characteristics as pointing to "husband" and "wife," respectively.[97] Referring to F. Sagnard, Ménard notes that "weakness," ϻⲛⲧϬⲟⲃ, is a technical term for the pneumatic seeds that should reunite with the angel.[98] This point allows Ménard to juxtapose husband and angel (power) with wife and weakness (fallen pneumatic seed).

At this point in scholarship, we seem to have no way of knowing whether the information "the form of the union is different" refers to anything sexual. Pondering this, E. Segelberg decides, "It can hardly have been anything carnal. *Gos. Phil.* has a fairly well-defined encratitic character."[99] I see no reason to designate the gospel "encratitic," however, since it contains no unambiguous condemnation of marriage, women, or earthly life.[100]

There is a further comparison between the material marriage and the bridal chamber in the text's description of the roles of the offspring from the two unions:

> In this world the slaves serve the free. In the kingdom of heaven the free will minister to the slaves: the children of the bridal chamber will minister to the children of the marriage. The children of the bridal chamber have [just one] name. Together they [share] rest. . . . They are numerous. . . . (72.15–30, p. 143)

The conditions in the aeon present an inversion of the usual arrangement. I think the service and the ministering here refer to the transformation of the marriage-produced children into spiritual entities. This means that there is no longer any real difference between the two "children"; all now have *one* name, which indicates that dualistic divisions have ceased. "Numerous" recalls the many children of Wisdom in *Gos. Phil.* 60, and these children now include those "served" by the bridal chamber children in 72.

Gos. Phil. 86–87 deals with the fire that burns in worldly as well as in otherworldly marriages.[101] This light "can be a symbol both of resurrection and of an ointment and it is connected to the spirit," says Giversen.[102] Eventually put out in the earthly marriages, the fire persists in the bridal chamber. "If anyone becomes a son of the bridal chamber he will receive the light. If anyone does not receive it while he is in these places, he will not be able to receive it in the other place" (86.1–10, p. 156).[103] Again, the gospel insists on accomplishments in *this* world ("in these places") in order to achieve the aeonic correlate.

"In the other place" does not refer to any postmortem goal, but to the ritual occasion of the bridal chamber wherein the partakers create the aeon *in place of* the world (86.10–15, p. 151).

Giversen allows that the bridal chamber metaphor may connote a ritual act, or it may involve "an evaluation of marriage as sacrament."[104] It might be both, for the bridal chamber constitutes both a parallel to and the goal for the mirrored bridal chamber, the material marriage. Viewed in this way, both kinds of marriage possess ritual value: the earthly marriage forms the prerequisite for the spiritual one. Further, worldly children parallel pneumatic ones; the latter are produced when the image and the angel unite. Such an offspring is the image's "own true (heavenly) self," as Meeks has it.[105]

Returning to Segelberg's query, it still seems premature to side with his decision on any possible carnal action in the bridal chamber. Gaffron agrees with Segelberg. But Gaffron has no high esteem for any Gnostic ritual, and he asserts that the bridal chamber sacrament belongs to the moment immediately before death.[106] This thesis has not found much support. If Jesus' kissing Mary Magdalene alludes—as I think it does—to some secret activity in the bridal chamber, the possibility of a "carnal" ritual does not seem precluded.[107] *Gos. Phil.* does not provide *one*, technical term for the bridal chamber, but uses three terms: νυμφών, παστός,, and κοιτών.[108] But these words also designate the earthly marriage, a fact that speaks for the sacramental value of this union, too.

J.-P. Mahé observes, "ce n'est pas à l'androgynie de la chair qu'aspire le gnostique, mais à celle de l'âme" ("the Gnostic does not aspire to bodily androgyny, but to that of the soul").[109] Receiving the angel, the image once more becomes one. For the bridal chamber aims at restoring the primordial unity of Adam and Eve: their division, which led to death, is now overcome. "When Eve was still in Adam, death did not exist. When she was separated from him, death came into being. If he again becomes complete and attains his former self, death will be no more" (68.20–30, p. 141).[110]

Another section explicitly connects this reuniting with the bridal chamber:

> If the woman had not separated from the man, she would not die with the man. His separation became the beginning of death. Because of this Christ came to repair the separation which was from the beginning and again unite the two, and to give life to those who died as a result of the separation and unite them. But the woman is united to her husband in the bridal chamber. Indeed those who have united in the bridal chamber will no longer be separated. Thus Eve separated from Adam because she was never united with him in the bridal chamber. (70.5–25, p. 142)[111]

As in 68, the emphasis here rests on Adam's, not Eve's, "healing" (68.1–15, p. 137). Resuscitation represents the unification. Jesus' kissing Mary Magdalene can again be brought up in this connection, as can *Gos. Phil.* 58–59 where the kissing connotes feeding with the Logos's nourishment. "Woman" and "husband" in 70 refer to the spouses on two levels: to earthly wife and husband, and to image and angel. *Gos. Phil.* deliberately uses the terms for the earthly spouses in order to convey what cannot really be revealed, for the bridal chamber ritual secrets must remain secrets.

The two marriages correspond to other patterns of complementary opposition in the text, such as the Holy Spirit/spirit of the world, angel/image, Adam/Eve. I think that for all these, unification is the ultimate goal, and thus the earthly marriage finds its higher image in the bridal chamber sacrament. The dualistic schemes are necessary in the world, but both world and its patterns are temporary. The aeonic goal is a third, unique state beyond the oppositional models. However, one of the elements in this pattern appears, sometimes, to be the envisioned goal: Adam both belongs in the oppositions and, when united, embodies the third state. This apparently is the case with the Spirit, too. But here there is a difference, for the Holy Spirit's aim is to become, simply, "Spirit," devoid of her attributes "Holy" or "of the world." The third element—"simply Spirit," united angel and image, and unified Adam—does away with the dualistic scheme and encodes the salvific state. *Gos. Phil.* intriguingly juggles both dualistic and tripartite patterns only to abolish both in the end.[112]

The most obvious company of three is, of course, the special instance, the trinity, which is frequently invoked in the text. But *Gos. Phil.* warns that the names of the trinity-members give rise to misunderstanding, for people fail to perceive the reality behind the names (53.20–54.10, p. 132). When Gaffron attempts to distinguish the Holy Spirit as trinity-member from the entity's role as *syzygos*,[113] he misses the gospel's deliberate play on the Holy Spirit's varied functions. She is one, two, and/or one of three.

Gos. Phil. 59 reveals:

> "The Father" and "the Son" are single names. "The Holy Spirit" is a double name. For they are everywhere: they are above, they are below; they are in the concealed, they are in the revealed. The Holy Spirit is in the revealed: it is below. It is in the concealed: it is above. (59.10–20, p. 136)

Why is the Holy Spirit singled out in the last sentence, even if she shares the characteristics of the Father and the Son? Because she differs from them by her double name. Double name conveys double nature; as argued, the transcendent Spirit may manifest herself as Holy Spirit or as spirit of the world.[114]

Now one may consider the passage, "[The Lord] said, 'I came to make [the things below] like the things [above and the things] outside like those [inside. I came to unite] them in that place' " (67.30–35, p. 141).[115] Aiming to render opposed entities equal by uniting them, the Lord may indeed include the double-named, double-natured Spirit in his salvation program. Her previous epithets "Holy" and "of the world" can be compared to the varied appearances of Truth in *Gos. Phil.* 67. Truth may be equated to the Spirit, for Truth is elsewhere called the Mother, while knowledge, gnosis, is the Father.[116]

When Jesus includes himself in the Thanksgiving prayer, he seeks his own salvation, unification.[117] His redemption is expressed in the gospel's notion that he has the Holy Spirit for both a mother and a spouse. As the Father's partner, the Holy Spirit is Jesus' mother, Mary. But, in his turn, the savior receives the Holy Spirit in the figure of Mary Magdalene, for an earthly and spiritual companion. In this respect—as in others discussed above—Jesus forms a parallel to Adam, whose mother and wife are both the Spirit.

But these roles of the Spirit come to an end at the completion of the salvation-work, that is, when the human being (= Adam)—and, by extension, Jesus—and the Spirit are unified. Like the children of the bridal chamber who all have one name, the Spirit, too, will become one: Echmoth merges with "Wisdom simply." As noted, the unifications take place both between a higher and a lower aspect of the same entity, and between entities of apparently opposite genders. I believe, however, that these two metaphors cover *one* unification, so that there is no question of two kinds of mergings. It is in the bridal chamber, by the actions of the human being, that the salvation comes about, *in this life*.

Finally, it is possible to add another identity for the Spirit in her "spirit of the world" aspect, namely, that of the male and female unclean spirits preying on humankind. The presence of the Holy Spirit deters these attacks, which means that the Spirit is depicted in combat with herself, her "Holy" aspect opposed to her lower one. The presence of the higher prevents the lower from advancing and conquering. As long as the Spirit remains set against herself, world, winter, and death reign. But Jesus' activities with Mary Magdalene/Sophia and Sophia/Holy Spirit—Janssens's recurring compounds—produce spiritual life and healing for both those partners and show the way for the human beings into the bridal chamber.

The Scope of Female Figures
in Gnostic Texts

THREE MODELS

Despite the variety in the portrayals of Gnostic female figures, certain categories for interpreting them may prove possible and useful. Initially, it seems to me pertinent to extract three typological patterns as regards these females. First, both Ruha in Mandaeism and Eden in *The Book Baruch* represent earth; both appear in a tripartite constellation in which the female is either the middle or the lowest of three entities. In Mandaeism, the female spirit hovers as middle constituent between soul and body. Capable of tilting either way, this middle entity—both as mythological figure and as element in the human being—will ultimately find redemption, union with the soul-companion.

Differing from the Mandaean model, *Bar.* assigns *its* female, Eden, to the lowest of three levels. Eden herself never attains to salvation. She is, at best, saved vicariously insofar as her element, the human soul, achieves redemption. Being earth, Eden does not appear able (or willing) to elevate herself in imitation of her eloped, "spiritual" husband, Elohim. In Mandaeism as well as in *Bar.*, the earth remains ambiguous. One notes, however, that both traditions evaluate earthly life and marriage positively, and that Ruha and Eden are never categorically repudiated qua females.

Two other Gnostic traditions that I have treated employ quite different tripartition schemes, and offer less mythologically colored solutions regarding the female. Both *The Gospel of Thomas* and *Excerpta ex Theodoto* posit the female as the lowest, initiatory stage beneath the male and the "living spirit"/ "angelic" level (*Gos. Thom.* and *Exc. Thdot.*, respectively). For these two texts, the dictum is that the female needs to be abolished, by absorption into the male. Only this middle, male position—in which the female is no longer female—makes possible an advancement to the third level. "Female" in *Exc. Thdot.* refers to the "psychic" condition of a group of believers, while the term in *Gos. Thom.* signifies the position of Jesus' female followers vis-à-vis that of his male companions.

In *Exc. Thdot.*, the progression from female to male is expressed as a gaining of form. This term denotes one's acquisition of the Savior for a father and entails a substitution for the previous imperfect, female parentage (compare *Gos. Phil.*). Insofar as Jesus acts as a spiritual guide for his female followers in *Gos. Thom.*'s bridal chamber initiation ritual, he furnishes them with the lacking male element. Thus, he becomes father as well as spouse for these females. The transformation from female to male and, in turn, from male to spirit leaves no place for earthly gender designations: female as well as male have been overcome.

The two remaining Gnostic texts I have chosen to deal with, *The Apocryphon of John* and *The Gospel of Philip*, show, on the surface, more interest in dualistic than in tripartite models. These documents allow the female to remain female by according her a split personality, a separation into a lower and a higher self. This solution brings into sharp focus the ambivalence of the female and may, at the same time, permit a sense of paradox to remain. Threatening to come apart into two distinct—and opposed—figures, the sinful, incomplete female personality and the elevated one barely manage to stay in one piece. The two texts handle the dilemma of dualism by allowing for paradox, resorting to negative theology, and advocating ultimate monism. The earthly state of things, which demands splits, multiplicities, and dichotomies, is not necessarily perceived negatively—for the present order expresses nothing less than the required condition on which the salvific goal depends.

So, the three basic categories for the female as I have presented them are: the female belonging in a tripartite, mythological scheme as the middle or lowest element (Mandaeism and *Bar.*); the female as a stage to be transcended (*Gos. Thom.* and *Exc. Thdot.*); and the female possessing a lower and a higher self (*Ap. John* and *Gos. Phil.*). Obviously, a number of the females could be made to fit more than one category, and the categories themselves are, admittedly, arbitrary. Nevertheless, this outline seems to me a useful point of departure for a specific task, namely, examining possible correlations between these females and the Gnostic exegeses of the Genesis creation accounts as these concern the female.

THE GENESIS TRADITIONS

The coming of human beings into the world and the consequences of this event constitute a central part of most Gnostic speculations. More or less openly stated, the creation accounts of Gen. 1 and 2 are assumed in the six traditions and texts treated in the chapters above. Gen. 2 is by far the more "popular," for Gen. 1 seems to lack conflict and therefore the capacity to provide material for the kinds of exegesis dear to the heart of Gnostic interpreters.

Still, both *Bar.* and Mandaeism evoke Gen. 1, even if they insert Adam and Eve into the story. Of course, it is significant that these two particular traditions should feel greater affinity with Gen. 1, for both of them testify to a certain optimism and to the idea of relative equality between the sexes. Neither of the two sources shows any interest in the Gen. 2 theme of Eve originating from Adam's rib. The two human beings are created in the same way, although Adam has priority in terms of sequence. Eve's creation is not tinged with negativity; marriage and procreation are givens.

In Mandaeism, both Adam and Eve (Hawwa) possess celestial counterparts; a balance of male and female is already present as a model in the Lightworld.[1] Certain Mandaean texts, such as *ATŠ*, seem more interested in stressing this Lightworld connection of the first human pair than in describing the earthly life of the two. The demiurge Ptahil creates earthly Eve on earthly Adam's model; according to another *Ginza* tradition, Eve has Ruha as her pattern—but one should take care not to impute any automatic negativity to this information, for Ruha is no unambiguously evil figure. And, despite the similarity between Hawwa's name, חַוָּה, and one of Ruha's demonic names, Ewat ('uat), there seems to be no formal, grammatical connection between the two.

In *Bar.*, Eden and Eve are associated, for "Eve is a seal of Eden to be preserved forever" (*Bar.* 26.9). Still, the text is only peripherally concerned with Eve. Like Adam, "a seal and love-token and eternal symbol of the marriage between Elohim and Eden" (26.8), Eve is created by the paternal angels. One assumes that she, like her husband, derives from the "human and civilized regions" (26.7) of Eden, the creation material. Both Adam and Eve are furnished with Elohim's spirit and Eden's soul. Like Mandaeism, *Bar.* is uninterested in the tradition that attributes sins to Adam and Eve. Sexual violations are perpetrated on the first human couple by Naas, the maternal, phallic angel characterized precisely by transgression.

Marriage and procreation are viewed positively both in the Mandaean tradition and in *Bar.*, and sexuality between spouses is not addressed as an acute moral and theological problem. In *Bar.*, Adam and Eve are outrightly told to multiply, in accordance with the command in Gen. 1. In Mandaeism, the "unevenness" between the two sexes appears as *the* issue when Ruha instructs Adam bar Adam, but the division of human beings into male and female is not repudiated. Even though it may be acknowledged that earthly, married life is not unequivocally easy, such a life still accords with the Lightworld's plan and model.

As soon as one moves to the other four examples in my investigations, however, the evaluation of the division between the sexes and of the earthly state of life changes drastically. In *Gos. Thom.*, the theme of Adam's and Eve's separation into distinct genders takes a central position. The gospel concentrates on Gen. 2's information that Adam was created as *one* being. *Gos. Thom.*'s very lack of a balanced, heavenly model for the two human genders has grave consequences for the text's view of the woman in the couple. Essentially responsible for severing Adam into two, Eve turns generic man (*prôme*) into male man (*arsēn*)—a fateful separation. Pre-Paradisial Adam (as I have termed him) is the salvific goal: the break between male Adam and his former, "living spirit" self must be healed. And the secondary division, that between the genders, also needs reparation. "On the day when you were one you became two" (logion 11) was a decisive day indeed. The woman is, then, twice removed from God: she needs to return to the male in order to become, finally, a "living spirit," which is her—and male Adam's—ultimate goal.

Ideologically, *Gos. Phil.* ties in with *Gos. Thom.*, for *Gos. Phil.* presents Eve as actively responsible for the break in Adam, and for death: "If the woman had not separated from the man, she would not die with the man" (*Gos. Phil.* 70.5). Division entails imperfection and mortality for both, but the emphasis is on Adam's predicament. This text remains ambivalent regarding the true identity of Adam's partner, for she is both corporeal and spiritual. Here, there is a marked difference between *Gos. Thom.* and *Gos. Phil.*: the former has no transcendental female figure corresponding to the Holy Spirit in *Gos. Phil.*, where the earthly woman's relationship to the higher female entity forms the foundation for a different conception of salvation. The interpretation of Eve in *Gos. Phil.* is intimately linked to the text's central interest in the female Holy Spirit. One could say that the Spirit is Adam's mother, spouse, and daughter. Such a solution closes two generation gaps: Adam is created—and is creative in relationship to—the same female. Originating from the Spirit, Adam internalizes it before he becomes separated from it.

This particular kind of solution to the problem of the female's role and identity is also discernible in *Ap. John.* Aeonic, androgynous Adam, Perfect Man, is born from Pronoia and possesses an invincible power. This power turns up again via Yaltabaoth, the demiurge, in earthly Adam, and is none other than the Spirit, Adam's wife-to-be. Both Adam and Eve are made on the model of First Man, that is, aeonic, androgynous Adam. One recalls, in contrast, the Mandaean tradition according to which both Adam and Eve (Hawwa) have separate, male and female Lightworld-models: Adam Kasia ("hidden" Adam) and Hawwa Kasia ("hidden" Hawwa). A gender-affirming system like Mandaeism does not need to posit an androgynous heavenly model.

In *Ap. John*, Yaltabaoth's entire career as demiurge centers on his attempt to obtain Adam's wife, as it were. Eve is both identical with and different from the pursued Spirit. She constitutes the element in Adam without which he could not stand—that is, without her he would not be fully human in the spiritual sense, but merely an earthbound soul. A portion of Adam's power is inserted into the fleshly woman; she is thus "born" out of Adam, "daughter" as well as spouse. Her task is not to aid Adam, but rather to help the archon attain the Spirit. However, the two females are essentially *one*. When Yaltabaoth is about to rape Eve, *Ap. John* takes care to separate the two females, because the spiritual principle must not be directly defiled. Physical Eve, on the whole, holds little interest for the text. For instance, it is Adam and Prognosis—not Eve—who are Seth's parents. The emphasis rests on the woman as the man's hidden, spiritual power.

This idea finds a unique expression in *Exc. Thdot.* Here, Wisdom puts both male ("elect") spirit and female ("calling") soul seeds into Adam. The female seed is extracted from him (as rib, one assumes) and becomes Eve. From her, the "females," the souls, subsequently derive; from Adam, the "males," the spirits. A potential male (that is, spirit), the female contains the soul that hides its marrow, the male spirit. Thus, the two elements are inextricably embedded in one another. It is, of course, imperative for Adam to regain his lost part, the bone containing the marrow. Upon retrieving it, Adam will become complete, and healed Adam implies healed humanity. In the Ogdoad, female *psuchē* is turned into male pneuma. To become an offspring of the male means to lose the female, Eve, for a mother. One's father is now Jesus, who represents a parallel to healed Adam. This required substitution of mother-parentage for father-parentage is also a prerequisite for salvation in *Gos. Thom.*, as noted above.

In sum, one may say that a system that allows for an already present female model—however ambiguous—accords a modicum of positive evaluation to Eve. Both Mandaeism and *Bar.* simply transfer the harmony between the sexes in Gen. 1 to Adam and Eve, who properly belong in Gen. 2. The notion of gender balance may also show up indirectly, as in *Exc. Thdot.*'s ideal of interdependent female soul and male spirit (but this text can hardly be said to advocate absolute equality between Adam and Eve).

Repudiation of Eve occurs when she is made responsible for Adam's "fall" from his pristine position, his pre-Paradisial self. His original status becomes the goal for both genders. However, this does not entail equality between the two; rather, it necessitates abolition of the female. In clear contrast, the woman who is Adam's partner can be interpreted so positively as to make her *the* spiritual, guiding principle in her husband. Again, this requires a separation of the female into several more or less autonomous personalities. A particularly profound psychological solution appears in the collapse of the three generations of the female into one. Such a view speaks eloquently of the ambivalence toward the female: her protective role as mother, the male resistance against her as autonomous spouse, and the male need to control her as daughter.

EVE AND THE GNOSTIC FEMALE FIGURES

What implications might the evaluative interpretations of the female and her place in the Genesis creation accounts have for the Gnostic female figures treated in the chapters above? Links between Eve and these females might be more or less openly stated; in any case, it is advisable not to assume any general, automatic parallels between them.

In *Ap. John*, one recalls, Sophia conspicuously neglects to ask for permission when she plans her autonomous creation. Previously, the narrative has stressed Barbelo's humble attitude: *she* petitions before bringing forth beings. Sophia is portrayed as the first violator of this "polite" pattern. It seems possible to interpret her arrogant behavior as a parallel to the Biblical tradition of Eve's transgression. In both cases, decisive acts of autonomy result in unprecedented creations. However, *Ap. John* emphasizes Sophia's being, at this point, deplorably unrelated to a male, whereas Eve obviously presupposes a male presence. Directly or indirectly, Sophia acts as an instigator to the human beings to taste "the perfect Knowledge" (*Ap. John* 23.25–30)—a parallel to Eve's traditional role beneath the tree. As in *Gos. Phil.*, Sophia is Adam's true, spiritual spouse and she seems to fulfil the expectations of several generations of women towards him.[2]

I have touched on the logical problem of *Ap. John*'s deploring Sophia's lack of a male partner and, at the same time, allowing for her identity as an androgyne who ought to have no need for a mate. *Ap. John* presents and, it seems, struggles with two distinct, opposed presuppositions: creative androgynes are affirmed (*except* for Sophia), and so are couples who create together in harmony. As an aeon, Sophia is identified with the higher, female androgynes in the text—and yet, *Ap. John* condemns her activity. This evaluation emerges at its most negative in BG where Sophia's invincible power is interpreted as lust (see above, p. 44).

Sophia's lack results not so much from her failure to acquire a (consenting) male partner as from the impossibility of satisfying diametrically opposed presuppositions in *Ap. John*, it seems to me. How can it be otherwise? Her goal is to be united with her *syzygos*: Christ/Adam/First Man/Holy Spirit—all of whom are, somehow, androgynes as well. At the same time, Sophia's aim is to merge with her own, same-gender self: Ennoia/Pronoia/Prognosis/Holy Spirit—also androgynes. The combination of these two models (I have called them "double syzygies") testifies to the tremendous problems posed by female, creative androgynes. It seems that androgynes allow for autonomy, partnership, and competition in the relationship between the entities incorporated in the composite being. When the androgyne is outspokenly female, negativity adheres to it, says W. O'Flaherty.[3] But for *Ap. John*, such an explanation seems insufficient, because other female androgynes "higher" than (or prior to) Sophia receive no negative evaluation. In all likelihood, it is the *result* of Sophia's creativity that demonstrates her previous lack, now present as something new and abhorrent, Yaltabaoth.[4]

Females capable of creating alone pose "a phallic threat to the male," according to O'Flaherty.[5] *Ap. John* eloquently expresses this threat, I think, precisely by describing Sophia's product, Yaltabaoth, as a serpent: his shape displays his mother's illegitimate, phallic capacity. She creates an objectified male power that by its very form manifests Sophia's "lack." The invincible spiritual power that Yaltabaoth steals from (or is given by) his mother cannot readily be distinguished from her creative sexual ability. Sophia needs to regain both aspects of this power in order to be restored, and her completion depends on Adam and Christ. But the latter, at least, is an androgyne, identified with female/androgynous Ennoia, who is Sophia's higher self. *Ap. John* seems consciously and jokingly to test a reader's discerning abilities: squinting with one eye, one sees androgynes; with the other, one perceives couples. Either way, Sophia's condition is one of simultaneous deficiency and excess of power.

A different kind of doubleness in the Wisdom-figure appears in *Exc. Thdot.* Characterized as "the Ennoia of Deficiency" (*Exc. Thdot.* 22.7)—one of the very few negative designations of Wisdom in this text—Sophia is none other than the female element *psuchē* bearing a male, pneumatic potential. Maleness is her goal, even when her role is primarily that of Christ's spouse. Male status implies her full realization and leaves behind anything "female." As in *Ap. John*, Wisdom seems capable of bringing forth beings by herself. Her lone, nonsyzygial emanation of male and female seeds in *Exc. Thdot.* 21 remains unreproached—but then, unlike Sophia in *Ap. John*, she gives rise to no monstrosity.

Soul and spirit are relational, not absolute, terms, as L. Schottroff has convincingly argued, and the two correspond to one another as do Wisdom and Christ. They are inseparable, as attested by the image of the marrow in the bone. That "[t]he visible part of Jesus is Wisdom and the Church" (*Exc. Thdot.* 26.1) may be interpreted as a circumlocution for the relationship of marrow to bone, spirit to soul: the Church and the borne-apart seeds form the casing for the invisible spirit. In a certain sense the bone equals Eve, for she represents the part Adam must regain in order to become whole. When he obtains it, he will again be able to "give birth," as he once did to Eve. However, it is not Adam himself, but the perfect Adam-figure, Jesus, who will fill the role as male birth-giver. *Exc. Thdot.*'s speculations on the necessity of acquiring male parentage thus link Adam's birth-giving capacity with that of the Savior. Eve and Wisdom parallel one another as "mothers," but ideally, as *Exc. Thdot.* sees it, it is the male, not the female, that ought to be the womb for the seed.

An inverse Adam-Eve parallel occurs in *Exc. Thdot.* 39, where the Mother emits Christ in complete form. He then deserts her (compare *Bar.*!), an act that renders her subsequent creations incomplete. As in *Exc. Thdot.* 21, the female has no problem accomplishing complete creations on her own, but in *Exc. Thdot.* 39 the disappearance of the pneumatic principle, Christ, leaves an asymmetry.

The theme of competition between the Mother (Wisdom) and Christ appears more acutely in *Exc. Thdot.* than in *Ap. John*, because it is explicitly tied to the ideas of birth and rebirth. At the eschatological moment, the male will once again become *the* parent and the seeds previously born of Wisdom will then acquire Christ for a father. Re-creation comes about solely in and on male terms. As noted, this requires two steps: first, the "public" wedding feast in the Ogdoad, where the females are turned into males—that is, Eve returns to Adam, as it were; and second, the final, "private," pleromatic bridal chamber in which the male syzygy reaches angelic status—that is, Adam regains his pristine position, *beyond* male and female (compare *Gos. Thom.*).

Wisdom's—the Mother's—salvation is portrayed in *Exc. Thdot.* 45, according to which Jesus "bestowed on her a form (μόρφωσιν)." This entails readying her for maleness, for achieving the pneumatic nature of the Savior. Her salvation parallels that of the *psuchē*-dominated human being who "is led into death and into the world" (80.1), as long as it remains the child of the

Mother. For both Mother and human being, "femaleness" is a stage to be overcome.

Gos. Thom. posits a virtual identification between Eve and the female disciples. Mary Magdalene, to whom Jesus promises maleness in logion 114, is linked to Eve because women signify the being who made Adam two. Jesus—himself a reconstituted Adam—acts as Mary's proper initiator. Twice removed from God, so to speak, Mary needs to lose her female identity, acquire male nature, and then gain spiritual status in the restored Adam. Except for Peter's ignorant judgment of Mary (which prompts Jesus' statement of his particular purpose for her), she is not directly reproached for being a woman.

Gos. Thom. deplores the division into genders; it does not repudiate sexuality as such. As I have argued, the gospel should not be taken to support ascetic views, but simply to present a cogent, "logical" solution to the initial separation of the *one* generic man into discrete, genderized beings. Because he is not "born of woman," Jesus is self-evidently suited to lead Mary, the woman, back to her spiritual origin. By so doing, he repeals female parentage and female nature (compare *Exc. Thdot.*).

The tripartition female–male–living spirit—respectively, female–earthly Adam–spiritual Adam—corresponds to another one in *Gos. Thom.*: likeness–lower image–upper image (see above, pp. 97–99). Likeness, ⲉⲓⲛⲉ, signifies the female. The last element in the "evolutionary" line, Eve must be reincorporated into pre-Paradisial Adam. The term "solitary," μοναχός, can be understood as the middle, male condition, which is both *arsēn* ("male" as opposed to "female") and *prôme* (that is, generic, male status combining both male and female).

Like *Gos. Thom.*, *Gos. Phil.* presents the bridal chamber as the ritual locus for the joining of the separated genders. But *Gos. Phil.*'s presupposition differs markedly from that of *Gos. Thom.*: the rectification of the fall implies no denial of the female. The bridal chamber in *Gos. Phil.* balances the genders and accords to each the other's spiritual powers, for the Holy Spirit protects the male in the female, and vice versa. The presence of the higher female entity, the Holy Spirit, guarantees an enduring salvific value in earthly females. According to *Gos. Phil.*, Eve's separation from Adam is due to her never having been "united with him in the bridal chamber" (*Gos. Phil.* 70.25). Thus, Adam's and Eve's earthly union fell short of its goal, which is the ritualized, spiritual joining that creates Pleroma in the Kenoma.

Just as Adam's true companion is the Spirit, so Jesus relates to Mary Magdalene. When Jesus kisses Mary, she becomes pregnant with spiritual children who will be "born" in the bridal chamber. This means that the partakers in the ritual achieve spiritual status: in their capacity as "spiritual parents" they themselves become "children of the bridal chamber." The kissing is a preliminary gesture that demonstrates the beginning of the healing of the first human couple who failed to accomplish their spiritual union. *Gos. Phil.* does not seem consciously to parallel Eve (mentioned by name only twice, in 68.23 and 70.20) and the Holy Spirit figure. One could, however, see in spiritualized Eve a Spirit finally having overcome her dichotomous aspects, "of the world" and "Holy."

As noted, Spirit Ruha as model for Eve is attested in Mandaeism. One of the few references to Ruha's direct dealings with Eve (Hawwa) appears in *GL* 3.1 (p. 438.24–35) where, at Adam's death, Ruha tempts Hawwa into noisy mourning, behavior disapproved of among the Mandaeans.[6] Ruha herself mourns when Hawwa dies, deploring the departure of the first female human being. This tradition seems to imply a special relationship between the two, but it also expresses, generally, the survivors' unavoidable grief at the departure of a relative from the earthly world. Hawwa can perhaps also be said to return to her Lightworld counterpart, Hawwa Kasia.

Common to both Mandaeism and *Bar.* is the lack of interest in Eve as a sinful being (see p. 128, above). *Bar.* states that Eve is a "seal" of the female entity Eden. But, as in Mandaeism, the concern with Eve dwindles because she plays no divisive part in the Gnostic interpretation of the Genesis traditions. Neither Mandaeism nor *Bar.* portrays a generic Adam torn asunder by the female, and an exegesis of Gen. 2 that simply leaves out any hint of Eve's derivative nature shows affirmation, not regret, regarding the earthly life of the two separate genders. Eve's relationship to her mate as well as to her own female "blueprint"—Eden and Ruha/Hawwa Kasia—poses no salvific problem for her as first human female. Moreover, Eve's fate is unrelated to Eden's and Ruha's redemption.

Thus, where there is no transgression connected specifically with Eve, the concern with her is minimal. On the other hand, in the traditions where she is portrayed as sinful, she and subsequent women may signify female "stages" that must be left behind. *Gos. Thom.* and *Exc. Thdot.* most directly associate Eve with their respective female figures. For these texts, the ideal is the reconstitution of Adam, but this restoration causes—perhaps counter to expectation—no central problem in terms of sexuality or androgyny.

In *Ap. John*, however, androgyny is a full-blown, principal issue. Sophia steps into prohibited action and territory and is therefore unavoidably correlated to the negative Eve-exegesis. In Sophia, deficiency and excess converge and are interpreted almost exclusively along sexual lines. The threat of a female acting in a male manner brings androgynous sexuality to the forefront in *Ap. John*'s portrait of personified Wisdom.

How differently *Gos. Phil.* handles *its* powerful female figure! Here, one of the Spirit's tasks is to guarantee the symmetry between male and female. They are equal partners in the world that they themselves turn into Pleroma as they perform the bridal chamber sacrament. *Gos. Phil.*'s positive attitude toward marriage and earthly life puts this text in close agreement with both Mandaeism and *Bar.* Predictably, these traditions show concern not only with the female mythological figure's role in the redemptive work, but also with the responsibility of human beings, be they male or female. Salvific work requires ritual, and it is to this dimension that I next turn.

THE RITUAL REQUIREMENT

Gos. Thom. speaks not of ordinary females, but of Jesus' two female disciples, Mary Magdalene and Salome. These exemplify the female becoming male and finally a unified, "living spirit." The bridal chamber is the setting for these transformations, and Jesus is the initiator. As long as he is present, the disciples have the opportunity to be transformed into reconstituted Adam. Replying to the issue of fasting, Jesus states, in logion 104, "But when the bridegroom leaves the bridal chamber, then let them fast and pray" (*Gos. Thom.*, p. 129). Concerned with the salvation of the disciples during Jesus' earthly lifetime, *Gos. Thom.* lays out no guidelines for how subsequent humanity might regain pre-Paradisial Adam's status. The reciprocity alluded to in logion 114, "*make her* male" and "*make herself* male" (my emphases), does show that the activity depends on both initiator and initiate, but there is no hint as to how the required change might be accomplished after Jesus' departure.

Gos. Phil. treats the ritual of the bridal chamber differently. The text does not mention Jesus as having any part in the ritual; in fact, Jesus merely alludes to the sacrament when he kisses his companion, Mary Magdalene. As I have argued, this "public" display can be understood as a calling attention to—but not as constituting an element in—the secret, "private" bridal chamber sacrament. "Conception" is effected when the believers kiss one another, an act that presumably precedes the actual "birth" of spiritual children in the bridal chamber. And these children are none other than the reborn partakers themselves. They emulate Jesus who, in his own baptism, was born in the bridal chamber. At the same time, they also imitate Jesus' parents, the virgin and the Father.

Unlike *Gos. Thom.*, *Gos. Phil.* stresses the sacrament of the bridal chamber as a duty enjoined upon married couples. Just as Jesus asked for the angel, his *syzygos*, in the Eucharist prayer and the apostles petitioned for their Sophia, so the believers need to join, spiritually, with their mates. Regarding material marriage, *Gos. Phil.* states: "Great is the mystery of marriage! For [without] it the world would [not have existed]. Now the existence of [the world depends on man], and the existence [of man on marriage]" (64.30–35, p. 139). Contracted on earth, material marriage—the "mirrored" bridal chamber—forms the condition for entering into the sacrament in which the union becomes an otherworldly marriage, a "true mystery" (see above, p. 120). The sacramental act transforms earth into Pleroma, and human partakers into spiritual ones. Significantly, the prescribed earthly union enables the couple to fight successfully against threatening, unclean spirits. One's true spouse *is*, indeed, the Spirit, who furnishes each spouse with this protective power against the aggressive spirits.

The bridal chamber's "healing" function occurs on two levels: first, in the earthly spouses who now accomplish what Adam and Eve did not, and secondly, in the Spirit herself who remedies her previous division into "worldly" and "Holy." Thus, according to *Gos. Phil.*, a great responsibility rests on human couples. Their own redemption as well as that of the higher, female principle depend not on external, divine intervention, but on a specific, human ritual activity. Salvation in the beyond is contingent on salvation in the present, says the gospel. Ritual, spiritual obligations fulfilled on earth turn this very earth into what can now be understood as *its* own higher image, Pleroma. The bridal chamber ritual dissolves separations on both the human and the spiritual level, a dichotomy that now becomes irrelevant. Also, what I have called the "double syzygies" (compare *Ap. John*), are transcended, as is the division of the female entity into a lower and a higher aspect.

The traditional question of realized vs. future eschatology might, in *Gos. Phil.*'s interpretation, merely demonstrate spiritual immaturity. Present *and* future merge in the actual, human performance of the bridal chamber sacrament, and redemption in the present provides eligibility for "future" salvation. "If anyone becomes a son of the bridal chamber he will receive the light. If anyone does not receive it while he is in these places, he will not be able to receive it in the other place" (*Gos. Phil.* 86.1–10, p. 156).[7] "In the other place" implies, it seems, a Pleromatic redemption outside the earthly realm turned into Pleroma. In all likelihood, this means that an earthly correlate for the postmortem Pleroma must be created on earth. The logic is, to borrow E. Goodenough's phrase, "by Light, Light."[8]

Gos. Phil.'s antidualistic statement (53.10–25) and its teachings about

Truth (see above, pp. 105–6 and 125) can be correlated with the emphasis on the necessity to "receive the light" while still on earth. The accomplished bridal chamber celebrant knows that the dualistic framework is a required foil for the one, yet many-faceted, Truth. Transformation of earth into Pleroma paradoxically still lets earth be earth, Pleroma Pleroma, in the sense that the initiate almost playfully both rejects and affirms the everyday division between "here" and "there." The gospel remains highly consistent in adhering to its philosophy of paradox.

Consequently, *Gos. Phil.*'s statement that "Truth did not come into the world naked, but it came in types and images. One will not receive Truth in any other way" (67.5–15) can, I think, be taken to imply that when the bridal chamber participants make the world no longer world, but aeon, this very act releases Truth from the straitjacket of dualism. As noted, Truth, identified with the Holy Spirit, symbolizes the female entity awaiting unification with herself through human activity in the bridal chamber.

Bridal chamber union is a concern for *Exc. Thdot.*, too. However, when holding forth about this notion, the text hardly speaks of any ritual required of human beings on earth. The "public" wedding feast between male pneuma and female *psuchē* in the Ogdoad creates a male syzygy eligible for ascent into the Pleromatic, "private" bridal chamber in which angelic entities emerge. Neither of these stages of unification appears to have any clear correlate on earth. The only parallel shows up in *Exc. Thdot.*'s allegorical interpretation of the priest's activities in the Holy of Holies (see above, pp. 67–68). Whether Clement knew of any "Theodotian" Valentinian ritual imitating the Jewish priest is, at this point, an unanswerable question.

The idea of a necessary, though largely difficult, relationship between pneuma and *psuchē* and the notion of the psychic as a condition for the "spiritual" work of salvation appear, as central themes, in *Ap. John.* But here, as in *Exc. Thdot.*, there is no concern with earthly, human ritual requirements toward redemption. Yaltabaoth, *psuchē* incarnate, ceaselessly attempts to capture the spiritual element that he unwittingly infused into Adam. I conclude, from my examination of *Ap. John*, that the text shows a certain inconsistency: the demiurgic soul-principle Yaltabaoth cannot look forward to final liberation, but human souls do have ample opportunity for salvation. According to Jesus' information to the inquiring John, only apostate souls remain beyond hope, but the three other kinds of souls will be saved. Adam and subsequent human beings possess both *psuchē* and pneuma and it is the latter element that makes salvation possible. Hapless Yaltabaoth displays a Nietzschean "spirit of vengeance" toward the element that eludes him, for the demiurge simultaneously desires and hates what he cannot obtain.

Bar. demonstrates a related, ironic inconsistency with regard to the salvation of the primary soul-bearer and of the resultant human being. Unable or unwilling to ascend in imitation of her eloped husband Elohim, Eden remains on and as earth, responsible for her element, the soul, in humanity. In contrast to Eden and to Jesus, human souls may possess the capacity for salvation. At least, this is one possible way to interpret *Bar.*'s adduced Isaiah passage, "Hear, O heaven, and *give ear, O earth*" (Isa. 1:2, my emphasis). According to *Bar.*'s exegesis, Elohims' spirit in human beings equals heaven, while earth is "the soul which is in man with the spirit" (*Bar.* 26.36), so that both elements appear able to grasp the message. If, indeed, both soul and spirit can be saved together, then their goal would seem to imply a vicarious, reconciled redemption of the two estranged spouses, Elohim and Eden.

Such an idea of the soul's chance of salvation differs markedly from *Bar.*'s information that both Jesus and Elohim left Eden behind—for Jesus, unperturbed by the maternal angel Naas, distanced himself from his Edenic part, leaving it on the cross (26.31–32). Human souls, then, appear able to attain a goal unavailable to either Elohim or Jesus. This seeming contradiction does, however, hide a kind of theological joke, for the initiate in the mystery discovers something unexpected in the course of the ceremony.

I have noted the mystery's two-part scheme: the oath provides the condition for the vision (see p. 12, above). Performed in imitation of "our Father Elohim" (27.1)—not of Jesus!—it expresses, perhaps, the ideal but unaccomplished form of the ascent as far as Elohim is concerned. For Elohim neglected to take his wife with him, and indeed, he seems subjected to doubts, perhaps precisely because he left Eden down below. If he doubts, he resembles his double-minded mate. Emphasizing Elohim's very lack of regret at having sworn the oath, however, the text merely underlines the ambivalent feelings regarding the mystery's desirability and efficacy. In the initiation ceremony, the neophyte drinks the pneumatic water, mimicking the "father's" spiritual baptism above; believers are assured that Elohim did not regret this act, either. The oath sworn in the name of "the Good" leads to the vision of this upper entity. It is likely that the sight produces a shock of recognition, for, as noted, "the Good" denotes fertility and procreation and is linked precisely to the element left behind, Eden. Finding that "the Good" shows far stronger affinities with Eden than with the spiritual Elohim, an initiate might indeed question the ritual he has just performed in imitation of Elohim.

Bar.'s positive evaluation of earth and marriage and its outright blaming of Elohim for the introduction of evil testify to an unresolved ambivalence toward the purported "salvation" from the earthly realm. The text allows the suspicion to crop up: perhaps it would have been better to stay on earth and serve "the

Good" and Eden there, instead of aspiring to "the Good" and Elohim above. The problem is, of course, that the supreme principle, "the Good," is both "up there" and "down here." But this truth is not revealed, except in the initiation ritual, which carries the requirement of silence—and by then it is too late, for "return to earth" is now impossible. Thus, the believers might easily find themselves in the position of Elohim, fighting thoughts of remorse about the whole spiritual adventure. All in all, stunned (or, perhaps, amused) silence appears to be the only solution; at any rate, it is preferable to the prohibited expression of regret.

In contrast to *Bar.*, the Mandaean tradition provides no ambivalent emotions regarding the efficacy of *its* ascension ritual, the *masiqta*. Barring serious sins on the part of the rising soul and spirit, successful ascent will result as long as the priests carry out their ritual duties in the prescribed manner. Seen from the earthly viewpoint, life in the Lightworld implies death, but it is, in reality, life in its fullest sense. The link, *laufa*, between the upper and lower worlds is created and upheld by the *masiqta* (among other rituals connecting the living and the dead). It is abundantly clear that the *laufa* "works" only insofar as the required rituals are performed. One might even say that the two worlds continue to exist solely because ritual work persists.

The *masiqta*'s goal is to join the soul (*nišimta*) and the spirit (*ruha*) of the deceased. Concentrating on this aim, the priests endeavor to create a Lightworld-body (*'uṣṭuna*) for the new member of the Mandaean community up above. Soul cannot rise without spirit; both constituents, frequently at war with one another while in the human, earthly body, are required for the *'uṣṭuna*. The spirit's goal is, more precisely, to acquire the nature of the soul, as this state marks complete salvation. It is important to note that, in contrast to other Gnostic systems, there is no sexual imagery involved here, no joining of "female" spirit to "male" soul, or the like.

Unlike *Bar.*, in which the lower entity—female soul, not female spirit, as in Mandaeism—is only indirectly granted the possibility to ascend, the Mandaean tradition regards the female spirit as positively eligible, despite this spirit's wobbly nature. Ruha, Eden, and Yaltabaoth are all hypostases expressing Gnostic speculations regarding the final fate of the human, middle/lower component. Neither Yaltabaoth nor Eden achieves salvation, but their respective soul elements do (with the exception of the apostate souls in *Ap. John*; see p. 56, above). In contraposition, Ruha will find final liberation at the end of time when there are no Mandaeans left on the earth and therefore no need for the earth. Thus, Mandaeism exhibits a "logical" consistency of thought between mythology and anthropology.

Every human spirit, *ruha*, foreshadows Ruha's final liberation as the spirit is raised into the Lightworld with the soul. As noted, this is accomplished through a cluster of three death-masses, *masqata*: the Mother-*masiqta* for sixty *fatiria*, the Father-*masiqta* for six *fatiria*, and finally, the annual *masiqta* of the Parents, the *Tabahata*, at the Panja festival. This three-stage sequence of *masqata* demonstrates the gradual erasure of the spirit's innate nature and powers in the process of acquiring "soul"-nature. Careful not to halt the soul on the spirit's level, the priests who perform the *masiqta* leave off certain oil-signings of the *fatiria* in the two first *masqata*. Finally, the open-ended acts in these two ceremonies are "closed" in the annual *Tabahata-masiqta*, which is, most fittingly, celebrated at the time of the year when hostile forces cannot block access to the Lightworld.

The three-part configuration of *masqata* may recall the required transformation of female to male to living spirit in *Gos. Thom.*, and the female-male-angel development in *Exc. Thdot.* Gender imagery in the Mandaean model of individual salvation does not, however, apply to the ascending soul and spirit, but to the Mother, earth, and to the Father, the Lightworld. These two paired (though opposed) realms first separately and then jointly, in the *Tabahata-masiqta*, assure the rising elements a full life in the above. The priests, moreover, act as this Mother and Father in the ritual, and so constitute the "parents" for the new *'ustuna*.

CONCLUSION

In the examples of ritual action treated in my chapters, the Mandaean *masiqta* presents the most scrupulously, almost excruciatingly detailed ceremonial steps. In contrast, one can barely guess what the actual proceedings may have been in, for instance, the bridal chamber ritual that *Gos. Phil.* alludes to. It is advisable, I think, to generally keep one's sight sharpened toward possible rituals in Gnostic traditions. Too often, students are unaccustomed to looking for them, or even to glimpsing them where they clearly do occur. It seems most likely that in Gnostic traditions, the human requirement for salvation not only includes lofty, metaphysical "saving knowledge," but implies ceremonials aimed at actively creating the desired goal, here on earth as well as in the beyond. Such a practical-ritual element in these religions can be referred to not just as "knowledge," but as "know-how."[9]

As a final summation, the three categories that I initially presented in this chapter should be taken as heuristic devices toward an interpretation of the selected Gnostic females. These devices seem to me particularly suited to highlighting Gnostic exegeses of the female in the Genesis creation accounts;

the placement and evaluation of the female entities as presented under the three rubrics show how seriously Gnostics take the problem of the two genders that constitute *one* humanity and, mysteriously, once indeed were *one* single being, according to the majority of the Gnostic examples. All the females treated here are in some sense interstitial: they do not keep to one place and refuse to conform to a specific set of expectations of character and behavior. Being divisive natures, they nevertheless connect and reconcile. In the latter capacity, they may be required to relinquish their femaleness altogether, or may, conversely, be allowed to remain female, albeit often on an otherworldly level. Lastly, the human role in the monumental task of bringing about the females' final destiny ought not to be underestimated. For Gnosticism as for other religions, the requirement enjoined upon human beings is to work toward achieving the desired result—"down here" as well as "up there"—by means of symbolic activity, not merely through philosophical speculation.

ABBREVIATIONS

AH   Irenaeus, *Adversus Haereses*

Ap. John   *The Apocryphon of John* (trans. F. Wisse, in J. M. Robinson, *The Nag Hammadi Library* [New York: Harper and Row, 1977], pp. 99–116)

ARR   *Alma Rišaia Rba* (in E. S. Drower, *A Pair of Naṣoraean Commentaries* [Leiden: Brill, 1963], pp. 1–53)

ATŠ   *The Thousand and Twelve Questions (Alf Trisar Šuialia)* (ed. and trans. E. S. Drower [Berlin: Akademie, 1959])

Bar.   The Book *Baruch* (in W. Foerster, ed., *Gnosis. A Selection of Gnostic Texts*, vol. 1 [Oxford: Clarendon, 1972], pp. 52–58)

BG   Berlin Gnostic Codex

C   Nag Hammadi Codex

CP   *The Canonical Prayerbook of the Mandaeans* (ed. E. S. Drower [Leiden: Brill, 1959])

Diw. Ab.   *Diwan Abatur or Progress through the Purgatories* (ed. E. S. Drower [Città del Vaticano: Studi e Testi 151, 1950])

Exc. Thdot. *Excerpta ex Theodoto of Clement of Alexandria* (ed. R. P. Casey, vol. 1 of *Studies and Documents*, ed. K. Lake and S. Lake [London: Christopher's, 1934])

G   S. Giversen, *Apocryphon Johannis* (Copenhagen: Munksgaard, 1963)

GL, GR   *Ginzā. Der Schatz oder das grosse Buch der Mandäer* (ed. M. Lidzbarski [Göttingen: Vandenhoeck and Ruprecht, 1925]) (*GL* is *Left Ginza*; *GR* is *Right Ginza*)

Gos. Phil. *The Gospel of Philip* (trans. W. W. Isenberg, in J. M. Robinson, *The Nag Hammadi Library* [New York: Harper and Row, 1977], pp. 131–51)

Gos. Thom. *The Gospel of Thomas* (trans. T. O. Lambdin, in J. M. Robinson, *The Nag Hammadi Library* [New York: Harper and Row, 1977], pp. 118–30)

H   R. Haardt, "The Apocryphon of John," in *Gnosis. Character and Testimony* (Leiden: Brill, 1971), pp. 182–206

J   Y. Janssens, "L'Apocryphon de Jean," *Le Muséon* 84.1,2 (1971): 43–64

JB   *Das Johannesbuch der Mandäer* (ed. M. Lidzbarski [Giessen: Töpelmann, 1915])

KL   M. Krause and P. Labib, *Die drei Versionen des Apocryphon Johannes im Koptischen Museum zu Alt-Kairo* (Wiesbaden: Harrassowitz, 1962)

T   W. Till, *Die gnostischen Schriften des koptischen Papyrus Berolinensis 8502* (Berlin: Akademie, 1955)

WW   E. S. Drower, *Water into Wine* (London: Murray, 1956)

ZRGG   *Zeitschrift für Religion in Geschichte und Gegenwart*

NOTES

PREFACE

1. Klaus Horn states that "[d]er Geist hat kein Geschlecht, deswegen hat auch der geistige Mensch kein Geschlecht" ("the spirit has no gender, therefore the spiritual human being has no gender, either") ("Geschlechtsfeindlichkeit in der Gnosis. Versuch einer Zusammenfassung ihrer Motive," in *Μελήματα. Festschrift für Werner Leibbrand zum siebzigsten Geburtstag*, ed. J. Schuhmacher [Mannheim: Boehringer, 1967], p. 46A).

CHAPTER I

1. *The Ante-Nicene Fathers*, vol. 5, ed. A. Roberts and J. Donaldson (Grand Rapids: Eerdmans, 1951), chap. 22, p. 73.
2. Justin's followers apparently had other books as well: see "The Book *Baruch*," in W. Foerster, ed., *Gnosis. A Selection of Gnostic Texts*, vol. 1, *Patristic Evidence* (Oxford: Clarendon, 1972), p. 58, 27.5 (hereafter cited as *Bar.* [Foerster]).
3. The account runs, roughly, from 26.1 to 27.4 in Hippolytos, *Refutatio* 5.
4. The reference is to the Heracles and Echidna myth in Herodotus 4,8–10.
5. Note that Eden and Paradise are separate entities.
6. Eden's name is, in the Greek text, Ἐδέμ, which recalls *'adamah*, "earth."
7. The reference is to Ps. 118(117).
8. This refers to 2 Cor. 2:9.
9. Here, the reference is to Ps. 110(109).
10. Observed by E. Haenchen, "Das Buch Baruch. Ein Beitrag zum Problem der Christlichen Gnosis," *Zeitschrift für Theologie und Kirche* 50 (1953): 147.
11. As Haenchen notes in his introduction to *Bar.* (*Bar.* [Foerster], p. 48).
12. Compare Elohim's desire for Eden in *Bar.* 26.2.
13. In his introduction (*Bar.* [Foerster], p. 51) Haenchen refers to Rev.
14. According to the narrative, however, the installation of the angels has not yet happened; *Bar.* is still in the process of telling how they came to their positions.
15. The Greek text does not have "of the father" in the last line.
16. This would answer the question as to whether Elohim is capable of suffering (above, p. 8).
17. See p. 9, above.
18. See p. 7, above.

19. Above, in *Bar.* 26.31, Jesus called Baruch "Lord."
20. Hippolytos (note 1, above), chap. 18, p. 69.
21. Ibid., chap. 19, p. 69.
22. Compare *Bar.* 26.16; see note 8, above.
23. Haenchen, *Bar.* (Foerster), pp. 48, 52.
24. Ibid., p. 50.
25. Haenchen, "Das Buch Baruch," pp. 145, 143.
26. Haenchen, *Bar.* (Foerster), p. 50.
27. R. M. Grant, "Gnosis Revisited," *Church History* 23 (1954): 44.
28. R. M. Grant, "Les Êtres intermédiaires dans le judaisme tardif," *Le Origini dello Gnosticismo, Colloquio di Messina 13–18 Aprile 1966*, ed. U. Bianchi (Leiden: Brill, 1967), p. 151.
29. M. Olender, "Le Système Gnostique de Justin," *Tel Quel* 82 (1979): 71–72, 86. Olender's article can hardly be distinguished from his work published a year earlier as "Éléments pour une analyse de Priape chez Justin le Gnostique," *Hommages à Maarten Vermaseren*, vol. 2, ed. M. B. de Boer and T. A. Edredge (Leiden: Brill, 1978), pp. 874–97. The author's statement that the *Tel Quel* article is "lightly modified" (p. 71) is not supported by the facts, for the two articles differ only in the short "Préliminaires" section. Otherwise, they are identical. Also, the *Tel Quel* publication is dedicated to Claude Royet-Journoud, while the other one appears in the volume honoring Vermaseren.
30. Olender, "Système," pp. 72 n. 2, 81; and see note 23, above.
31. Ibid., p. 86. One may also recall Irenaeus's Bythus-figure who impregnates Sige, in Irenaeus, *Adversus Haereses* 1.1.1 (*The Ante-Nicene Fathers*, vol. 1 [1951], p. 316; hereafter cited as *AH*).
32. Olender, "Système," p. 86. Here, he refers to M. Tardieu, *Trois mythes gnostiques. Adam, Éros et les animaux d'Égypte dans un écrit de Nag Hammadi (II,5)* (Paris: Études augustiniennes, 1974), p. 166.
33. Olender, "Système," pp. 77–79.
34. M. Simonetti, "Note sul Libro di Baruch dello gnostico Giustino," *Vetero Christianorum* 6 (1969): 74 n. 12.
35. H. Jonas, *Gnosis und spätantiker Geist*[3] 1.1 (Göttingen: Vandenhoeck and Ruprecht, 1964), pp. 340, 337 n. 2. One may note that this pattern clearly comes out in Mandaean mythology where the demiurges Yušamin, Abatur, and Ptahil all incur guilt and sin for their roles in creation. Their final rehabilitation into the Lightworld, however, does not happen until the end of the world. Up to that moment they are forced to carry out their duties as toll-house watchers in the purgatories, the *maṭarata*. (See my two studies, "The Mandaean Šitil as an Example of 'the Image Above and Below,'" *Numen* 26.2 [1979]: 185–91, esp. p. 188, and "A Rehabilitation of Spirit Ruha in Mandaean Religion," *History of Religions* 22.1 [1982]: 60–84, esp. pp. 74, 82, with n. 129.)
36. Jonas, *Gnosis*, p. 341.
37. Haenchen, "Das Buch Baruch," p. 147.

38. K. Kvideland, "Elohims Himmelfahrt," *Temenos* 10 (1974): 70, 71, 73, 77, 78.
39. Haenchen, "Das Buch Baruch," p. 148.
40. Ibid., p. 157.
41. See note 26, above.
42. Grant, "Gnosis Revisited," p. 39.
43. Ibid., p. 44.
44. Simonetti, "Note sul Libro di Baruch," p. 84.
45. Ibid., pp. 75, 78, 83, 89.
46. Ibid., pp. 77, 84, and n. 33.
47. R. van den Broek, "The Shape of Edem According to Justin the Gnostic," *Vigiliae Christianae* 27 (1973): 43.
48. Simonetti, "Note sul Libro di Baruch," p. 86.
49. Grant, "Gnosis Revisited," pp. 39, 43. To my knowledge, Grant is the first scholar to have identified the Elohim-Eden story as dependent on the treatise by Pherecydes of Syros (see ibid., p. 41).
50. Haenchen, "Das Buch Baruch," p. 147.
51. Haenchen, *Bar.* (Foerster), p. 52.
52. Simonetti, "Note sul Libro di Baruch," pp. 83 n. 32, 84, 85.
53. G. C. Stead, "The Valentinian Myth of Sophia," *Journal of Theological Studies* 20.1 (1969): 96.
54. Ibid.
55. Simonetti, "Note sul Libro di Baruch," pp. 80, 82. G. Quispel, too, notes that "Edem is not intrinsically evil. It is only when her husband leaves her that she makes herself up in order to make him return to her" ("Jewish Gnosis and Mandaean Gnosticism," in *Les Textes de Nag Hammadi*, ed. J.-É. Ménard [Leiden: Brill, 1975], p. 98.)
56. Haenchen, "Das Buch Baruch," p. 158.
57. Ibid., p. 157, referring to *Bar.* 26.18.
58. Grant, "Gnosis Revisited," p. 43.
59. See Olender's article on Priapus in *Dictionnaire des mythologies et des religions des sociétés traditionelles et du monde antique*, ed. Y. Bonnefoy (Paris: Flammarion, 1981), 311A–314A.
60. Olender, "Système," p. 83. Compare van den Broek's identification of Eden ("Shape of Edem," pp. 37–38).
61. See note 21, above.

CHAPTER 2

1. See entry "ruh, ruha" in E. S. Drower and R. Macuch, *A Mandaic Dictionary* (Oxford: Clarendon, 1963), pp. 428B–429A.
2. One of the first such interpretations is Th. Nöldeke, *Mandäische Grammatik* (Halle: Buchhandlung des Waisenhauses, 1875), p. xx; one of the more recent is E.

Yamauchi, "Some Alleged Evidences for Pre-Christian Gnosticism," in *New Dimensions in New Testament Study*, ed. R. N. Longenecker and M. C. Tenney (Grand Rapids: Zondervan, 1974), p. 64.

3. E. S. Drower, *The Canonical Prayerbook of the Mandaeans* (Leiden: Brill, 1959), p. 74 (hereafter cited as *CP*). Drower's translation of *alaha* as "Allah" is incorrect (see *Mandaic Dictionary*, p. 18B), for the word means, simply, "god."

4. H. Jonas, *Gnosis und spätantiker Geist*[3], 1.1 (Göttingen: Vandenhoeck and Ruprecht, 1964), p. 277 n. 4.

5. V. Schou-Pedersen, *Bidrag til en Analyse af de mandaeiske Skrifter* (Aarhus: Universitetsforlaget, 1940), p. 85.

6. See E. S. Drower, *The Mandaeans of Iraq and Iran* (1937; reprint, Leiden: Brill, 1962), pp. 184–86, 197. For a rare ambiguity on this point, see M. Lidzbarski, *Ginzā. Der Schatz oder das grosse Buch der Mandäer* (Göttingen: Vandenhoeck and Ruprecht, 1925) (the work is separated into *Right* and *Left Ginza* [hereafter cited as *GR* and *GL*, respectively]), *GL* 1.2, p. 430.22–29.

7. E. S. Drower, *The Haran Gawaita and the Baptism of Hibil Ziwa* (Citta del Vaticano: Studi e Testi 176, 1953), pp. 34–35. ('*Uthras* [the correct plural is '*utria*] are Light-beings, and sometimes messengers or defective Light-beings.)

8. Ibid., p. 34; and E. S. Drower, *The Thousand and Twelve Questions (Alf Trisar Šuialia)* (Berlin: Akademie, Veröff. d. Inst. f. Orientforschung 32, 1959), p. 183 (265) (hereafter cited as *ATŠ*).

9. *GR* 5.1, p. 170.35–37; cf. *GR* 3, p. 82.5–12, where Ruha informs 'Ur that the Lightworld is stronger than he is.

10. This seems to imply that the "Evil Spirit" came from the Lightworld.

11. *Contra* Rudolph (see K. Rudolph, *Theogonie, Kosmogonie und Anthropogonie in den mandäischen Schriften* [Göttingen: Vandenhoeck and Ruprecht, 1965], pp. 283 and 346; but see his modification on this point in W. Foerster, ed., *Gnosis. A Selection of Gnostic Texts*, vol. 2, *Coptic and Mandaic Sources* [Oxford: Clarendon, 1974], p. 139 [Rudolph's introduction to the Mandaean material]).

12. Cited in E. S. Drower, *The Secret Adam* (Oxford: Clarendon, 1960), pp. 47–48. (See my "The Making of a Mandaean Priest: The Tarmida Initiation," *Numen* 32.2 [1985]: 194–217. I am now working on the scroll *Diwan malkuta 'laita*.)

13. Drower, *Secret Adam*, p. 48.

14. See also *CP*, p. 123 n. 1; Drower's view, here, of the lament as irony, is not supported by Drower and Macuch, *Mandaic Dictionary*, p. 341B, as regards this interpretation of '*dilma* ("[O] would").

15. M. Lidzbarski, *Das Johannesbuch der Mandäer* (Giessen: Töpelmann, 1915), pp. 166–67 (hereafter cited as *JB*).

16. See my article, "Two Female Gnostic Revealers," *History of Religions* 19.3 (1980): 259–69, for a treatment of Ruha as revealer.

17. E. S. Drower, *Diwan Abatur or Progress through the Purgatories* (Città del Vaticano: Studi e Testi 151, 1950), p. 38 (hereafter cited as *Diw. Ab.*).

18. See *GR* 5.1, p. 159.11–16.

19. *ATŠ*, pp. 264–65 (307) ("Body" = *ʿuṣṭuna* refers to the celestial body, "body" = *pagra* to the material, human body).
20. K. Rudolph (*Die Mandäer*, vol. 2, *Der Kult* [Göttingen: Vandenhoeck and Ruprecht, 1961], p. 157 n. 5) expresses astonishment that the "sign of the left" is a prerequisite for the "sign of the right."
21. This also recalls Ruha's "escape" in *GR* 5.1, p. 173.16–17.
22. Here, in n. 1, Drower confuses the identity of Hibil's companion; cf. also E. S. Drower, *Šarh d-Qabin d-Šišlam Rba* (Rome: Pontificio Instituto Biblico, Biblica et Orientalia 12, 1950), p. 107.
23. "*CP* 75" refers to the number of the prayer, not to the page number.
24. See references in my unpublished Ph.D. dissertation, "Spirit Ruha in Mandaean Religion" (University of Chicago, 1978), pp. 101–12.
25. Drower, *Šarh d-Qabin*, p. 106.
26. Rudolph, *Theogonie*, p. 238 n. 2.
27. Drower and Macuch, *Mandaic Dictionary*, p. 280A: " 'the sublimated of truth'—a world of ideas in which the prototypes of all earthly things and beings exist." I would include the middle beings, too, not just the earthly ones, as having such prototypes.
28. For the ambiguity of Ptahil, see Jonas, *Gnosis*, p. 269 n. 2; of Abatur, *JB*, pp. 232–34; *CP*, pp. 22, 54, 56, 89, 106; *ATŠ*, pp. 174 (245), 233 (116), 285 (414); and *Diw. Ab.*, p. 7; of Yušamin, *JB* pp. 240–41; *GR* 14, p. 292, and 15, p. 311; and Drower, *Haran Gawaita*, p. 52. See also my article, "The Mandaean Šitil as an Example of 'the Image Above and Below,'" *Numen*, 26.2 (1979): 185–91.
29. Jonas, *Gnosis*, p. 341.
30. Ibid., p. 337 n. 2. (See chapter 1, p. 14, above.)
31. Drower, *Secret Adam*, p. 47.
32. E. S. Drower, *Water into Wine* (London: Murray, 1956) pp. 243–44 (hereafter cited as *WW*; in the following, I will rely on Drower's account of the *masiqta* in *WW*). For greater detail on the *masiqta*, see my article, "The Mandaean Ṭabahata Masiqta," *Numen* 28.2 (1981): 138–63.
33. See p. 21, above.
34. Drower's field-work accounts are the main sources for our knowledge of these secrets. Although she was not allowed to watch any of the secret rituals, her informants' explanations, together with the esoteric texts on the subject of the *masiqta*, make for a reasonably dependable picture of the ritual; in fact, the informants' accounts and the secret texts agree to a remarkable degree.
35. These prayers contain the letter "N" wherever the name of the deceased is to be inserted (this insertion is called a "*zhara*").
36. For the necessity of Mandaean laypeople as "witnesses," see *ATŠ*, pp. 257–58 (206).
37. E. S. Drower, *A Pair of Naṣoraean Commentaries* (Leiden: Brill, 1963), pp. 12–13 (the first commentary is *Alma Rišaia Rba*, hereafter cited as *ARR*). Note Drower's queasiness with the fact of sacrifice in Mandaeism (*Secret Adam*, p. 32).

38. See *WW*, illustration p. 250, and p. 246.
39. See *ATŠ*, p. 240 (143).
40. *GL* 3.38, pp. 566.20–567.20. Note that there is no strict consistency with respect to the gender of the spirit and soul. Even if both are grammatically feminine, this does not prevent the brother and sister imagery; moreover, the relationship between the two is never sexual.
41. See Drower, *Mandaeans*, p. 31, and *ATŠ*, p. 242 (148).
42. See *GL* 3.15, p. 532.30f., and *GL* 3.44, p. 571.25f., for the soul's fears at ascending.
43. See also *GL* 3.52, p. 582.34–583.4, and 3.56, p. 587.20–23. Recall Ruha in Abatur's house (above, p. 26)!
44. *WW*, p. 251.
45. Ibid. (see Drower and Macuch, *Mandaic Dictionary*, p. 411A).
46. Ibid.
47. E. S. Drower, *The Coronation of the Great Šišlam. Being a Description of the Rite of the Coronation of a Mandaean Priest According to the Ancient Canon* (Leiden: Brill, 1962), p. 28.
48. Except for the sixtieth *faṭira* during the recitation of *CP* 52; see my "Mandaean Ṭabahata Masiqta," pp. 145 and 155–56.
49. *WW*, p. 252.
50. Ibid., p. 253; see also Drower, *Secret Adam*, pp. 79–80.
51. *WW*, p. 253.
52. Again, see my "Mandaean Ṭabahata Masiqta," pp. 155–56.
53. See also *ARR*, p. 50.
54. Recall the required "sign of the left" before "the sign of the right"; see notes 19 and 20, above.
55. See my "Mandaean Ṭabahata Masiqta," pp. 149–50; Drower, *Secret Adam*, p. 75; and Rudolph, *Der Kult*, p. 266 n. 1.
56. See Drower, *Mandaeans*, pp. 210–11, 214, and *WW*, p. 242.
57. See, e.g., W. Oliver, "The Mandaean Tarmid. The Growth of a Priesthood" (Ph.D. dissertation, Hebrew Union College, Cincinnati, 1967), pp. 91–93; and Rudolph, *Der Kult*, p. 134 n. 5 and p. 267 n. 8.
58. See above, p. 33.
59. See above, ibid.
60. Rudolph is surprised that the priests do not eat the faṭiria (*Der Kult*, p. 135).
61. For the reciprocity of prayers—another indication of the two-way system of communication—see *GR* 3, p. 119.9–19, and *GR* 16.4, p. 389.29–32.
62. *Contra* M. V. Cerutti, who in her article "Ptahil e Ruha: per una fenomenologia del dualismo mandeo," *Numen* 24.3 (1977): 186–206, assigns Ruha to condemnation, *ruha* to redemption (p. 198).
63. See my article, "Two Female Gnostic Revealers" (above, note 16), pp. 266–69; and see notes 18 and 19, above.

64. Drower, *Mandaeans*, p. 271.
65. See note 4, above.

CHAPTER 3

1. *Ap. John* exists in two longer and two shorter versions. The shorter are, respectively, BG (= Berlin Gnostic Codex) 8502.2, and C (= Nag Hammadi Codex) III.1; the longer, C II.1 and C IV.1. My basic text will be F. Wisse's translation of C II.1 in J. M. Robinson, *The Nag Hammadi Library* (New York: Harper and Row, 1977) pp. 99–116. Other editions/translations of the C II.1 text include S. Giversen, *Apocryphon Johannis* (Copenhagen: Munksgaard, 1963) (hereafter, G), and M. Krause and P. Labib, *Die drei Versionen des Apocryphon Johannis im Koptischen Museum zu Alt-Kairo*, Abhandlungen des Deutschen Archäologischen Instituts Kairos, Koptische Reihe Bd. 1 (Wiesbaden: Harrassowitz, 1962) (hereafter, KL). I have also made use of the following editions/translations of the BG text: A. Kragerud, "Versjonen av Apocryphon Johannis i Papyrus Berolinensis 8502," *Norsk Teologisk Tidsskrift* 63.1 (1962): 1–22; W. Till, *Die gnostischen Schriften des koptischen Papyrus Berolinensis 8502*, Texte und Untersuchungen zur Geschichte der alt-Christlichen Literatur (Berlin: Akademie, 1955) (hereafter, T); and R. Haardt, "The Apocryphon of John," in *Gnosis. Character and Testimony* (Leiden: Brill, 1971), pp. 182–206 (hereafter, H).
2. *Contra* A. Kragerud, "Apocryphon Johannis. En formanalyse," *Norsk Teologisk Tidsskrift* 66.1 (1965): 21.
3. All *Ap. John* references are to Wisse, unless otherwise indicated. Square brackets mark lacunae.
4. Parentheses mark additions by editor/translator.
5. Krause and Labib have "Er erkennt," ("he understands," or "he knows") (ⲉϥⲉⲓⲙⲉ), for "[he] gazes upon" (KL, pp. 119–20, 4.22). For the corresponding BG-passage, see T, pp. 94–95, 27.1.
6. See KL, p. 120, 4.31 (*Νοῦς* shows up later).
7. Giversen translates *μήτρα* as "Mother" (G, p. 55, 53.5).
8. This term is no longer translated "Grossvater" ("grandfather"), as in KL, p. 121, 5.6–7. S. Arai has "väterliche Mutter" ("fatherly mother") ("Zur Christologie des Apocryphon Johannes," *New Testament Studies* 15.3 [1969]: 307, and n. 1).
9. See Y. Janssens, "L'Apocryphon de Jean," *Le Muséon* 84.1 and 2 (1971): 46, 59 (hereafter, J).
10. In BG, the section corresponding to "This is the first thought" reads, "Sie ist die erste *ἔννοια*, sein Abbild (*εἰκών*), sie wurde zu einem ersten Menschen . . . der Äon (*αἰών*), der nicht altert, der mann-weibliche, der aus seiner *πρόνοια* hervorging" ("She is the first *ἔννοια*, his image (*εἰκών*), she became a first human being . . . the aeon (*αἰών*) that does not change, the male-female that emerged

from its πρόνοια) (T, pp. 95–97, 27.18–28.40). H.-M. Schenke reacts negatively to the androgyny in BG 28.3 ("Nag-Hamadi Studien III," *Zeitschrift für Religion in Geschichte und Gegenwart [ZRGG]* 14 [1962]: 359). Along with H, p. 186 n. 2; T, p. 140; and Kragerud, "Versjonen," p. 19 n. 22, Janssens believes that the text here—and in what immediately follows—implies a creation of a second Ennoia (J, p. 44). She admits, however, that such a distinction remains fluid (J, p. 47); see also the second part of her article (*Le Muséon* 84.3 and 4 [1971]: 412), about "Forethought" (Pro-noia) and "Afterthought" (Epi-noia).

11. J, p. 46; H, p. 186; but T has "Erste Erkenntnis" ("first cognition") (ⲚⲞⲨⲚⲞⲨⳛⲞⲣ︤ⲡ︥ Ⲛ̄ⲤⲞⲞⲨⲚ), pp. 96–97, 28.6. Note that all three scholars speak of the BG version.

12. Note a slightly different list in BG: T, pp. 97–99, 28.5–29.15.

13. In their recension of *The Nag Hammadi Library* R. Kraft and J. Timbie have criticized Wisse's inconsistencies in his translations and transliterations of the terms *pronoia* and *prognosis* here ("The Nag Hammadi Library: In English," *Religious Studies Review* 8.1 [1982]: 46.2).

14. T, p. 99, 29.15.

15. See for instance, KL, p. 121, 5.11 and 5.20, who give first a male, and then a female, pronoun. Wisse does not render this inconsistency.

16. See note 6, above.

17. G, pp. 60–61, 56.32.

18. Here I follow G, p. 61.34–35, and not Wisse's construction "Pigeraadama (s)" (p. 103, 8.30–35).

19. That Adam's invocation of the Father, the Mother, and the Son "contradicts" Christ's self-predication, as Arai has it ("Zur Christologie," p. 316), seems a misguided judgment.

20. G, p. 192 (see also p. 198).

21. L. Schottroff, *Der Glaubende und die feindliche Welt*, Wissenschaftliche Monographien zum Alten und Neuen Testament, no. 37 (Vluyn: Neukirchen, 1970), p. 47; compare G, p. 197.

22. See T, p. 42 n. 1; R. Haardt, "Schöpfer und Schöpfung in der Gnosis. Bemerkungen zu ausgewählten Aspekten gnostischer Theodiceeproblematik," in *Altes Testament–Frühjudentum–Gnosis*, ed. K.-W. Tröger (Gütersloh: Mohn, 1980) p. 46; S. Giversen, "The Apocryphon of John and Genesis," *Studia Theologica* 17.1 (1963): 67; and G, p. 192.

23. See J. Sieber, "The Barbelo Aeon as Sophia in *Zostrianos* and Related Tractates," in *The Rediscovery of Gnosticism*, vol. 2, *Sethian Gnosticism*, ed. B. Layton (Leiden: Brill, 1981), p. 794.

24. G, p. 63, 57.26–28; see also Kragerud, "Versjonen," p. 20 n. 39.

25. G, p. 193.

26. J, p. 62.

27. Giversen translates this as "her male element" (G, p. 63, 57.32). For the problem of Sophia's *syzygos* in general, see Schenke, "Nag-Hamadi Studien III," pp. 356–

60. The BG version implies that Sophia has looked for her mate, but not found him (see T, pp. 114–15, 37.6–7), and *therefore* she creates independently.

28. See Schottroff, *Der Glaubende*, pp. 43–44 n. 4. Janssens sees πνεῦμα παρθενικόν as Sophia's consort (J, p. 62).

29. It is *not*, as N. A. Dahl says ("The Arrogant Archon and the Lewd Sophia: Jewish Traditions in Gnostic Revolt," in *The Rediscovery of Gnosticism 2: Sethian Gnosticism*, ed. B. Layton [Leiden: Brill, 1981], p. 710 n. 51), "invisible power."

30. T, p. 115, 37.11.

31. Dahl, "Arrogant Archon," p. 709 (see also p. 708 n. 47, and compare Schottroff, *Der Glaubende*, p. 46).

32. J, p. 62 (see also p. 63, Janssens's reference to Hippolytos, *Phil.* 6.30.6f.). About C II.1, see G, p. 199.

33. Dahl, "Arrogant Archon," p. 708.

34. G. C. Stead, "The Valentinian Myth of Sophia," *Journal of Theological Studies* 20.1 (1969): 78.

35. Note the phallic image which, in some sense, indicates Sophia's lack.

36. Schottroff emphasizes the distance between Yaltabaoth and his mother (*Der Glaubende*, p. 49).

37. As noted by Haardt, "Schöpfer und Schöpfung," p. 47; see also Schottroff, *Der Glaubende*, p. 47.

38. G. MacRae, "The Jewish Background of the Gnostic Sophia Myth," *Novum Testamentum* 12.2 (1970): 89.

39. H, p. 190, 36.

40. Schottroff, *Der Glaubende*, p. 43 n. 4.

41. Krause and Labib have a very different translation: "er war erstaunt in sein Unverstand" ("he was astonished in his ignorance") (KL, p. 138, 10.26).

42. See Schenke, "Nag-Hamadi Studien III," p. 360.

43. See G, p. 231. Compare the Mandaean demiurge Ptahil, who loses his light when he becomes involved with the lower powers (*GR* 3, p. 98.28–32).

44. See, for instance, Giversen, "Apocryphon of John," pp. 75–76, regarding the positive view of Moses.

45. Schottroff disagrees (*Der Glaubende*, p. 51 n. 7).

46. Giversen has a slightly different view (G, p. 233).

47. *Where* is unclear; see W. Foerster, "Das Apocryphon des Johannes," *Gott und die Götter, Festgabe für Erich Fascher zum 60. Geburtstag* (Berlin: Evangelischer Verlagsanstalt, 1958), p. 137, and n. 15.

48. Giversen (G, p. 233) connects the oblivion (ⲁⲩⲃϣⲉ) with Sophia creating Yaltabaoth "in ignorance." Krause and Labib translate it as "Erkenntnisunfähigkeit" ("incapability of understanding") (KL, p. 146, 13.24).

49. See Giversen's translation: G, p. 67, 59.10.

50. Ibid., p. 71, 61.23–26.

51. See Giversen's comments, ibid., p. 235.

52. H.-M. Schenke ("Nag-Hamadi Studien I," *ZRGG* 14 [1962]: 60) says of Sophia's

shame about her lacking consort: "Diese Scham der Sophia ist der Beginn der Rettung für sie selbst und die verlorene Lichtkraft" ("This shame of Sophia is the beginning of salvation for herself and for the lost Light-power").

53. Note that in Krause and Labib's translation the Pleroma and the Spirit are not seen as subject and object (KL, pp. 147–48, 14.1–5).

54. For the problem of capitalized or uncapitalized "Spirit," see R. McL. Wilson, "The Spirit in Gnostic Literature," in *Christ and Spirit in the New Testament: In Honour of C. F. D. Moule*, ed. B. Lindars and S. S. Smalley (Cambridge: Cambridge University Press, 1973), p. 346.

55. Compare G, p. 73, 62.8, and L, p. 148, 14.6; see also Schottroff, *Der Glaubende*, pp. 57–59.

56. G, p. 73, 62.7–9.

57. Ibid., p. 236. See also Schottroff, *Der Glaubende*, p. 51; and W.-D. Hauschild, *Gottes Geist und der Mensch* (Munich: Kaiser, 1973), pp. 231, 234.

58. G, p. 73, 62.11, and explanation p. 236; also KL (p. 148, 14.11) translate against Wisse's "above."

59. H, pp. 193–94, 47; compare T, p. 135, 47.6–7.

60. J, pp. 408–9; see also G, pp. 237–38.

61. J, p. 409.

62. G, p. 237.

63. J, p. 409.

64. G, p. 239.

65. H.-M. Schenke, *Der Gott "Mensch" in der Gnosis* (Göttingen: Vandenhoeck and Ruprecht, 1962), p. 41. B. Pearson draws attention to the pun involved in the similarity between φώς: "man" and φῶς: "light" (*Philo and the Gnostics on Man and Salvation*, The Center for Hermeneutical Studies, Colloquy 29, 17 April 1977, ed. W. Wuellner [Berkeley: Graduate Theological Union, 1977], p. 11 n. 60).

66. Giversen, "Apocryphon of John," p. 69. Schenke says that the story of heavenly Adam foreshadows what is to come ("Nag-Hamadi Studien I," p. 69).

67. T, p. 139, 49.2; see also Kragerud, "Versjonen," p. 9, who affords a question mark. B. Pearson ("Gnostic Biblical Exegesis," in *Armenian and Biblical Studies*, ed. M. Stone [Jerusalem: St. James Press, 1976], p. 72) has, "They created it (fem. sg., i.e. the soul). . . ."

68. For the problem of Wisdom in general in *Ap. John*, see R. McL. Wilson, "The Trials of a Translator: Some Translation Problems in the Nag Hammadi Texts," in *Les Textes de Nag Hammadi*, ed. J.-É. Ménard (Leiden: Brill, 1975), pp. 36–37, where the author draws special attention to this passage and to *Ap. John* 15.22.

69. About the parallel passage in BG, Janssens observes that this is the first time the expression "Epinoia of Light" is used (J, p. 412). Schenke notes how Sophia and the Father—as usual—work together in harmony ("Nag-Hamadi Studien III," p. 357).

70. See Giversen, "Apocryphon of John," p. 70.

71. Note Janssens' comments (J, p. 412).

72. See p. 46, above; G, p. 257.

73. Ibid.

74. Giversen uses "fulfilment" (G, p. 85, 68.21); see also G, pp. 258–59.

75. Wilson, "The Spirit," p. 350 n. 14. Note that "teaching him about the descent of his seed" evokes Adam's coming down from his Pleroma-life into the lower world.

76. T, p. 147, 53.14.

77. For Sophia, see Schottroff, *Der Glaubende*, p. 48.

78. See, for instance, K. Rudolph, "Ein Grundtyp gnostischer Urmensch-Adam— Spekulation," *ZRGG* 9 (1957): 20.

79. Foerster, "Das Apocryphon des Johannes," p. 138.

80. Hauschild, *Gottes Geist*, pp. 231, 232.

81. Ibid., pp. 231, 233.

82. Consult A. Böhlig, "Zum Antimimon Pneuma in den koptisch-gnostischen Texten," in *Mysterion und Wahrheit. Gesammelte Beiträge zur spätantiken Religionsgeschichte* (Leiden: Brill, 1968), pp. 163–65.

83. Pearson (*Philo*, p. 15) notes that this is expressly opposed to the statement of "Moses" in Gen. 2:7.

84. See p. 46, above.

85. Giversen notes that because Adam does not eat, he is disobedient to the archons ("Apocryphon of John," p. 71 n. 15).

86. Giversen translates that the archons remained in front of *Adam*, not of the tree (G, p. 89, 70.6).

87. Schenke, *Der Gott "Mensch,"* pp. 79, 83. Giversen (G, p. 259) claims that *Ap. John*'s author seems to have forgotten that Epinoia already entered Adam, but this is beside the point (see note 2, above, for Kragerud's parallel prejudices).

88. See p. 46, above.

89. G. MacRae, "Sleep and Awakening in Gnostic Texts," in *Le Origini dello Gnosticismo*, Colloquio di Messina 15–18 Aprile 1966, ed. U. Bianchi (Leiden: Brill, 1967), p. 498 n. 3.

90. See p. 50, above.

91. Giversen is hardly correct when he says that part of the power is removed from the Invisible Spirit (G, p. 262).

92. Ibid., p. 263; compare this to his earlier judgment in "Apocryphon of John," p. 72.

93. See pp. 46 and 53, above, and G, pp. 71, 61.33 and 91, 71.7. The terms are ϫⲃⲱ and ⲕⲁⲗⲩⲙⲙⲁ; Giversen translates both "veil."

94. G, p. 91, 71.9. BG has οὐσία; see Janssens's comment (J, p. 418).

95. G, p. 91, 71.14–21.

96. *Contra* G, p. 263, for *Ap. John* does not identify Sophia with the mother in the clause "his father and his mother."

97. H, p. 199, 60 (and observe his n. 1!).

98. J, pp. 418–19.

99. See p. 43, above. Giversen says with respect to C II.1, 58.18 and 68.19, that Epinoia is Zoe (G, p. 257).

100. A. Orbe, "'Sophia Soror.' Apuntes para le teología del Espíritu Santo," in *Mélanges d'histoire des religions offerts à Henri-Charles Puech* (Paris: Presses Univ. de France, 1974), p. 355; see also his reference to C III (ibid.).

101. Wilson, "The Spirit," p. 353. See also Schottroff (*Der Glaubende*, pp. 60–62), who tries valiantly but unsuccessfully to keep apart the untainted Epinoia and the faulty Sophia and consequently has trouble with Sophia as savior.

102. G, p. 91, 71.23–25. Note Schottroff's comments on Sophia in BG 60.12f. (*Der Glaubende*, p. 66).

103. See Kraft and Timbie, "Nag Hammadi Library," p. 46B.

104. J, pp. 415–16.

105. For the theme of competition between Epinoia and Christ, see Arai, "Zur Christologie" (above, note 8).

106. H, p. 199, 60–61; and see J, pp. 419–20.

107. This is the first time Eve is mentioned by name. Inexplicably, Giversen omits "out of Eve" in his translation (G, pp. 92–93, 72.15).

108. G, p. 264.

109. Both Wisse (*Ap. John*, p. 112, 24.25–30) and Giversen (G, pp. 92–93, 72.29) have Eve as the bearer of sexual desire, while Krause and Labib see Adam as the culprit (KL, p. 178, 74.29).

110. Again, Wisse's inconsistency in translation becomes evident (*Ap. John*, p. 112, 24.35); compare Giversen (G, pp. 92–93, 72.35).

111. See p. 42, above.

112. Schottroff wavers with respect to the fault in Pleroma. First, she decides against any imperfection in it (*Der Glaubende*, pp. 49, 57), then she says that the Pleroma is "tangiert" ("touched") by the fall (p. 67); she seems to return to her initial position on p. 68. See also her comments on pp. 63–64; on the latter page she speaks of the "andere Mutter" ("other mother"), a dubious construction, which Krause and Labib also assume (KL, p. 179, 25.3).

113. G, p. 267; see also J, pp. 422–24.

114. G. Quispel, "The Demiurge in the Apocryphon of John," in *Nag Hammadi and Gnosis. Papers read at the First International Congress of Coptology (Cairo, December 1976)*, ed. R. McL. Wilson (Leiden: Brill, 1978), p. 22.

115. Compare Giversen's translation (G, p. 99, 75.33–76.4); for the BG version, see J, p. 426.

116. See p. 43, above.

117. H, p. 204, 76; compare T, p. 191, 75.10–13.

118. Arai, "Zur Christologie," p. 308, echoed by Schenke, "Nag-Hamadi Studien III," p. 356.

119. See J, p. 428.

120. Arai, "Zur Christologie," p. 308.

121. Ibid., p. 315.

122. H, p. 204, 76. Foerster finds the "again" incomprehensible ("Das Apocryphon des Johannes," p. 140); but see J, p. 429.

123. H, p. 204.
124. Arai, "Zur Christologie," p. 311.
125. For this section, see the following: MacRae, "Sleep and Awakening," pp. 498–502, and "Jewish Background," p. 92; Arai, "Zur Christologie," p. 312; and J. Turner, "The Gnostic Threefold Path to Enlightenment. The Ascent of Mind and the Descent of Wisdom," *Novum Testamentum* 22.4 (1980): 326, 331. Compare BG (T, p. 191, 75.14–15) for Christ's ascent.
126. H, p. 204, 76; observe his n. 1.
127. J, p. 428, supported by T, p. 193, 76.4–5.
128. See p. 56, above.

CHAPTER 4

1. O. Dibelius, "Studien zur Geschichte der Valentinianer I," *Zeitschrift für die neutestamentliche Wissenschaft* 9 (1908): 230.
2. See F. Sagnard, *Extraits de Théodote (Sources Chrétiennes* 23) (Paris: Les Éditions du Cerf, 1970), p. 5f.
3. See Sagnard, *Extraits*, pp. 7–21, 28–49; R. P. Casey, *The Excerpta ex Theodoto of Clement of Alexandria*, vol. 1 of *Studies and Documents*, ed. K. Lake and S. Lake (London: Christopher's, 1934), pp. 3–33; E. Pagels, "Conflicting Versions of Valentinian Eschatology: Irenaeus' Treatise vs. The *Excerpts from Theodotus*," *Harvard Theological Review* 67 (1974): 35; J. F. McCue, "Conflicting Versions of Valentinianism? Irenaeus and The *Excerpta ex Theodoto*," in *The Rediscovery of Gnosticism*, vol. 1, *The School of Valentinus*, ed. B. Layton (Leiden: Brill, 1980). Compare L. Schottroff's caution as regards *Exc. Thdot.* 43–65 and its relationship to Irenaeus's source for *Against the Heresies* 1.1–8.4 ("Animae naturaliter salvandae," in *Christentum und Gnosis*, ed. W. Eltester [Berlin: Töpelmann, 1969], p. 97).
4. *Contra* F. Sagnard (*La Gnose Valentinienne et le Témoignage de Saint Irénée* [Paris: Vrin, 1947], p. 302, and *Extraits*, pp. 26 and 112.1), who sees the Valentinian church as consisting of "elect" only.
5. In the following, Casey's translation of *Exc. Thdot.* will be referred to, unless otherwise indicated.
6. Sagnard, *Extraits*, pp. 98–99 and n. 3.
7. Pagels, "Conflicting Versions," pp. 41–42.
8. Casey, *Exc. Thdot.*, pp. 57, 115.
9. Sagnard, *Extraits*, p. 99.
10. Ibid., n. 1; see also Sagnard, *La Gnose*, p. 549.
11. For instance, *Exc. Thdot.* 39, pp. 66–67.
12. Pagels, "Conflicting Versions," p. 42.
13. Compare *Exc. Thdot.* 39, pp. 66–67. Rather than relying on subsequent paragraphs of *Exc. Thdot.*, 39 and 40, to explain 21, one might, in this case, see discrepancies between 21 and 39–40 as an example of rivalry between Sophia and

Christ, for 21 voices a competing tradition to that of 39–40.

14. Casey, *Exc. Thdot.*, p. 18.
15. McCue, "Conflicting Versions," p. 409.
16. Sagnard translates this as "male element" (*Extraits*, pp. 98–99).
17. Sagnard translates συνεστάλη, not as "drawn together," but as "concentrés" ("concentrated"), although he suggests Casey's solution (ibid., p. 99 n. 6). Casey's seems the better choice, because the "elect" are not yet "concentrated in" the Logos, but are "drawn to" the Logos in their salvation.
18. Casey, *Exc. Thdot.*, p. 18.
19. See McCue's observation ("Conflicting Versions," p. 411).
20. Casey, *Exc. Thdot.*, p. 18.
21. Sagnard, *La Gnose*, p. 302 (see note 4, above).
22. Pagels, "Conflicting Versions," p. 39.
23. *Exc. Thdot.* is quite uninterested in portraying "pneumatics"; one exception is the section on Seth, paragraph 54 (pp. 76–77).
24. *Contra* Sagnard, *La Gnose*, p. 557.
25. I use the terms "pneumatics" and "psychics" within quotation marks, since such "classes" of people do not strictly exist, according to *Exc. Thdot.*
26. Pagels, "Conflicting Versions," p. 41.
27. McCue seems to muddle the terminology when he speaks of "non-incarnate angels" ("Conflicting Versions," p. 409) in *Exc. Thdot.* 22.1. I assume he means the preexistent angels, not the "pneumatics" on earth. See also his comments on the relationship between angels and "psychics" in the ritual of baptism (ibid., p. 410).
28. Sagnard, *Extraits*, p. 33.
29. K. Rudolph, speaking of *Exc. Thdot.* 79, notes that the Greek term for "angel" is of the male gender (*Die Gnosis* [Leipzig: Koehler and Amelang, 1977], p. 290). In *Exc. Thdot.* there is never any indication that angels may be female.
30. See Sagnard's appendix C, *Extraits*, pp. 217–19.
31. Casey, *Exc. Thdot.*, p. 18.
32. Ibid., p. 19; see also note 28, above.
33. Ibid.
34. See Pagels, "Conflicting Versions," p. 49, for a slightly different emphasis.
35. Casey, *Exc. Thdot.*, p. 20; see also his further references to *Exc. Thdot.* 1.1 and 2.2.
36. Notice that in *Exc. Thdot.* 38.3, where Jesus stays with Space, the Demiurge, so that the elements may not rise before he, Jesus, does, Sagnard and Casey both substitute *pneumata* for *pragmata* as terms for these elements (Sagnard, *Extraits*, pp. 142–43 [see his n. 1, p. 42!]; Casey, *Exc. Thdot.*, pp. 66–67). Both scholars think that only pneuma can rise (compare Sagnard, *Extraits*, p. 112.1).
37. See Sagnard's appendix D, *Extraits*, pp. 220–24; Casey, *Exc. Thdot.*, pp. 122–24.
38. Sagnard, *Extraits*, p. 11.
39. See ibid., pp. 113–19, for Sagnard's opinion on this.

40. For a different view, see ibid., p. 119 n. 2.
41. Ibid., p. 11. Compare C. Oeyen's comments on the *protoktistoi*, the "First-Created," in his article, "Eine frühchristliche Engelpneumatologie bei Klemens von Alexandrien," *Internationale Kirchliche Zeitschrift* 55 (1965): 107 n. 16.
42. Dibelius, "Studien," pp. 245–46. The thesis is P. Ruben, *Clementis Alexandrini excerpta ex Theodoto* (Leipzig: B. G. Teubneri, 1892) (Dissertatio Philologa, Bonn).
43. Or: in the Ogdoad?—see *Exc. Thdot.* 63.1. The Mother is another name for Wisdom.
44. J. Leipoldt and H.-M. Schenke, *Koptisch-gnostische Schriften aus den Papyrus-Codices von Nag-Hamadi* (Hamburg-Bergstedt: Reich, 1960), p. 36.
45. A. Szabo, "Die Engelvorstellungen vom Alten Testament bis zur Gnosis," in *Altes Testament-Frühjudentum-Gnosis*, ed. K.-W. Tröger (Gütersloh: Mohn, 1980), p. 149.
46. Sagnard, *Extraits*, p. 137 and n. 4.
47. Ibid., n. 6. Compare similar misunderstandings of the relationship between angels and different seed in Casey, *Exc. Thdot.*, p. 18, and G. Quispel, "La conception de l'homme dans la gnose valentinienne," *Eranos Jahrbuch* 15 (1947): 263.
48. McCue, "Conflicting Versions," p. 411.
49. Pagels, "Conflicting Versions," p. 43.
50. See *Exc. Thdot.* 22.6–7 for the meaning of baptism for Jesus (see p. 66, above).
51. Sagnard (*Extraits*, p. 139 n. 3) interprets the division as that of the Jordan waters!
52. Quispel, "La conception de l'homme," p. 264.
53. Sagnard (*Extraits*, p. 139 n. 2) equates the original and final unity as that of the male angelic seeds with female, pneumatic ones. This thesis, again, depends on Sagnard's faulty identification of different seeds with "pneumatics."
54. Compare this with chapter 1, above, where Elohim, in *Bar.*, leaves Eden for the higher realms (pp. 6–7).
55. Sagnard, *Extraits*, pp. 143–45 n. 5; Casey, *Exc. Thdot.*, p. 133.
56. Pagels, "Conflicting Versions," p. 42 (my emphasis).
57. Ibid., p. 43.
58. Sagnard, *Extraits*, pp. 143–45 n. 3.
59. McCue, "Conflicting Versions," p. 411.
60. *Contra* Sagnard, *Extraits*, p. 145 n. 2.
61. Again, *contra* Sagnard (ibid.; see also ibid., p. 144, Sagnard's reference to *Exc. Thdot.* 35.1).
62. Compare Pagels, "Conflicting Versions," p. 48.
63. Ibid., p. 43.
64. McCue, "Conflicting Versions," p. 411.
65. Ibid.
66. Pagels, "Conflicting Versions," p. 43, notes the affinity with the Light, but does not deal with the passionlessness. Sagnard's translation (*Extraits*, p. 147) has

"parenté" ("parentage") for "affinity" (οἰκειότης), which gives a slightly different impression.

67. Compare Chapter 3, p. 50, above.
68. Pagels, "Conflicting Versions," p. 49.
69. Schottroff, "Animae," p. 90 (see note 3 above).
70. Ibid., p. 91; but compare *Exc. Thdot.* 44 and 45! See chapter 3, pp. 46–48, above.)
71. Schottroff, "Animae," pp. 90–91.
72. Pagels, despite her insights ("Conflicting Versions," pp. 46f.), continues to use the terms *psychics* and *pneumatics* in her article. More unabashedly, Sagnard (*Extraits*, p. 174) speaks of "trois races" ("three races").
73. Schottroff, "Animae," p. 94 n. 52.
74. Ibid., p. 93.
75. See Sagnard, *Extraits*, p. 171 n. 5, for a different view.
76. McCue, "Conflicting Versions," p. 413.
77. *Exc. Thdot.* 59.1. Compare p. 74, above, as regards McCue's conception of "formation" in *Exc. Thdot.* 40 and 41.
78. See Casey's discussion of Christology, *Exc. Thdot.*, p. 24.
79. See Sagnard, *Extraits*, p. 181 n. 2.
80. Compare the ritual in *Exc. Thdot.* 27 (see pp. 67–69, above).
81. See McCue, "Conflicting Versions," p. 413 n. 19. (Compare chapter 2, above, pp. 33, 35–36.)
82. Sagnard, *Extraits*, p. 185 and n. 1.
83. J.-D. Kaestli, "Valentinianisme italien et valentinianisme oriental: leurs divergences à propos de la nature du corps de Jésus," in *The Rediscovery of Gnosticism*, vol. 1, B. Layton, ed. (Leiden: Brill, 1980) p. 400.
84. W. Foerster, "Die Grundzüge der Ptolemäischen Gnosis," *New Testament Studies* 6 (1959–60): 30 n. 1.
85. Sagnard, *Extraits*, p. 185 n. 2.
86. *Exc. Thdot.* 61.8; and see Schottroff, "Animae," p. 91.
87. Sagnard (*Extraits*, p. 187 n. 2) interprets the passage as dealing with the equality of the pneumatic elements, an obvious misreading.
88. Ibid., p. 187 n. 1.
89. Pagels, "Conflicting Versions," pp. 44–46, 50.
90. Ibid., p. 44. This is tricky: *Exc. Thdot.* 63.1 and 34.2 may not quite agree with respect to the Demiurge-souls' final redemption; see further discussion.
91. Pagels, "Conflicting Versions," p. 46.
92. Ibid.
93. McCue, "Conflicting Versions," pp. 414–15; Sagnard, *Extraits*, p. 184.1; Casey, *Exc. Thdot.*, pp. 151–52.
94. McCue, "Conflicting Versions," p. 415.
95. Ibid., p. 414, and see p. 75, above. Also see *Exc. Thdot.* 54–56, pp. 76–79.
96. See p. 74, above.

97. Schottroff, "Animae," p. 92.
98. Compare this with the ritual in *Exc. Thdot.* 27.
99. See p. 74, above. Speaking of *Exc. Thdot.* 54–56, McCue states ("Conflicting Versions," p. 413) that the "pneumatic race" is formed; but it is the psychic, not the pneumatic entity that requires formation here. Compare also *Exc. Thdot.* 45, 67, 68, and 79.
100. Sagnard, *Extraits*, p. 187 n. 4; see also Casey, *Exc. Thdot.*, p. 25.
101. *Exc. Thdot.* 21.6 and 45; in the latter, Wisdom becomes *truly* Wisdom when saved by Christ. (However, the theme of competition emerges later, in *Exc. Thdot.* 68; see pp. 80–81 below!)
102. Leipoldt and Schenke, *Koptisch-gnostische Schriften*, p. 36.
103. Compare Casey's derogatory comments, *Exc. Thdot.*, p. 16 n. 2.
104. Pagels, "Conflicting Versions," p. 46.
105. Ibid., p. 51.
106. *Contra* Casey (*Exc. Thdot.*, p. 25). See Sagnard, *Extraits*, pp. 35 and 189 n. 2, and *La Gnose*, p. 536; McCue, coming to the same conclusion, does not recognize Sagnard's insight, however ("Conflicting Versions," p. 415).
107. Not the pneumatic seed, as Sagnard (*Extraits*, p. 191 n. 2) has it.
108. Compare this with the utterance in *The Gospel of the Egyptians* (*New Testament Apocrypha* 1, ed. E. Hennecke and W. Schneemelcher [Philadelphia: Westminster, 1962], p. 166 [with further references]), and in "The Gospel of Thomas" (*The Nag Hammadi Library*, J. M. Robinson, ed. [New York: Harper and Row, 1977], p. 127, logion 79).
109. Sagnard, *Extraits*, p. 190.1.
110. Ibid., p. 193 n. 2.
111. Compare the similar thought in "The Gospel of Philip" 52 (*The Nag Hammadi Library*, p. 132).
112. Sagnard, *Extraits*, p. 193 n. 2.
113. *Contra* Sagnard, *Extraits*, p. 190.2.
114. Schottroff, "Animae," pp. 92–93 (see pp. 74–75 and 78, above).
115. See Szabo, "Die Engelvorstellungen," p. 149 (see note 45, above).
116. See p. 63, above.
117. See p. 76, above.

CHAPTER 5

1. See, e.g., the material in O. Cullmann, "Das Thomas-evangelium und die Frage nach dem Alter der in ihm enthaltenen Tradition," *Theologische Literaturzeitung* 85.5 (1960): cols. 320–34; G. Quispel, *Makarius, das Thomasevangelium und das Lied von der Perle* (Leiden: Brill, 1967); *idem*, "The Gospel of Thomas Revisited," in *Colloque International sur les textes de Nag Hammadi* (Quebec, 22–25 Août 1978), ed. B. Barc (Quebec: Les Presses de l'Université Laval; Louvain:

Éditions Peeters, 1981), pp. 218–66; H. Koester's two studies, "GNOMAI DIA-PHOROI. The Origin and Nature of Diversification in the History of Early Christianity" and "One Jesus and Four Primitive Gospels," in J. M. Robinson and H. Koester, *Trajectories through Early Christianity* (Philadelphia: Fortress, 1971), pp. 114–57 and 158–204.

2. "The Gospel of Thomas," in J. M. Robinson, ed., *The Nag Hammadi Library* (New York: Harper and Row, 1977), p. 130 (the translation is by T. O. Lambdin, and references are to this one, unless otherwise indicated).

3. See references in, e.g., B. Gärtner, *The Theology of the Gospel According to Thomas* (New York: Harper and Row, 1961), pp. 253–55.

4. *Contra* R. M. Grant (in collaboration with D. N. Freedman), *The Secret Sayings of Jesus* (New York: Doubleday, 1960), p. 87; K. H. Rengstorf, "Urchristliches Kerygma und 'gnostische' Interpretation in einigen Sprüchen des Thomasevangeliums," in Ugo Bianchi, ed., *Le Origini dello Gnosticismo. Colloquio di Messina 13–18 Aprile 1966. Testi e Discussioni*, Studies in the History of Religions, Supplement to *Numen* 12 (Leiden: Brill, 1967), p. 567; and J.-É. Ménard, "Repos et salut Gnostique," *Revue des Sciences Religieuses*, 51.1 (1977): 85. These scholars see the new creation as being that of Gen. 1: the male and the female created in God's image. In his book, *L'Évangile selon Thomas* (Leiden: Brill, 1975), however, Ménard links *Gos. Thom.* to Gen. 2.

5. Compare W. Meeks, "The Image of the Androgyne: Some Uses of a Symbol in Earliest Christianity," *History of Religions* 13.3 (1974): 195 n. 133. Meeks does not draw the full conclusion, however.

6. Ph. de Suarez, *L'Évangile selon Thomas* (Montélimar: Marsanne [Éditions Metanoia], 1974), p. 315 (de Suarez is not explicit with respect to the androgyny here, but elsewhere in his work, treating logion 22, he refers to Gen. 2 [p. 267]); Ménard, *L'Évangile*, p. 20.

7. Ménard, *L'Évangile*, p. 210 (and see chapter 4, above, pp. 62, 70, 78–82).

8. Ibid., pp. 210, 43.

9. Gärtner, *Theology*, pp. 255–56; see also Quispel, *Makarius*, pp. 104–5.

10. Grant, *Secret Sayings*, pp. 197–98. See also Grant's references to Naassene material in the second ed. of his *Gnosticism and Early Christianity* (New York: Columbia University Press, 1966), pp. 197–98.

11. A. F. J. Klijn, "The 'Single One' in The Gospel of Thomas," *Journal of Biblical Literature* 81 (1962): 273; Cullmann, "Thomas-evangelium," col. 329; R. Kasser, *L'Évangile selon Thomas* (Neuchâtel: Delachaux & Niestlé, 1961), p. 120.

12. Kasser, *L'Évangile*, p. 120 (Kasser's n. 1 here betrays a certain sentimental view of women; moreover, he judges logion 114 to be a late addition to the gospel).

13. P. Perkins, "Pronouncement Stories in The Gospel of Thomas," *Semeia* 20 (1981): 130.

14. E. Haenchen, *Die Botschaft des Thomas-Evangeliums* (Berlin: Töpelmann, 1961), p. 69; J. Doresse, *Les Livres Secrèts des Gnostiques d'Égypte. L'Évangile selon Thomas ou les Paroles secrètes de Jésus* (Paris: Plon, 1959), p. 205.

15. Meeks, "Image," p. 196 n. 137; it is worth noting that Paul did not like Thecla's appearing as a man.
16. P. Vielhauer ("*ANAΠAΥΣIΣ*," in *Apophoreta. Festschrift E. Haenchen*, ed. W. Eltester, *Beiheft, Zeitschrift für die neutestamentliche Wissenschaft 30* [Berlin: Töpelmann, 1964], p. 298), notes that the transformation to maleness is to be made in *this* life, not after death.
17. H.-C. Puech, *En quête de la Gnose, 2: Sur L'Évangile selon Thomas* (Paris: Gallimard, 1978), p. 280.
18. Rengstorf, "Urchristliches Kerygma" (see note 4, above), p. 565.
19. Ibid., pp. 566, 567–68, 569.
20. Ibid., p. 569; and see H. Kees, "Ägypten," in A. H. Bertholet, *Religionsgeschichtliches Lesebuch* 10 (Tübingen: Mohn [Siebeck], 1928), p. 30.
21. Rengstorf, "Urchristliches Kerygma," pp. 569, 570.
22. Ibid., p. 573.
23. See W. Spiegelberg, "Varia," *Zeitschrift für aegyptische Sprache und Altertumskunde* 53 (1917): 95.
24. See Kees, "Ägypten," p. 29; Th. Hopfner, *Plutarch. Über Isis und Osiris* 1, Monographien des *Archiv Orientalni* (Prague: Orientalisches Institut, 1940), pp. 82–84; and J. G. Griffiths, *Plutarch. De Iside et Osiride* (Cardiff: University of Wales Press, 1970), pp. 284, 353. For Osiris's lost male member—of which Isis makes a replica to be revered—see Plutarch, *Moralia 5, Isis and Osiris*, trans. F. C. Babbitt, The Loeb Classical Library (1936), 358B and 365C.
25. E. Pagels, *The Gnostic Gospels* (New York: Random House, 1979), p. 49.
26. Ibid., p. 67. M. Meyer's "Making Mary Male: The Categories 'Male' and 'Female' in the *Gospel of Thomas*," *New Testament Studies* 31.4 (1985): 554–70, is general and comparative.
27. Ménard divides the heavens into the lower, "created" one and the upper one (*L'Évangile*, pp. 37, 96).
28. Ibid., p. 37; see also his references to Naassene and Manichaean material, and to *Gos. Phil.*, about "eating the dead." Compare Puech, "En quête," p. 39 n. 1 and p. 87.
29. Kasser, *L'Évangile*, p. 45.
30. For instance, Quispel, *Makarius*, p. 32, and B. Lincoln, "Thomas-Gospel and Thomas-Community: A New Approach To A Familiar Text," *Novum Testamentum* 19.1 (1977): 74.
31. This is Quispel's phrase (*Makarius*, p. 32).
32. Compare logion 19 (p. 120), where Jesus says, "If you become my disciples" (a possible exception is logion 13, p. 119).
33. Puech, "En quête," p. 107.
34. J.-É. Ménard, "Beziehungen des Philippus- und des Thomas-Evangeliums zur syrischen Welt," in *Altes Testament–Frühjudentum–Gnosis*, ed. K.-W. Tröger (Gütersloh: Mohn, 1980), p. 321. Quispel suggests that logion 18 may be an amplification of the Syrian *Didaskalia* 26 (*Makarius*, p. 33).

35. Quispel, *Makarius*, p. 33.
36. Ibid., p. 32.
37. See the article by H. C. Kee, "'Becoming a Child' in The Gospel of Thomas," *Journal of Biblical Literature*, 82 (1963): 307–14.
38. Or, "to make the two a single one," as in the ed. and trans. by A. Guillaumont et al., *The Gospel According to Thomas* (Leiden: Brill; New York: Harper & Brothers, 1959), p. 17. The Coptic term is Ⲙ̄ⲡⲓⲟⲩⲁ.
39. Guillaumont et al. has "as" instead of "like" (ibid.); see also Gärtner, *Theology*, p. 220.
40. Lincoln, "Thomas-Gospel," pp. 69, 70–76.
41. Ibid., p. 75. Note Quispel's judgment of the *Gos. Thom.* author: "an encratite, rejecting women, wine and meat . . . taught that only bachelors could go to heaven" ("Gospel of Thomas," p. 234 [see note 1, above]); I find no explicit support for this in the gospel.
42. Lincoln, "Thomas-Gospel," p. 75 and n. 27.
43. Gärtner, *Theology*, p. 256. (Note Grant [*Secret Sayings*, p. 144] about "cutting off" members in order to gain spiritual ones.)
44. Gärtner, *Theology*, p. 256; see also Ménard, *L'Évangile*, p. 115, and "Repos," p. 87.
45. Puech, "En quête," pp. 278–80.
46. Meeks, "Image," p. 195.
47. Vielhauer, "*ΑΝΑΠΑΥΣΙΣ*," p. 298.
48. Rengstorf, "Urchristliches Kerygma," pp. 565–66.
49. J. Z. Smith, "The Garments of Shame," in *Map is Not Territory*, Studies in the History of Religions (Leiden: Brill, 1978), p. 19.
50. Compare p. 89, above.
51. The logion has nothing to do with lack of "worry about clothes," as Gärtner says (*Theology*, p. 86).
52. De Suarez refers to Freud's theories (*L'Évangile*, p. 309). Ménard makes an incomprehensible distinction between the spiritual parents and those who are "d'en haut" ("from above"): the first set of parents are to be detested, the second set to be loved (*L'Évangile*, p. 202). Gärtner wonders if Jesus' heavenly mother is "the Spirit, Sophia?" (*Theology*, p. 138). See also Klijn, "The 'Single One,'" p. 278.
53. Quispel, *Makarius*, p. 95 (and see his comments on logia 55 and 101 in "Gospel of Thomas," p. 257); Puech, "En quête," p. 247. (See chap. 4, p. 81, above.)
54. Kasser, *L'Évangile*, p. 112.
55. Ibid., p. 115.
56. Ménard, *L'Évangile*, p. 204.
57. Koester, "One Jesus and Four Primitive Gospels," p. 171 n. 35 (the reference is to Gärtner, *Theology*, p. 246). One should note that the expression "the sons of men" in logion 28 (*Gos. Thom.*, p. 121) obviously refers to earthly, unsaved people.
58. *Gos. Thom.*, p. 127; compare Puech, "En quête," p. 239 (such capitalization is, of

course, due to the translator's choice).

59. Puech, "En quête," p. 243.
60. Puech distinguishes between *arsên* ("male") and *anthrôpos* ("man") (ibid., p. 239).
61. Ibid., pp. 282–83.
62. See pp. 92–93, above.
63. Ménard, *L'Évangile*, pp. 28, 101; see also Quispel, *Makarius*, p. 99.
64. Kasser, *L'Évangile*, p. 50.
65. Gärtner, *Theology*, p. 137.
66. R. M. Grant, "Notes on The Gospel of Thomas," *Vigiliae Christianae* 13 (1959): 174.
67. Lincoln, "Thomas-Gospel," p. 74. Kee, " 'Becoming a Child,' " p. 309, supports my view here.
68. Lincoln, "Thomas-Gospel," p. 74.
69. Ménard, *L'Évangile*, p. 146; Puech, "En quête," p. 99.
70. Kee, " 'Becoming a Child,' " p. 309.
71. For this term see A. Baker, O.S.B., " 'Fasting to the World,' " *Journal of Biblical Literature* 84 (1965): 293–94.
72. Ménard, "Beziehungen," p. 324 (see note 41, above, for Quispel's view).
73. Gärtner, *Theology*, p. 252.
74. Ménard, *L'Évangile*, p. 180.
75. Perkins, "Pronouncement Stories," p. 126. Kasser's view (*L'Évangile*, p. 101), that Jesus' first utterance means that the church is more important than the Son's bodily resurrection, appears too much like fantasizing.
76. See p. 94, above.
77. Ménard, *L'Évangile*, p. 17 (see his references here; and see Grant, *Secret Sayings*, p. 191). Quispel notes that "marriage" is "πορνεία" (*Makarius*, p. 99). Ménard also notes that parents equal dualism (*L'Évangile*, p. 204).
78. Kasser, *L'Évangile*, pp. 114–15.
79. See pp. 92–93 and 94, above.
80. See p. 93, above.
81. Puech wonders if one may identify Jesus with "the image of the light of the Father" ("En quête," p. 156).
82. Ménard, *L'Évangile*, p. 41.
83. Klijn, "The 'Single One,' " p. 277.
84. Puech, "En quête," p. 112.
85. Compare with logion 19, *Gos. Thom.* (p. 120).
86. Puech, p. 114.
87. Gärtner, *Theology*, pp. 204–5.
88. See Ménard, *L'Évangile*, pp. 42 and 185; compare with *Gos. Phil.* 67 (Robinson, *Nag Hammadi Library*, pp. 140–41).
89. Ménard, *L'Évangile*, p. 186 (Ménard refers to *Gos. Phil.* here).

90. Grant, *Secret Sayings*, p. 181.
91. G. Quispel, "Genius and Spirit," in *Essays on the Nag Hammadi Texts*, ed. M. Krause (Leiden: Brill, 1975), p. 159.
92. See note 89, above.
93. Compare my articles, "The Mandaean Šitil as an Example of 'the Image Above and Below,'" *Numen* 26.2 (1979): 185–91, and "Two Female Gnostic Revealers," *History of Religions* 19.3 (1980): 259–69, for discussions of the "image."
94. Gärtner, *Theology*, p. 195.
95. Ménard, *L'Évangile*, p. 18 (my emphasis); but on pp. 70 and 145 Ménard uses "richesse," not "chute."
96. See note 71, above.
97. Quispel, *Makarius*, pp. 26, 27; Quispel also refers to logion 22 here. In "The Gospel of Thomas," Quispel interprets the bridal chamber as the sacrament of baptism (p. 236), but I see no reason for this equation; he observes (p. 237) that Aquila and Symmachos—the Bible translators—used "monachos" to translate "*labado*," "alone" (as in "It is not good that man be alone . . ." [Gen. 2:18]). *Gos. Thom.* would say precisely the opposite of what God said in Gen. 2:18!
98. See pp. 95 and 96, above (and compare chapter 4, above).
99. Ménard, *L'Évangile*, p. 204.
100. Perkins, "Pronouncement Stories," p. 127.
101. Quispel, *Makarius*, p. 92; Guillaumont et al., *Gospel*, p. 35 (this translation also has "from the Same," not "from the Undivided"); Gärtner, *Theology*, p. 135.
102. For "male" brides, see chapter 4, above, esp. pp. 62, 70, and 78–82.
103. See p. 89, with note 32, above.
104. Koester, "One Jesus," pp. 178–79.
105. Ménard, *L'Évangile*, p. 162.
106. Kasser, *L'Évangile*, p. 33.
107. Puech, "En quête," p. 177.
108. R. Schippers, *Het evangelie van Thomas* (Kampen: J. H. Kok, 1960), pp. 111–12; the reference is to *The Acts of Thomas* I, 11f. (see W. Foerster, ed., *Gnosis. A Selection of Gnostic Texts*, vol. 1, *Patristic Evidence* [Oxford: Clarendon, 1972], pp. 347–48).
109. De Suarez, *L'Évangile*, pp. 289, 290.
110. Klijn, "The 'Single One,'" p. 272; the term is ογⲁ or ογⲱⲧ.
111. See ibid., pp. 271–72; and compare pp. 94–96, above.

CHAPTER 6

1. *Gos. Phil.* is in *The Nag Hammadi Library*, ed. J. M. Robinson (New York: Harper and Row, 1977), pp. 131–51 (here p. 136); edition and translation is by W. W. Isenberg, and, unless otherwise indicated, I use his version.

2. Eve is another, though negatively evaluated, figure.

3. G. S. Gasparro, "Il personaggio di Sophia nel vangelo secondo Filippo," *Vigiliae Christianae* 31 (1977): 245, 252 n. 29, 270, 280–81; Y. Janssens, "L'Évangile selon Philippe," *Le Muséon* 81 (1968): 93, 99, 132; B. Barc, "Les noms de la Triade dans l'Évangile selon Philippe," in *Gnosticisme et monde hellenistique. Actes du Colloque de Louvain-la-Neuve (11–14 mars 1980)*, ed. J. Ries (Louvain-la-Neuve: Publications de l'Institut Orientaliste de Louvain 27, 1982), pp. 369–70, 373–75 (Barc's is an excellent article).

4. Two perceptive examples are: S. Giversen, *Filipsevangeliet* (Copenhagen: Gad, 1966), p. 27; and J.-M. Sevrin, "Les noces spirituelles dans l'Évangile selon Philippe," *Le Muséon* 87 (1974): 163.

5. H.-M. Schenke, "Das Evangelium nach Philippus," in J. Leipoldt and H.-M. Schenke, eds., *Koptisch-gnostische Schriften aus den Papyrus-Codices von Nag-Hamadi* (Hamburg-Bergstedt: Reich, 1960) (= "Das Evangelium nach Philippus," *Theologische Literaturzeitung* 84 [1959]: cols. 1–26), p. 34. Note, however, that the term "Ogdoad" does not appear in *Gos. Phil.* Schenke is echoed by R. McL. Wilson, *The Gospel of Philip* (London: Mowbray, 1962), p. 96; by J.-É. Ménard, *L'Évangile selon Philippe* (Strasbourg: Université de Strasbourg, 1967), pp. 14–15; and by Sevrin, "Les noces spirituelles," p. 163.

6. See J.-É. Ménard, "L'Évangile selon Philippe et l'Exégèse de l'âme," in *Les Textes de Nag Hammadi*, ed. J.-É. Ménard (Leiden: Brill, 1975), pp. 61–62; and my study, "A Cult-Mystery in *The Gospel of Philip*," *Journal of Biblical Literature* 99.4 (1980): 570–73.

7. See, again, "Cult-Mystery," pp. 570–73, 575–81.

8. I have coined this term to refer to the undivided Adam *before* he was put in Paradise (see p. 89 in Chapter 5, above). As a "living soul," not yet needing a helper, Adam is autonomous and self-sufficient. His "Paradisial" state, however, causes his downfall.

9. See p. 103, above.

10. References are in Ménard, *L'Évangile*, p. 136.

11. Giversen, *Filipsevangeliet*, p. 47.27–30 (my transl.); see also his n. 7.

12. For Gnostic parallels, see Ménard, *L'Évangile*, pp. 125–26, and Wilson, *Gospel*, p. 68. In the Mandaean *ATŠ*, the Mandaeans make puns on *Yahuṭaiia* (Jews) and *iahṭa* (abortion): *ATŠ*, pp. 255 (198) and 276 (358).

13. Schenke, "Das Evangelium," p. 41 n. 3.

14. Ménard, *L'Évangile*, p. 136.

15. Janssens, "L'Évangile," p. 86; on the next page, she credits Joseph with giving Jesus a human body without blemishing Mary.

16. J. Lagrand, "How was the Virgin Mary 'Like a Man' (ܐܝܟ ܓܒܪܐ)? A Note on Mt. i 18b and Related Syriac Christian Texts," *Novum Testamentum* 22.2 (1980): 104, 105.

17. B. McNeil, "New Light on Gospel of Philip 17," *Journal of Theological Studies*

29. I (1978): 144–46. Attempting to read the Arabic text's view into *Gos. Phil.*, McNeil admits that he may be trying to explain "obscurum per obscurius" (p. 144).

18. Ibid., p. 145. See also Janssens, "L'Évangile," p. 87.

19. Ménard, *L'Évangile*, p. 150; see also chapter 5, above, pp. 85 and 101.

20. Giversen, *Filipsevangeliet*, p. 53 n. 3.

21. Wilson's translation of the last line seems to bring this out: "For Mary was his sister and his mother and his consort" (*Gospel*, p. 35.10–11). A. Orbe sees three Marys in heaven corresponding to those on earth: the three earthly ones reflect "la triple eficacia de María, la virgen incontaminada" ("the triple efficacy of Mary, the uncontaminated virgin") ("'Sophia Soror.' Apuntes para la teología del Espíritu Santo," in *Mélanges d'histoire des religions offerts à Henri-Charles Puech* [Paris: Presses Univ. de France, 1974], p. 360).

22. J.-É. Ménard, "Le milieu syriaque de l'*Évangile selon Thomas* et de l'Évangile selon Philippe," *Revue des sciences religieuses* 42.3 (1968): 264.

23. R. M. Grant, "The Mystery of Marriage in The Gospel of Philip," *Vigiliae Christianae* 15 (1961): 138.

24. Giversen leaves the text broken (*Filipsevangeliet*, p. 62) while others emend it: Schenke, "Das Evangelium," p. 47; Ménard, *L'Évangile*, pp. 71–73 and K. H. Kuhn, "The Gospel of Philip," in *Gnosis. A Selection of Gnostic Texts*, vol. 2, *Coptic and Mandaic Sources*, ed. W. Foerster (Oxford: Clarendon, 1974), p. 86.

25. See W. Meeks, "The Image of the Androgyne: Some Uses of a Symbol in Earliest Christianity," *History of Religions* 13.3 (1974): 190 n. 111 (compare note 20, above).

26. See, e.g., references in E. Pagels, *The Gnostic Gospels* (New York: Random House, 1979), pp. 64–65.

27. Schenke, "Das Evangelium," p. 38. Gasparro, discerning the parallel Savior-Achamoth in the couple Jesus–Mary Magdalene ("Il personaggio," p. 270), does not interpret the kiss. Ménard sees in Mary Magdalene "le prototype du parfait réuni au Soter dans un baiser" ("the prototype of the perfect one who is reunited to the Savior by a kiss") (*L'Évangile*, p. 150).

28. Meeks, "Image," p. 190 n. 111; Janssens, "L'Évangile," p. 99; Sevrin, "Les noces," p. 185 n. 112. Compare *Gos. Phil.* 70.25–30 (p. 142), where the "powers" envy the Spirit-endowed Adam who speaks words incomprehensible to them.

29. Sevrin, "Les noces," pp. 185–86, 191–92, 185 n. 112, 163 n. 63.

30. Ménard, *L'Évangile*, pp. 61.33–63.2; consult Ménard's commentary, p. 149, and see also Kuhn's translation, "Gospel," p. 83.

31. H.-G. Gaffron, "Studien zum koptischen Philippusevangelium unter besonderer Berücksichtigung der Sakramente" (Theol. Diss., Rheinische Friedrich Wilhelms-Universität, 1969), pp. 214, 216. See also Giversen regarding the "pregnancy of grace" (*Filipsevangeliet*, p. 27).

32. Meeks, "Image," p. 190 n. 111.

33. Sevrin submits parallels to Irenaeus' works ("Les noces," pp. 184–85), but warns

against relying on Irenaeus' terminology, which is different from that in *Gos. Phil.* Sevrin thinks both passages about kissing refer to a rite (ibid., p. 183).

34. Janssens draws attention to the fact that the masc. Coptic word for summer, ⲡϣⲱⲙ, has here turned fem., ⲧϣⲁⲙⲏ, in order to accord with the Holy Spirit's feminine character ("L'Évangile," p. 119).

35. See Gasparro's comments ("Il personaggio," p. 263 n. 73).

36. See p. 106, above.

37. Recall the spiritual begetting in 58–59 (see p. 110, above).

38. "Wind" = πνεῦμα.

39. Janssens, "L'Évangile," p. 104.

40. Ménard, *L'Évangile*, p. 155.

41. Compare chapter 2, p. 27, above! (See also my study, "A Rehabilitation of Spirit Ruha in Mandaean Religion," *History of Religions* 22.1 (1982): 60–84, esp. 73–84.)

42. Consult my treatment in "Cult-Mystery," pp. 570–71, and see p. 103 above, regarding "Truth."

43. See Ménard, *L'Évangile*, p. 167, for references to other Gnostic material where similar imagery occurs.

44. Janssens, "L'Évangile," p. 97.

45. Ménard, *L'Évangile*, p. 85 (my emphasis). Janssens, too, has "compagnon" ("companion"), ("L'Évangile," p. 109), and Schenke translates, "Die Seele (ψυχή) des Adam ist entstanden aus einem Hauch. Ihr Paargenosse ist der [Geist. Die] ihn ihm gegeben hat, ist seine Mutter, und mit seiner Seele (ψυχή) gaben sie ihm einen [Geist an] ihrer (sc. der Mutter) Stelle"—"The soul (. . .) of Adam comes about by breath. Its mate is the [spirit. The] one who has given it to him, is his mother, and together with his soul (. . .) they gave him a [spirit] in her (that is, the mother's) stead ("Das Evangelium," p. 80). Both Giversen (*Filipsevangeliet*, p. 74) and Kuhn ("Gospel," p. 91) leave some lacunae in their translations (see Gasparro, "Il personaggio," p. 278 n. 123, for her emendations).

46. W.-D. Hauschild, *Gottes Geist und der Mensch* (München: Kaiser, 1973), refers to *Gos. Phil.* 63 in this connection (pp. 184–85 n. 11). He notes that "Wiedergeburt und Geistesverleihung hängen zusammen" ("Rebirth and spirit-endowment are related") (p. 186).

47. Hauschild draws the connection to the Valentinian doctrine, according to which the demiurge transmits both pneuma and *psuché*; as no demiurge appears in the present context, Hauschild determines the passage to be pre-Valentinian (*Gottes Geist*, p. 185).

48. See p. 106, above, and consult my articles, "The Mandaean Šitil as an Example of 'the Image Above and Below,'" *Numen* 26.2 (1979): 185–91, and "Two Female Gnostic Revealers," *History of Religions* 19.3 (1980): 259–69, esp. pp. 266–69. (See also the introduction to Chapter 3, above.)

49. Till observes that the Coptic ⲕⲁϩ, "earth," is masc., but Greek γῆ is fem., which speaks for a Greek original (T, p. 6).

50. Ménard, *L'Évangile*, p. 204.
51. This corresponds well to the Mandaean notion that the Jordan (that is, running water fit for baptism) constitutes the upper Lightworld as reflected on earth.
52. See Wilson's interpretation, *Gospel*, p. 147.
53. See Gasparro, "Il personaggio," p. 281.
54. The bridal chamber has both a preexistent and an eschatological dimension, says Ménard in "L'*Évangile selon Philippe*," p. 59.
55. For "When that Spirit blows . . . ," see note 34, above.
56. Janssens, "L'Évangile," pp. 100, 133, 118.
57. Wilson, *Gospel*, p. 137. Till's translation (T, p. 69, 117.4–8) agrees with Wilson's. See also Giversen, (*Filipsevangeliet*, p. 71), and Ménard's comments (*L'Évangile*, p. 193).
58. See note 12, above.
59. See p. 113, above.
60. See p. 109 and note 24, above.
61. See Janssens' comments, "L'Évangile," p. 99.
62. Gaffron, *Studien*, p. 215.
63. See above, pp. 107–8 for *Gos. Phil.* 55 and p. 109 for *Gos. Phil.* 63–64.
64. Gasparro, "Il personaggio," p. 260 (see also her nn. 61–63); for additional references, consult Wilson, *Gospel*, p. 100.
65. Ménard, *L'Évangile*, p. 63, 36.31–32.
66. Ibid., p. 171.
67. The text repeats "the Wisdom of death which is," indicated by ellipsis points.
68. See Barc, "Les noms," p. 373 n. 20!
69. Janssens, "L'Évangile," p. 93; Gasparro, "Il personaggio," pp. 267–68; see also Barc, "Les noms," pp. 372–73.
70. Wilson, *Gospel*, p. 103.
71. Sevrin, "Les noces," p. 163.
72. Janssens has "nourrit" ("nourishes") for "shepherds" (the verb is ᴍᴏᴏɴᴇ) ("L'Évangile," p. 93).
73. See p. 113 and note 41, above.
74. See Gasparro's comments on the relationship of the perfect man to the Holy Spirit ("Il personaggio," p. 257 n. 55).
75. So Wilson (*Gospel*, p. 99), *contra* Janssens ("L'Évangile," p. 92) for whom the "alien" is "materiél, chose de ce monde" ("material, something worldly"). Gasparro concurs with Wilson ("Il personaggio," p. 257).
76. Both Schenke ("Das Evangelium," p. 44 n. 4) and Janssens ("L'Évangile," p. 92) identify the Holy Spirit as the mother.
77. Gaffron, *Studien*, p. 184.
78. Compare introduction to Chapter 4 above. Sevrin feels that Jesus should not need to ask for salvation, for he has already achieved it in his tripartition as Logos, angel, and human being ("Les noces," p. 152).

79. See Schenke, "Das Evangelium," p. 43 nn. 3–4.
80. See pp. 109 and 111 above for *Gos. Phil.* 63.30–35.
81. A. H. C. van Eijk comments on this ("The Gospel of Philip and Clement of Alexandria. Gnostic and Ecclesiastical Theology on the Resurrection and the Eucharist," *Vigiliae Christianae* 25.2 [1971]: 104).
82. In 63.20–25, Jesus is said to be the eucharist. Consult van Eijk for other references to the eucharist within *Gos. Phil.* ("Gospel of Philip," p. 102), and see E. Segelberg, "The Coptic-Gnostic Gospel According to Philip and Its Sacramental System," *Numen* 7 (1960): 189–200, for a discussion on the ranking and interrelationships of the gospel's sacraments.
83. See pp. 110–11, above.
84. See pp. 115–16, above; and compare Janssens, "L'Évangile," p. 132.
85. Van Eijk, "Gospel of Philip," p. 105; on p. 103 he refers to *Gos. Phil.* 61.25–35, which declares that he who sees the Spirit, becomes Spirit. Gaffron observes, "die himmlische Syzygie ist im Kelch geheimnisvoll gegenwärtig. Sonst könnte *Ph* schliesslich nicht behaupten, dass man den vollkommenen Menschen empfängt" ("the heavenly syzygy is secretly present in the cup. Otherwise, *Gos. Phil.* could certainly not claim that one receives the perfect man") (*Studien*, p. 175); compare Hauschild, Gottes Geist, p. 189, and Ménard, *L'Evangile*, p. 218, for pertinent comments.
86. See pp. 109–11, above.
87. See above, notes 72 and 41 and p. 118, respectively.
88. Ménard, *L'Évangile*, p. 142.
89. Van Eijk, "Gospel of Philip," p. 104.
90. See *Gos. Phil.* 65.20–25 (p. 139).
91. E.g., Schenke, "Das Evangelium," p. 38, and Sevrin, "Les noces," p. 181.
92. See also 64.30–35 (p. 139).
93. Ménard, *L'Évangile*, p. 29; Grant, "Mystery," p. 138. See also my "Cult-Mystery," pp. 576–77.
94. Gaffron, *Studien*, pp. 109–10.
95. Pointed brackets indicate translator's correction. (See chap. 5, above, note 89.)
96. T, pp. 52–53; see also Wilson, *Gospel*, p. 164.
97. *Contra* J.-P. Mahé, "Les sens des symboles sexuels dans quelques textes hermétiques et gnostiques," in Ménard, *Les Textes de Nag Hammadi*, p. 137.
98. Ménard, *L'Évangile*, p. 221.
99. Segelberg, "Coptic-Gnostic Gospel," p. 198.
100. G. S. Gasparro ("Aspetti encratiti nel 'Vangelo secondo Filippo,' " in *Gnosticisme et monde hellénistique*, ed. J. Ries [see note 3, above], pp. 394–423) gives a negative evaluation (e.g., pp. 400–401). In line with this judgment, she equates the division of the genders with sexual transgression (pp. 406–7) and (e.g., pp. 422–23) speaks of a "pneumatics" *vs.* "psychics" distinction—but these are not technical terms in *Gos. Phil.*

101. See p. 112, above.
102. Giversen, *Filipsevangeliet*, p. 37 (my transl.). Consult *Gos. Phil.* 74.10–25 (p. 144) for the place of the anointment in the bridal chamber.
103. For "son of the bridal chamber," see Ménard, *L'Évangile*, p. 125.
104. Giversen, *Filipsevangeliet*, p. 24 (my transl.); compare Ménard, *L'Évangile*, p. 29.
105. Meeks, "Image," p. 190 n. 111, here confronts Gaffron, *Studien*, p. 214.
106. Gaffron, *Studien*, pp. 213, 218, 225. See my "Cult-Mystery," p. 576, for a brief discussion of Gaffron's theory, and consult Sevrin, "Les noces," pp. 165, 186–88.
107. See my discussion, pp. 120–21, above, and Gaffron, *Studien*, pp. 109–10, who says that the bridal chamber is the only sacrament termed μυστήριον.
108. Gaffron, *Studien*, p. 200; Sevrin, p. 165.
109. Mahé, "Les sens des symboles," p. 137.
110. Note Ménard's translation (*L'Évangile*, p. 81.25): "et s'il la prend en lui-même" ("and if he takes her to himself").
111. E. Pagels discusses this passage in "Adam and Eve, Christ and the Church: A Survey of Second-Century Controversies Concerning Marriage," in *The New Testament and Gnosis: Essays in Honour of Robert R. McL. Wilson*, ed. A. H. B. Logan and A. J. M. Wedderburn (Edinburgh: T. & T. Clark, 1983) p. 164 (the reference is wrongly given: it should be to *Gos. Phil.* 70, not to 78–79). In light of Eph. 5:32 and other documents, Pagels sees *Gos. Phil.* 70 as referring to Jesus and the Church: an interesting, but to me unconvincing, thesis.
112. E.g., *Gos. Phil.* 60.15–35 (p. 136) (see note 87, above). Note that the tripartition in 66.5–25 (p. 140) is of a different kind, for here the evaluation of the third element is the most negative.
113. Gaffron, *Studien*, pp. 180–81.
114. See Ménard, *L'Évangile*, p. 222; Gasparro, "Il personaggio," pp. 258–59; and Barc, "Les noms," pp. 372–73.
115. Compare Chapter 5, p. 89, above!
116. See p. 105, above, and *Gos. Phil.* 77.15–20 (p. 146).
117. That even Jesus was divided is hinted at in *Gos. Phil.* 63.20–25 (p. 138) and 68.25–30 (p. 141).

CHAPTER 7

1. See, for instance, E. S. Drower, *The Secret Adam* (Oxford: Clarendon, 1960), pp. 21f.; 36; 40.
2. See the interpretations of A. Orbe ("'Sophia Soror.' Apuntes para la teología del Espíritu Santo," in *Mélanges d'histoire des religions offerts à Henri-Charles Puech* [Paris: Presses Univ. de France, 1974], p. 355) and R. McL. Wilson ("The Spirit in Gnostic Literature," in *Christ and Spirit in the New Testament*, ed.

B. Lindars and S. S. Smalley [Cambridge: Cambridge University Press, 1973], p. 353).

3. W. O'Flaherty, *Women, Androgynes, and other Mythical Beasts* (Chicago: Chicago University Press, 1980), p. 284.

4. Compare B. Lincoln, *Emerging from the Chrysalis. Studies in Rituals of Women's Initiations* (Cambridge: Harvard University Press, 1981), p. 26.

5. O'Flaherty, *Women*, p. 333.

6. E. S. Drower, *The Mandaeans of Iraq and Iran* (1937; reprint, Leiden: Brill, 1962), pp. 180–81.

7. *Gos. Phil.*'s statements on resurrection express the same idea: see 56 (p. 134) and 57 (p. 137).

8. E. Goodenough, *By Light, Light* (New Haven: Yale University Press, 1935).

9. As I have termed it in "The Mandaean Ṭabahata Masiqta" (*Numen* 28.2 [1981]: 158).

INDEX